Social Interaction and Consciousness

P. D. ASHWORTH

Sheffield City Polytechnic

JOHN WILEY & SONS

Chichester · New York · Brisbane · Toronto

Library of Congress Cataloging in Publication Data:

Ashworth, P. D.
  Social interaction and consciousness.

  Bibliography: p.
  Includes indexes.
  1. Social psychology — Methodology. 2. Social interaction.
  3. Symbolic interactionism. 4. Awareness. I. Title.
HM251.A83   301.11   78-27252

ISBN 0 471 27567 0
ISBN 0 471 27566-2 pbk.

Typeset by Photo-Graphics, Honiton, Devon and
printed at Unwin Brothers Ltd., The Gresham Press, Old Woking.

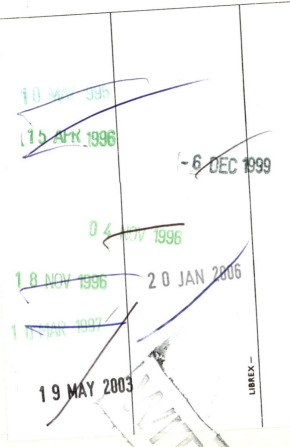

To Marilyn
and our parents

CONTENTS

Consciousness is the problem, the solution of which cannot too variously be reworded, too manifoldly be illustrated....Almost all is yet to be achieved.

This state and growth of reflex consciousness...is not conceivable without the action of kindred souls on each other, i.e. the modification of each by each, and of each by the whole.

S. T. Coleridge

Introduction

Social psychology is that part of psychology that deals with how the thought, feeling and behaviour of individuals are influenced by the actual, imagined or implied presence of others (G. Allport, 1968), and that part of sociology that deals with the relationship between individuals and social structure (Lindesmith, Strauss and Denzin, 1975). This being so, the focus is generally taken to be social interaction — a phenomenon which links the person to others and to which we must look for the evidence of social structure. There is no need to make an issue of this definition. The intention is merely to give a general impression of the topics that social psychologists are concerned with, and also indicate the intimate connection between the neighbouring disciplines. In fact the boundaries are often no more than conventions for the purpose of academic administration.

The two parts of the definition map out the area of social psychology from the contrasting viewpoints of psychology and sociology. But it is as if the area were symmetrical, for the different points of view do not give rise to different impressions of the shape of the field. By including both perspectives in the definition, then, the same thing has been said twice. However, it is also the case that the two parts are worded in a manner which reflects the different reasons that psychologists and sociologists have for their interest in social psychology. The sociologist wishes to people his social institutions and historical descriptions of societal development. The psychologist realizes that the individuals with which his science is concerned are bound up in society and that their social nature cannot be ignored. We must now take a closer look at these sciences and their relationship to social psychology.

It is clear from the definition that social psychology is an area of interest shared by the 'parent' disciplines of psychology and sociology/social anthropology. Rationally, this surely must be so: as human sciences, both psychology and sociology are faced with the fact that individual human beings, even in isolation, are essentially social; their thoughts, feelings and actions the product of social experience. Without society, a biological member of *Homo sapiens* would not be recognizable as psychologically human. It appears certain that individual psychology must take note of man's social nature. On the other hand the study of society is incomplete without an understanding of the individual biological beings which enact the roles and people the institutions. A social theory necessarily implies the existence of

1

individual members of society who have personal characteristics. The two disciplines, sociology and psychology, can be seen to intersect, then. At their intersection or interface is the area of concern of social psychology.

This notion of man as essentially social, and of society as 'peopled', is merely stated here as an assertion. It is introduced, prior to evidence, as an orienting idea, which sets the perspective of the book as a whole. The following chapter provides a detailed account of many of the arguments which relate to the social nature of man and the human basis of society.

Social psychology, then, is the interface discipline which treats the relationship of man and the social world to detailed analysis.

The ways in which interface disciplines can occur include the following (cf Cherns, 1975). First of all, a technique used in one science can be applied to a quite different one — as when anthropological techniques involving the analysis of cultures began to be applied to the study of religions including Christianity. This was an *invasion of technique*. An anthropological technique was applied to a theological area, giving rise to the interface discipline of comparative religion. An invasion of technique has also given birth to an important part of social psychology. That is, the area of attitude research (see Chapter 8) relies to a large extent on techniques of scaling by which individuals are put in a rank order indicating their approval or disapproval of an attitude. Scaling originates in the psychological study of sensation. Thus social psychology owes at least a part of its existence to the invasion of a technique from the psychology of the senses.

Another way in which an interface discipline can emerge is by *reductionism*. This involves the attempt to deal with complex phenomena normally thought of as the province of a particular science by regarding them as the result of more basic processes belonging to the area of concern of a different science. For instance, the complex phenomena of biology — living objects — can be regarded as the result of chemical processes, so that biology is reduced to chemistry and the interface discipline of molecular biology emerges. In the human sciences we see reductionism in operation when the phenomena of psychology — mental processes — are thought of as the outcome of biological events. This tendency has given rise to the interface discipline of physiological psychology. Reductionism is one source of social psychology, too. Authors such as Skinner (see Chapter 2) have wanted to explain sociological phenomena in terms of relatively simple principles of social interaction between individuals. In that chapter the adequacy of such an approach is debated.

A third reason for the emergence of an interface discipline — again one that is very relevant to social psychology — is when a particular problem of one science requires a *partial synthesis* with another.

For instance many problems of psychology, such as the question of how a child acquires the use of language, demand a careful consideration of the very nature of language. This is the sphere of linguistics, and from such sources a synthesis, an interface discipline, has arisen: psycholinguistics. It has already been hinted that this sort of process is a major factor in the emergence of social psychology. Sociology and psychology have problems that require a partial synthesis between them. This shared area has its focus in the study of interaction.

Other processes giving rise to an interface discipline are somewhat less important for social psychology. Sometimes an interface discipline emerges when a body of scientific knowledge begins to be applied to problems that require other specialisms — the *new context* is the major factor. Industrial metallurgy is an instance of this. Again, a discipline might expand to the extent that a *split* occurs. Or a rather *distinct body of knowledge* might be newly generated by a research group, and this becomes accepted as a different discipline. These latter three ways by which interface disciplines can arise may be set aside as far as social psychology is concerned.

From the perspective of this book, the most pertinent reason for the development of social psychology as an interface discipline mediating between psychology and sociology is the need for a partial synthesis of the disciplines in order to conduct detailed analysis of the nature of man as social and the nature of society as human.

It must not be thought that the two aspects of social psychology as an interface discipline can be separated. In order to develop an understanding of the social nature of man which is adequate for the purposes of psychology, the view of this 'social nature' must be sufficiently sophisticated to be tenable sociologically. And at the same time, in developing an account of the human actor in society for the elaboration of sociological theory, the 'humanity' must be defensible psychologically. Thus a social psychology which is built up by scientists who are fully aware of its function as an interface discipline would be expected to be unified, with a single perspective, but 'Janus faced', turned towards both psychology and sociology.

In pursuit of this object, several considerations are immediately apparent. Most important amongst these is the fact that the parent disciplines undoubtedly exert a pull, as it were, on the interface. We may label the assimilative force from the direction of psychology *reductionism,* and that from sociology, *sociological determinism.*

Psychological reductionism, then, is the attempt to treat the objects of social psychological interest in terms of individual psychological processes. Thus, Skinner (1953) analyses the 'social episode' by considering each participant in the interaction in turn, and using the principles of operant conditioning to explain his behaviour. Thus, his reaction to a certain 'stimulus' is taken as being due to earlier experience with 'similar' stimuli. Skinner does not erect any special model to cover the phenomena of social interaction: the laws of individual behaviour can accommodate behaviour in settings where the stimuli and reinforcement come from other people. This view is discussed critically in the next chapter. But the general reductionist approach is not to be summarily rejected.

Sociologists have from time to time advocated the summary rejection of reductionist approaches to social behaviour, simply because they are reductionist. Durkheim (1964) is the classical source: 'Every time that a social phenomenon is directly explained by a psychological phenomenon, we may be sure that the explanation is false'. Lévi-Strauss (1968) invokes this assertion in argument against the reductionism of Homans (1962), a sociological adherent of Skinner's behaviourist school. In defence of Homans, Heath (1976) states the entirely valid argument: 'In assessing an explanation we should first look to see if the conclusion can be derived logically from the premises. If it can. . .our next step is to check whether the premises are factually sound. If our explanation passes both of these tests, then it is very hard to see how it can be rejected. To introduce some third criterion dealing with the character of the premises tells the audience about the nature of one's prejudices but little else' (pp.163f).

Reductionism has been a source of social psychology as an interface discipline. Yet there are dangers in the enterprise. Whorf (1956) took psychologists to task for neglecting those aspects of psychological functioning which are only part of an individual's mental equipment because of his membership of society — especially society as a verbal community. The study of the individual must be aware of social factors in behaviour if it is to be true to the phenomena it intends to explain. Reducing social interaction to the effects of individual psychology stands in danger of neglecting the broader perspective.

In this vein, Moscovici (1972) and Tajfel (1972) are among the large number of recent social psychological writers who have commented on the lack of an understanding generally in social psychology that social interaction takes place within a social and historical context. But unless this is in the forefront of the scientist's awareness, the full meaning of the social psychological processes involved will not be understood — since the actors are inevitably enacting roles which find their meaning in the social structure in which they are embedded.

Husband (1977) has speculated that the use of social psychological concepts by sociologists may tend to be more fruitful than their use by social psychologists, since sociologists are likely to pay attention to the broader context. However, the assimilative force from sociology must now be considered. Sociological determinism is an 'imperialistic' tendency whereby social interaction is seen as roleplaying — the actors being nothing other than exemplars of a certain social category. Here psychology is not considered; rather, explanation of social psychological phenomena is sought in the structure of society. A mental patient, for instance, may be seen as the player of a certain social role. Again, the perspective is not to be immediately dismissed. Indeed, Watt (1963) has argued that the novel, as a realistic account of persons in their diversity, rose historically with the rise of economic individualism, and Bromley (1977) has discussed the possibility that such an ideological source may underly the study of human personality. Thus the effect of individual tendencies ('personality') on interpersonal processes may be quite weak, and the main effects may be due to social and historical factors.

If so, the current concentration by many social psychologists on individual differences and their manifestations in social behaviour may be ideological.

This is speculative. The central issue is that neither social nor individual aspects of interpersonal behaviour should be excluded from consideration merely because of theoretical and methodological biases. In the same way that psychologists have been criticised for neglect of the social, Inkeles (1959) and Wrong (1961) are among the sociologists who have complained of a lack of concern with psychological processes amongst sociologists.

An adequate, 'Janus faced' social psychology, then, requires an awareness in its practitioners both of the social and the individual. This in its turn appears to demand a certain cautiousness in the face of reductionism and sociological determinism.

SOCIAL INTERACTION AND CONSCIOUSNESS

The theme of this book is the consciousness/social interaction nexus. This is a focal concern of social psychology, for it covers both the source in social experience of the individual's awareness of the world, and the way in which social interaction among human beings is patterned through the active participation of conscious social actors.

The sense in which the term 'consciousness' is being used in this book is 'awareness'; the individual's experience of a relation between himself and some 'thing' (which includes the various clusters of notions treated in later chapters, such as thinking; perceiving things, people and self; experiencing emotions and motives, and attributing emotions and motives to others, and holding attitudes). Thus 'states of consciousness' are not our present concern (although the unexplored area of a social psychology of mental states is indeed inviting, cf. Ornstein, 1973).

The relationship between social interaction and consciousness is investigated in the chapters of this book by, firstly, introducing a theoretical framework which, it is claimed, is adequate to the task of structuring our exploration of the area. The chosen theory is symbolic interactionism, which has as central features the notions that human interaction depends on conscious, 'symbolic' functioning, yet that the capacity for symbolic functioning is itself the outcome of very rudimentary interaction in infancy. The account of symbolic interactionism in Chapters 1 and 2 should be read in the light of the views expressed in this Introduction concerning social psychology and its interface position.

In Chapter 3, the place of language use in thinking is discussed. Language is not only a means of communication (and thereby important in interaction); it is also a symbol system basic to human thinking. Thus the relationship between interaction and consciousness is particularly focal in consideration of language behaviour. There is a direct connection between Chapter 3 and Chapters 4 to 8, since in all of them language is found to be a potent influence on the aspects of conscious awareness treated.

Chapters 4 and 5 are concerned with perceiving. A pivotal consideration here is to impress on the reader the idea of perception being in terms of *meanings*. Language as a 'vehicle' of meanings is thus related to perceiving. Objects, other people and self are perceived in terms of categories of which linguistic categories are especially pervasive. Obviously, perceiving is an essential component of social interaction. The attribution of characteristics of personality, etc., guides the process of interpersonal communication.

Chapter 4 treats the perception of emotional states in other people; in Chapter 6 the focus of attention is on awareness of emotional states in oneself. Again, verbal labelling of the emotion is found to be a feature of one's awareness of it. Social factors are paramount in emotional awareness — not only in providing the vocabulary for such labelling, but also in enmeshing the individual in the interpersonal situations which occasion emotional reactions.

Chapter 7 deals with the attribution of motives to other people and to oneself. Scientific theories of motivation are considered less important for our purposes than the study of how we ordinarily commonsensically account for other's actions or our own — since it is supposedly these which guide interaction. In this context, aspects of the theory of 'causal attribution' are outlined, and the social influences on the categories available for accounting for behaviour are discussed.

The treatment of social attitudes has deservedly been a major theme in social psychology — a correct emphasis because individual attitudes concerning social objects seem to provide an approach to the study of the relationship between individual and society. In Chapter 8 this area is reviewed, necessarily selectively. The idea of 'symbol' is not unrelated to the idea of 'attitude' — both notions point to a structuring of awareness which derives from social experience and influences the course of social interaction.

The Conclusion briefly reviews and comments on the preceding material, suggesting that the book takes various conceptual 'packages' (eg 'perceiving') and uses them to 'lift' or isolate certain phenomena out of the total social-psychological context in a life situation, in order to understand that social-psychological context better. But 'perceiving' is not to be understood in isolation. The actual meaning of 'perceiving' is 'existential' — i.e. immersed in ongoing consciousness/social interaction.

The book ends with the suggestion that a developed symbolic interactionist social psychology has connections with recent trends in psychoanalysis, and also that it has a particular affinity with certain types of psychology and sociology.

This book is obviously a most elementary introduction to the topic. But the elementariness is not merely because the book is intended for readers new to social psychology. It is the case that the field of study is relatively undeveloped. Coleridge's words have not yet been outdated, almost all is yet to be achieved.

CHAPTER 1

A Theoretical Framework: Symbolic Interactionism

The chapter opens by summarizing the main arguments of G.H. Mead's approach to social psychology: human interaction depends on symbolic functioning in that one acts on the basis of the meaning ascribed to the behaviour of the other — yet the very capacity for symbolic functioning is regarded as the outcome of interaction, albeit interaction of a limited sort. In childhood, Mead postulates a development from gestural to symbolic interaction.

The implications of the idea of 'symbolic interaction' for the understanding of playing social roles is then discussed, relying not only on Mead's own account, but also on interpretations in the work of M. Natanson, H. Blumer and others. The view of the general nature of society which seems to be demanded by the interactionist approach is discussed.

The following chapter is devoted to various debates about this approach, and is much more detailed than this general outline.

GEORGE H. MEAD: MIND AND SOCIAL INTERACTION

Mead's work is not the only source of interactionism. Among the other writers cited by Meltzer, Petras and Reynolds (1975) in their study of the school of thought are W.I. Thomas and William James (who dealt in an interactionist vein with the 'definition of the situation' as a basis for action, and the social self, respectively). However, his work, especially the book *Mind, Self and Society* (1934), remains the most developed, consistent and insightful body of ideas from which the later interactionists trace their intellectual roots.

In point of fact, the books bearing Mead's name were published after his death and consist of a carefully edited collection of lecture notes, rough drafts of papers and so on. Hence *Mind, Self and Society* is inevitably a repetitive and patchy book, and the newcomer would be advised to begin with secondary sources before reading Mead himself. Such sources include Blumer (1966), Meltzer (1964), Meltzer, Petras and Reynolds (1975), Natanson (1973) —

though perhaps Natanson's approach is rather difficult as an introduction to Mead — and Rose (1962).

Mead (1934) took as his starting point the failure of the various schools of psychology of the time to take account of the relationship between self-conscious mental activity and social interaction. This failure he attributed to the adoption of a false starting-point: psychologists began by assuming that people were capable of self-conscious thought, and then had the task of attempting to explain how social interaction occurred, and also how these mental processes people exhibited in interaction had arisen in the individuals. Mead proposed a very startling alternative approach, that we should not assume mental activity led to interaction, but the reverse: *interaction led to mental activity*. He writes (p. 50): 'If you presuppose the existence of mind at the start, as explaining or making possible the social process of experience, then the origin of minds and the interaction among minds become mysteries. But if, on the other hand, you regard the social process of experience as prior (in a rudimentary form) to the existence of mind and explain the origin of minds in terms of the interaction among individuals within that process, then not only the origin of minds, but also the interaction among minds...cease to seem mysterious or miraculous. Mind arises through communication by a conversation of gestures in a social process or context of experience — not communication through mind'. Thus, society was to be regarded as prior to the development of mental processes in the individual.

The question for Mead now becomes, 'How is it that the human being, the physiological individual, is transformed into a person capable of reflection and also, incidentally, capable of being aware of himself and reflecting on himself?' This takes place, according to Mead, through the 'internalizing' of social interaction (which occurs even at this stage in a rudimentary way by means of 'gestures'). And this internalization is possible through the agency of meaningful symbols — e.g. language.

Now I have just introduced several concepts which require elaboration and definition: gestures, symbols, self and reflection. Reflection is my term, not Mead's. He uses the word *mind* to refer to the ability to reflect on one's actions and those of others and, eventually, to reflect on quite abstract acts such as possible modes of attack on a mathematical problem. So mind is a process for Mead, not a structure vaguely associated with the brain — which is the general use of the word. Mind takes place through the use of meaningful, or *'significant' symbols* by which, for instance, outer reality may be represented. *Self* is also a process for Mead. It partly refers to the capacity adult human beings have of thinking about their own actions and thereby drawing conclusions about 'me' — the author of the actions. *Gestures* are the basic communicative elements in interaction prior to the development of mind and the concomitant ability to regulate behaviour symbolically. These terms will be developed more clearly in looking at Mead's theory.

Prior to the development of mind, interaction takes place. Yet this is of a rudimentary, gestural form: it is non-symbolic interaction (Blumer, 1966). At this level, individuals may participate in a social activity using the early stages of each other's actions as 'gestures' (Wundt's concept) which are guides to the nature of the act as a whole and cause action in other participants leading to the completion of the act. These gestures in a sense are meaningful symbols of the acts of which they are early fragments, and presumably the apparently cooperative but stereotyped social activity of animals are guided throughout by such gestures. By way of illustration, Mead gives the particular example of a dog fight. In preparing to attack the other dog, one adopts the posture of readiness to spring at the other's throat. The attacked dog's response is to change position in some way, maybe to adopt a stance of readiness for counter attack. There is a 'conversation of gestures', a piece of gesturing by one dog being the stimulus for a reply in the form of a responding gesture from the other.

Mead points out that, in the conversation of gestures, imitation is not involved. The one dog does not mimic the bodily attitude of the other, but rather adopts a different stance in the making of a response to the attacking move. Neither is an imaginative adoption of the role of the other attempted and used to understand the intention of the other dog in making the attacking gesture. Rather the response is a direct one, called forth by the original gesture.

In this example, Mead tries to show that the dog fight is not interaction in the human sense. A dog does not imagine what response its gesturing will bring forth in the other dog. To bring this idea out more clearly: suppose a team of dogs were taught to play a game akin to football — what sort of performance would they put up? Mead would say that animals would certainly have no tactical sense. Behaviour like passing a dummy ball would be impossible, because it requires the player to imagine the response that a gesture will bring out, and then act in a way deliberately to mislead. To imagine means to be able to understand the role expectations of the other. This dogs cannot do, Mead claims. Dog footballers would merely run all over the pitch — the stimulus provided by the behaviour of the one dog calling forth a relatively automatic response in the others.

Such activity is not indicative of mind, in Mead's sense. For the individuals to be consciously-communicating selves, the individuals must be able to interpret the meaning of their gestures for the other individuals, and choose their actions in terms of such meanings. This is possible in human interaction of an adult, conscious type, by means of internal use of 'significant symbols', of language. Mind is the presence in behaviour of significant symbols, internalized as an inner forum within which thought goes on by assuming the roles of others and controlling behaviour in terms of such role-taking.

The distinction between the 'conversation of gestures' of animals and the symbolic interaction of adult humans is clearly drawn by Mead. Rose (1962a) and Lindesmith, Strauss and Denzin (1975) are among those interactionists who point out that man 'lives in a symbolic environment' — he does not act in terms of automatic response to stimuli, but on the basis of the meanings the environmental circumstances have for him. Mead also points out that people actively organize their perception of the world, *presupposing* the meanings that they intend to encounter. He writes (countering the viewpoint of a forerunner of Skinner): 'Spencer conceived of the central nervous system as being continually played upon by stimuli which set up certain paths, so that it was the environment which was fashioning the form...[However] our attention enables us to organise the field in which we are going to act. Here we have the organism as acting and determining its environment. It is not simply a set of passive senses played upon by stimuli that come from without. The organism goes out and determines what it is going to respond to, and organises that world. One organism picks out one thing and another picks out a different one, since it is going to act in a different way' (pp 24f).

Clearly, Mead's model of man is cognitive, picturing as he does a being who actively organizes his perception of the world, and acts on the basis of the meanings of the objects and events encountered. And as far as interaction is concerned, it is not a matter of responding directly to the activities of others. Rather it involves such phenomena as responding to the inferred future *intentions* of others. All this, of course, involves 'mind'.

Prior to the development of mind, interaction is a conversation of gestures. After mind has developed in the child, interaction can be symbolic — based on mutual interpretations of the meanings of each other's actions, and having a continuous mental representation, so that my talk can continually be monitored by me, and a choice can be made between alternative possible things to say. We have the 'before' and 'after' situations: How is non-symbolic interaction transformed into symbolic interaction?

The early stage of development of the child involves interaction with parents, etc., at the level of a *conversation of gestures*. Note that it is incorrect to conclude from what has gone before that gestures are equivalent to non-verbal behaviour and speech is required for significant symbolic functioning. Clearly in the case of a parrot, the words spoken are meaningless, whereas when an adult human being talks 'he is saying it to himself as well as to everybody else within reach of his voice' (Mead, 1934, p.67). So the first stage of development towards symbolic interaction comes when the child begins to internalize the conversation of gestures; for instance this is beginning when he slaps his own hand when about to open the biscuit barrel. Here we have a *significant gesture*. Natanson (1973): 'The significant gesture involves two fundamental elements: first, the individual making the significant gesture places himself in the position of the individual to whom the gesture is addressed; second, from the point of view of the other, the individual then regards the content of his own gesture' (p. 8). In the case of the child slapping himself when tempted, the process of development has obviously gone far enough for the child to be able to act both roles — the person addressed in the gesture and the person making the significant gesture.

Thus significant gestures are attained. The process of *internalization* moves ahead now, so that the child develops through the stage when he converses externally with himself (exhibiting behaviour such as slapping himself to control anticipated action) to the stage where the conversation of significant gestures can be carried out entirely mentally. The child is now able to consider possible actions and their consequences prior to acting, and for this purpose the use of language as a system of significant symbols is vital. (It ought to be pointed out here that Mead tends to treat spoken-and-heard language as *the* example of a system of significant symbols, but that the term 'language' in Mead must be understood broadly as indicating any form of symbolic interpersonal communication.)

Language (in this broad sense) has many attributes which show its instrumentality in both internal and external conversation: words and other units of communication symbolize events and objects and thus these can be referred to and thought about even when out of sight (or when entirely imaginary); the language is shared so internal thought and external communication can exactly match; the grammatical structure of a language allows the possibility of thought-manipulations of events and actions in a unique sense, and so on (Chapter 3 elaborates on these facts and introduces others).

Language use involves mind, and with the development of *symbolic interaction* through internalization of the conversation of significant gestures, mind also evolves. Hence the original argument of Mead that mind does not precede, but results from interaction. And also, very importantly, awareness of self results from the same process. Although much of Chapter 5 is devoted to the development of self, it must be noted here that there is additional evidence about the development of mind to be gleaned from a study of Mead's account of the growth of self during childhood.

MEAD: SOCIETY AND SOCIAL ROLES

What, then, are the essential characteristics of human social interaction? Blumer (1962) writes: 'Human beings interpret or define each other's actions instead of merely reacting to each other's actions. Their response is not made directly to the actions of one another but instead is based on the meaning which they attach to such actions. Thus, human interaction is mediated by the use of symbols, by interpretation, or by ascertaining the meaning of one another's actions' (p. 180).

Symbolic interaction involves, not responding to physical stimuli emanating from the other person merely, but interpreting the meaning of their actions and in turn acting in a way that one believes will be interpreted in a certain way by the other. One monitors one's own actions and can check a particular action and replace it with a better alternative — bearing in mind the meaning that the other will read into it. Similarly, these capacities allow one to lie (acting in a way that the other, you expect, will interpret in a certain way which you believe to be false), and — as we saw earlier — also allow the possibility of acting 'tactically'.

In all this, a key analytical concept is *taking the role of the other*. In the example I have referred to of a child attempting to control his behaviour by slapping himself, taking the role of the other is quite explicit. But also in everyday interaction with real other people we act in terms of the meaning we expect them, from their perspective, to infer from our behaviour. This imaginative act is taking the role of the other. Within a quite different tradition of social psychology, G.A. Kelly (1955) has an exactly parallel view of role enactment. It involves, he says, 'construing the construction processes of the other' — imagining the process of interpretation that they will go through, given their different point of view.

Mead began with the fact that social roles are *there;* interaction takes place, and this involves roleplaying. M. Natanson (1972) and T. Sarbin (1954) have, in their different ways developed some of the esential characteristics of social roles. For instance, Sarbin argues that '...taking the role of the other is not possible without the *as if* ability' that human beings have (p. 236). Consciousness must be capable of the organization necessary to develop hypotheses and use these, acting as if they were true. Presumably this characteristic of roleplaying is an aspect of mind, and is dealt with by Mead.

Natanson points out that, not only has consciousness to be organized in a certain way that allows role-playing, society, too, is organized in such a way that particular roles are 'playable': 'That I am able to take the role of judge means that both social and psychological aspects of reality permit me to stand outside of myself, to represent the law, to fulfill a set of complex obligations in a typified manner' (p. 226). By 'permitted' here, Natanson means that, for instance, the society has a legal system including the role of judge and that it provides that suitable people may set aside whatever might be their own standpoint and act as if purely 'judges' — and that such behaviour is understood as a mode of legitimate action by others in the society. This involves: (1) Historicity — roles are *not* to be viewed as the spontaneous creation of individuals at a given time, but the culmination of a long development (this as against some ahistorical representations of symbolic interactionism criticized by Lichtman, 1970; Meltzer, Petras and Reynolds, 1975, among others); (2) Intersubjectivity — as suggested earlier in the discussion of the emergence of significant gestures, the possibility that one can act in such-and-such a manner must be understood by all concerned: there must be shared understanding; (3) Identity — there must also be an understanding that, in any instance, a person 'may distinguish between his idiosyncratic needs and preferences and the requirements of a formal role' (pp. 227f). In a way, this last factor is part of the *as if* ability. All understand that the individual can 'step back' from the role, and inspect it from another vantage point. Natanson's discussion does no more than make explicit some of the background assumptions of Mead's approach.

Mead's cognitive emphasis in his treatment of role-playing has several important repercussions, and leads in particular to an approach to social roles which is rather different to that normally adopted in sociology and social psychology. The usual view of role-playing is that the person experiences his role as pregiven by society, and performs in accordance with its prescriptions — role determines behaviour (Urry, 1970). This view pictures society as a structure of roles, people acting in passive conformity to the roles in which they are found (Turner, 1962). As against this, an interactionist interpretation of role-playing would emphasize that it is a *process*, constructed by the mutual interpretations involved when each takes the role of the other consciously into account in devising a line of action. As Blumer (1966) points out, roles are important, not as social categories which determine behaviour, but as cognitive categories which enter into the process of interpretation and definition out of which joint action arises.

Within the interactionist understanding of role, the 'minded' individual is characterized as able to be aware of what they are doing and to control and modify their actions thereby (Harré and Secord, 1972). Moreover, the very fact that people can do social science, 'stepping back' and inspecting the process of role-playing, indicates the human capacity to monitor the act of monitoring behaviour. (A certain form of this ability is what Goffman has treated under the rubric of 'role distancing' — where, for instance, the person outwardly enacts a role but wishes to indicate to others that he is not to be fully identified with the role, and subtly mocks the role: a child of a particular age who rides the fairground roundabout sitting backwards on the horse; the lecturer who has to discipline a student whom he regards as of an age when such a disciplinary situation is unwarranted, and who adopts a tone of voice which indicates 'what I am having to say is only a form-of-words'.) The social-structural view of role precludes discussion of such phenomena (cf. Linton, 1945, for the classic source on the structural view), although for purely sociological purposes it may be that the structural approach has its uses — as in the study of role conflict between, let us say, professional groups with overlapping spheres of interest.

Unfortunately it is possible even for interactionist authors to revert to a structural view of role whereby societal action results in individuals conforming to role. For instance Rotenberg (1974) points this out in Becker's (1963) 'labelling theory' of deviance, in which certain actions are socially designated as deviant — resulting in a particular probable future career for the individual — while other forms of behaviour are not specifically designated in this way (e.g. the difference in the treatment of male homosexuality and lesbianism up to the present time). Rotenberg's point is that, whilst it is no doubt correct to view deviant behaviour as in some sense labelled by society at large, and that deviant behaviour is treated as such as a consequence of such societal reaction, nevertheless the individual and his mental activity is left out of Becker's theory. The individual may or may not accept the categorization of his activities: the process of 'self-labelling' deserves treatment. In general we may say that Becker is covertly re-introducing a structural view of role.

Mead's approach is one which does not set role-playing apart, but 'at the mid-point of everyday routine in which roles and roletakers are, in the language of Alfred Schutz [1962], simply taken for granted' (Natanson, 1972, p. 223). This is a further repercussion of the interactionist view of role. This emphasis on the absolutely natural human necessity for role-taking as a skill that is essential for social interaction to take place at all is very different from the pejorative language which is often used to make role-playing appear abnormal, fraudulent, inauthentic in character. Sartre (1958) regards role-playing as inauthentic — a means by which the individual, by acting a role, assumes a sort of identity which is merely a mask covering his essential freedom to act in any way he chooses not just in ways in keeping with the role. In an odd way Goffman (1969), though writing within an interactionist tradition, and regarding role-taking as an essential element of social life, nevertheless adopts a style that makes role-playing appear inauthentic, calculating. When Goffman's subjects weep, they are doing so in the context of a self-display. Their emotion is not described with an air of reality: they weep crocodile tears. In contrast, as Natanson (1972, p. 220) writes: 'Perhaps the major motif in Mead's account of role is his insistence on the necessity and desirability of taking roles..., a process which is as vital to the genesis of human beings as language is. Further, role taking is desirable because it enables the individual to advance beyond provinciality, to sophisticate his life by learning to see things from variant perspectives. Finally, for Mead, there is a humanising dimension to role taking, for through the kind of empathy roles demand, we are able to appreciate each other more fully and to understand the needs of larger communities of human organization in the realms of politics, history and law'.

How do the concepts of symbolic interactionism, especially role-taking, affect our view of society? 'Human society as we know it could not exist without minds and selves, since all its most characteristic features presuppose the possession of minds and selves by its individual members; but its individual members would not possess minds and selves if these had not arisen within or emerged out of the human social process in its lower stages of development — those stages at which it was merely the resultant of, and wholly dependant on, the physiological differentiations and demands of the individual organisms implicated in it' (Mead, 1934, p. 227).

Blumer (1966) points out two important elements of the concept of symbolic interaction — interaction where, as we have seen, the individual interprets a significant gesture and acts on the basis of its meaning. The first is that, in contrast to the usual approaches — psychology accounting for interaction in terms of reinforcement or motives, and sociology referring to structural pressures such as social roles — in the scheme of symbolic interaction, the participants have to build up their respective lines of conduct by constant interpretation of each other's ongoing acts. The second important element of the symbolic interaction concept is that human group life takes on the character of an ongoing process. Established patterns of group life exist and persist only through the continued use of the same schemes of interpretation;

and such schemes are maintained only through their continued confirmation by the defining acts of others.

In an earlier paper, Blumer (1962) points out that 'sociological thought rarely...treats human societies as composed of individuals who have selves. Instead, they assume human beings to be merely organisms with some kind of organisation, responding to forces which play upon them' (pp. 184 f). This is a similar point to that of Wrong (1961) whose work was mentioned in the Introduction. However, note must be taken of the dual nature of the relationship between the individual and society: society is a precondition for the emergence of mind and self, so interactionism cannot be reductionist, even if (on the other hand) social processes are possible only insofar as individuals engage in significant communication.

Natanson (1973, p. 17) points out the impact of the preexisting social situation: 'Born into a world he did not create, destined to live and die under the shadow of institutions and social structures he did not order, and, finally, reared within the limitations of a language or of languages taught to him by elders, the individual cannot be held "responsible" for the objective situation in which he finds himself as a human being living among other human beings in societal reality.'

CHAPTER 2

Elaborations and Criticisms of Mead's Position

In this chapter, both empirical findings and theoretical refinements are discussed in the attempt to elaborate Mead's basic position, and thereby mark out lines of defence against various criticisms. The material is arranged under three heads:

1. *Conversation of gestures, in which empirical work in developmental psychology which has a bearing on the sketchy account of the transformation from gestural to symbolic interaction given by Mead is paraded.*

2. *Defining the situation, where the notion of W.I. Thomas which has so central a place in contemporary interactionism is discussed. This discussion centres about the ambiguity of interactionist treatment of determinism, and the problem of the place of history, social structure and power in the interactionist account of everyday social experience.*

3. *Mead as a 'social behaviorist', in which a comparison between Mead and behaviourist psychologists enables the approach of interactionist social psychology to be further elucidated.*

This chapter, taken together with the previous one, is designed to specify a theoretical framework within which to locate the various arguments of later chapters concerning the relationship between social interaction and awareness.

CONVERSATION OF GESTURES

Mead's distinction between gestural interaction, based on a 'reflex' reaction to the movement of the other (which is taken as a sign of the completed act), and symbolic interaction, in which the actor is capable of formulating the intention of the other and framing an action with that in mind, is of course insufficiently detailed to be considered a full-blown theory of this aspect of child development. There are many questions unanswered. However, research in developmental psychology over the past decade indicates that Mead's viewpoint is substantially accurate. The outline he provided no doubt glosses over some complications — in particular the child seems to be a real

16

participant in interaction very early on so that the distinction between gestural and symbolic interaction may be too strictly drawn. Yet Mead's thought on the development of mind and interaction constitutes, all in all, a magnificent speculation, justified by empirical evidence which has only become available some forty years after his death. We shall review some of this evidence now. (For detailed accounts see Lewis and Rosenblum, 1974; Schaffer, 1971, 1977 a,b; Stern, 1977.)

The emphasis of recent research has been on the child's earliest development as proceeding through experiences of interaction with (usually primarily) his mother. The infant is viewed as an active participant, even from the earliest days, in such interaction. It appears that the infant is in some ways biologically prepared for rudimentary interaction, as indeed would be required by Mead's view that gestural interaction is within the infant's capacity at a very young age.

Early capacities of the infant

Mead presented gestural interaction as simple. Perhaps this is relatively true, in that symbolic interaction is far more complex. Yet, carefully considered, the conversation of gestures demands an extensive set of capacities, which the child must presumably be innately equipped to acquire.

Richards (1971) is among a number of authors who have pointed out that phasing of interaction seems to require a rhythmical sensitivity. It was made plain earlier by Lashley (1951) that any sort of serially-ordered behaviour (e.g. 'the control of trotting and pacing in a gaited horse') could not be explained in terms of the effect of sequences of external stimuli. He postulated an innate rhythmic capacity — a set of internal oscillators which would be linked to the control of the serial behaviour.

In the earliest mother-infant interaction, such serial ordering occurs at several levels, not only in the behaviour of the infant viewed merely as individual behaviour unrelated to the mother's activity (e.g. crying), but also in his behaviour when seen as part of an interaction with her. Richards notes that the temporal phasing of each partner's behaviour is central to the growth of mother-infant interaction. The mother phases in her contributions with the activity of the infant; but rhythmic capacity in the infant seems a prerequisite for his own development of the ability to 'converse gesturally'.

Evidence for the existence of rhythmic sensitivity is provided by Condon and Sander (1974), who found that even in the first days of life, the baby moves in 'precise and sustained segments of movement' in time with adult speech patterns. All sixteen infants studied showed this behaviour, and most were only a day old. Condon and Sander suggest that this might help to explain the extremely perplexing problem of language acquisition. Considering the fact that *speech* patterns are perceived in this way by the infant, it is indeed suggestive that the child seems innately primed for sensing gross linguistic patterning. But the more general consideration is that detection of rhythms is within the neonate's capacity.

The infant finds himself in a rhymthic world, then, and has at least one of the prerequisite skills for moving in a serially-ordered way in it. Trevarthen (1977) finds that infant movements are indeed temporally regulated, and that the basic elements of limb movement are comparable to those of adults. He sees no reason for not attributing 'intentions to move in a controlled manner' to infants. However, this demands that the child also sees the world as a spatial unity. One cannot move in a controlled manner without somehow being aware of a unified space within which all body parts act. Trevarthen argues that the fact of controlled movement is evidence of such awareness, and also that this fact is evidence that the various senses are all taken by the child as providing information about one unified world — the same world as that within which movement occurs. Separate studies confirm Trevarthen's view. Aronson and Rosenbloom (1971) found that infants as young as thirty days exhibited signs of distress when they were subjected to a discrepancy between sight and sound, seeing their mother talking in one place while the apparent location of the voice is elsewhere. Auditory and visual information is about a common space. (This concords with the view expressed in Chapter 4 that perception does not take place by means of the analysis and integration of sense data from the separate senses. Even at one month of age, a child is using the senses as concerted perceptual systems for gleaning meaningful information about the world.)

Beyond the elementary awareness of temporal and spatial features of the world, recent research has led to the general acceptance (Collis, 1977) that the very young infant attends selectively to the sort of stimuli that come typically from human beings. In particular, the face is of early interest.

Fantz (1961) found evidence that preference for faces could be demonstrated in infants as young as one week old. His experimental studies compared the time babies spent viewing a schematic face (black features painted on a pink card of face size and shape), with the time spent looking at 'scrambled' and 'control' faces (the one having the features moved about the card so as to lack 'faceness'; the other merely having a black area at the top of the card equal in size to the sum of the features on the other cards). The preferences found in his study were particularly marked in the third month of life. The control card excited least interest, and there was a small preference for the face over the scrambled card. However, there is conflicting evidence as to the precise age at which this discrimination can be observed (Koopman and Ames, 1968; Fantz and Nevis, 1967; Haaf and Bell, 1967). There is also a question which remains unanswered as to whether the Fantz phenomenon is explained by the fact that the face combined a number of simple stimuli to which the infant is biologically primed, or whether 'faceness' itself involves something other than an amalgam of stimuli for the infant (Haaf and Bell, 1967; Schaffer, 1971; Stern, 1977). Despite these outstanding matters, the very early responsiveness of the infant to the face is not in dispute. Early patterns of behaviour such as crying, smiling and looking are also contributed by the infant to interaction. Wolff (1969) has shown that crying is actually a set of distinct signals, which the mother is intuitively able to distinguish. A basic pattern indicative of such factors as hunger is differentiable from the angry cry and the pain cry in terms of rhythm, suddenness and intensity of onset, and overall pattern. Here again we have evidence of controlled serially-ordered behaviour. But the control is not at first conscious: early on, crying is elicited almost automatically in given circumstances, and it is the action of the mother in endowing the cry with meaning that enables the child to use it as an intentional signal later.

Smiling is, similarly, a 'reflex' initially. Spitz (1946) showed that the face could elicit smiling. But recent work indicates that more elementary stimuli are sufficient early on. The eye configuration seems to be crucial in the first two months, and gradually other features of the face become necessary for smiling. The effect of the train of development is that there is an initial stage in which smiling does not seem to be reliably linked to any particular visual stimulus; later, faces in general will serve; and after seven months or so, only actual, familiar faces will elicit a smile. Thereafter, of course, smiling becomes a part of the infant's repertoire of conscious signals.

Greatest interest has been aroused in the last decade or so by the study of patterns of looking, and particularly by the process of interaction between mother and infant as reflected in the child's looks, glances and gaze. This behaviour develops towards a conversational mode of interaction, and we shall consider it is those terms after reminding ourselves of the contribution of the mother to early interaction.

Mother behaviour towards the infant

Although much of the mother's contribution to the interaction is best mentioned in discussion of mother-infant interaction rather than as separate phenomena, Stern (1977) points out what is self-evident: the behaviour of the adult to an infant is very different from their behaviour to other adults. To rehearse the most manifest points of difference is instructive.

Facial expressions elicited by the infant tend to be exaggerated, both temporally and spatially, and limited in repertoire. Stern suggests that there are only five common expressions exhibited by the mother for the benefit of the child: mock surprise, smile, concern-and-sympathy, frown, and the neutral, expressionless face. The four active expressions are displayed almost in slow motion, very distinctly. Consider the mock surprise expression as an example. Here, the catching of the infant's attention may occasion an expression where the eyes are opened wide, the brows raised, mouth opened (though this element varies), head raised and slightly tilted. And the mother may say 'oooooh'.

Stern further suggests that the five expressions are signals which regulate early mother-infant interactions. Mock surprise initiating contact — marking the event; maintenance of the interaction is performed by head movement and the smile or concern-and-sympathy face; frown may mark the momentary termination of interaction. The neutral face, combined with gaze aversion under certain circumstances, serves to avoid interaction, as when the infant is sucking during feeds. This analysis of Stern's is in line with Bruner's (1977a) insistence on the centrality of the marking of social episodes for the learning of their rule structure. Doubtless it can also be viewed as illustrating the earliest approximation to gestural interaction, with the infant's contribution apparently limited to signals interpretable by others as registering attention or a switch of attention away from them.

Adult vocalizations (which are mentioned in greater detail later in the context of language acquisition) are of a particular type in interaction with infants. Baby talk (Ferguson, 1964, 1969; Snow, 1972, for instance) is simplified in certain ways, repetitive, with short utterance length and including nonsense sounds. Again we find exaggeration, but particularly of gross characteristics such as vowel length, pitch (a falsetto is typically adopted), and the overall 'contour' of the utterance — with marked crescendos, diminuendos and glissandos. The function of this behaviour in the mother's interaction with the child is possibly to emphasize the contour of the utterance, since it is argued (Bruner, 1977a) that the overall shape of, say, a demand utterance is distinct from an interrogative utterance, and the child may perceive this feature and use such contours as matrices within which to site words.

The mother's behaviour is apparently perceived as a whole by the infant — the work of Aronson and Rosenbloom (1971) shows that this is likely. Moreover, Tronick (see Stern, 1977) and Tatum and Murray (cited in Trevarthen, 1977) have shown that infants are distressed by maternal behaviour when the mother alternates normal and deadpan expressions, or acts paradoxically in other ways.

Aspects of mother-infant interaction

Robson (1967) has singled out eye contact as especially significant in mediating maternal response to the infant. Let us consider at this point patterns of glances and gaze in the infant-mother interaction, and the significance of these in indicating a line of development in gestural interaction.

Visual fixation and following are among the very first actions which are subject to the control of the infant. As we have seen, Fantz (1961) and later authors concerned with the infant's attraction to the face have been able to use the length of visual fixation as an index of interest in even the very young child. But it is during the second month that perception of the face and control of fixation is such that the mother suddenly becomes aware of an apparent change in the quality of the relationship that is due to the child being able to fixate on her eyes, and holding the fixation with eyes widening and brightening (Stern, 1977; Robson, 1967). In addition, the smiling response follows quickly on the development of mutual gaze.

Simmel (1969) pointed out the importance of mutual gaze in signalling affiliation, and this is the meaning with which mothers endow the event (although there are alternative interpretations of gaze, e.g. as signalling dominance: Sartre, 1958). It is to be underlined that it is the mother's interpretation of gaze that it signifies an affectionate bond. On the side of the infant it is the unfolding of a biological programme of development, albeit one which is meshed with a social environment which, doubtless, occasioned its evolution. This is a typical maternal activity — to give a social meaning to the actions of the infant, and thereby to set up situations for him which have the structure (though not yet for him the meaning) of social interaction.

By the fourth month of life, the visual-motor system is functionally mature, allowing voluntary control of gaze and following on a par with the capacity of adults (Robson, 1967; Jaffe, Stern and Peery, 1973). The development of so important a sensory-motor system at so early a stage in life is only paralleled by sucking (Stern, 1971). At this point mutual gaze seems to signal reciprocal attachment for both members of the dyad, not just the mother. Indeed, Peery and Stern (1976), on analysing videotapes of interactions between mother and child found that the statistical properties of eye contact events were such as to allow the implication to be drawn that gaze at this stage has the same significance as it does in adult interaction.

If the conclusions of these various authors are sound, patterns of gaze may be expected to have wide consequences in the mother-infant conversation of gestures. Some evidence that this is indeed so is provided by Robson (1967), who reports individual differences in infants in eye contact patterns. However his suggestion that this affects the interaction between mother and child, though highly likely, is only supported by anecdote. In contrast, Stern (1971) presents a detailed study of the interaction of a mother and her twins, in which the basis of analysis is a frame-by-frame breakdown of filmed sequences made from videotapes. The interest in this study lies in the fact that the mother-child interactions were of a different type in the two cases. In the one case, with Mark, the interaction proceeds smoothly; in the other, with Fred, the mother's behaviour is described by Stern as insensitive overstimulation, which did not take sufficient note of the infant's behaviour and attempt to attribute wants or see the childs behaviour as reactions to her own.

These discriptions of the apparent situation were substantiated by the analysis of the videotapes. Mark typically held the face-to-face position five times as long as Fred. The two participants in the Mark-mother interaction were equally likely to terminate exchange by averting the head whereas this was done nine times as frequently by Fred than his mother. When placed facing away from mother, Fred turned back to face her more frequently than did Mark. Apart from these observations of general tendencies in interaction, Stern detected patterns in the interaction process itself. There appeared to be a difference in infant responsiveness to maternal movements such that the mother acted in an 'overstimulating' way to Fred to produce the required reaction. But at the same time, the mother seemed to need more cuing from Fred, for example to register a termination of interaction. Overall, Stern concluded that the maternal behaviour which seemed 'controlling' and 'overstimulating' might profitably be viewed as mutual, interactive event. It was not possible to decide whether individual differences between the twins were responsible for the patterns of interaction, or whether differences in attitude of the mother towards them might account for the tendencies.

In a follow-up of the twins in his study, Stern (1971) found that Fred was more dependent on his mother than Mark, suggesting that, at least in that case, a disturbance of early interaction had had an effect on behaviour. Here Stern's work links with that of Bennett (1971), who suggests that a characteristic of the infant, or even a transitory piece of behaviour, may lead adults to attribute a 'personality' to the child. There are tendencies such as alertness, patterns of gaze, facial movements, activity level, which may indeed be affected by styles of interaction set up by adults under the guidance of personality attributions. Bennett presents case studies in which such a sequence of events seemed to have occurred, and it might be that Stern's observations were of a part of a process of this sort.

Gaze patterns have been studied, not merely as elements in gestural interaction, but also because of the light that could be shed by such studies on the development of symbolic interaction. Thus, Jaffe, Stern and Peery (1973) have drawn an analogy between patterns of mother-infant gaze and the structure of adult verbal interaction, to the extent that verbal interaction may be facilitated by prior experience of glancing. This form of argument is quite widespread amongst psychologists interested in the precursors of symbolic interaction. Exchanging glances is like exchange of talk — *turn-taking* is a skill which is surely required in more developed forms of interaction, and so practice at turn-taking using capacities that might be acquired as the result of an unfolding biological programme, could prepare the child for talk.

Kaye (1977) has similarly argued that the burst-pause sequence in sucking in the earliest months of infancy might be a basis of the turn-taking sequence in dialogue. Studied as a dyadic performance, feeding is structurally akin to talking. Mothers tend to jiggle babies during pauses in feeding in the belief, opposed by experimental evidence, that this keeps them awake and elicits a resumption of sucking. The evidence is that pauses are actually longer if jiggling occurs. The pause is not a pause for breath, nor is it a sign of fatigue. Kaye suggests that pauses are 'designed' to elicit a response from the mother, so the interaction has the conversational form: baby sucks while mother waits, then baby pauses while mother jiggles baby or bottle or taps the infant's feet, etc.

Perhaps the most direct approach to the study of the genesis of turn-taking as the conversational form in earliest infancy is to observe the pattern of vocalizations during gestural interaction. Bateson (1975) presents some evidence for such turn-taking in interactions with infants of seven to fifteen weeks. Interestingly, it was also found that the time for one utterance to follow another was faster when the 'floor' had been exchanged (mother followed by child or vice-versa) than when one speaker was following his own utterance.

This perhaps further indicates the expectation of turn-taking. (Further evidence on this is provided by Stern, Jaffe, Beebe and Bennett, 1975.)

Schaffer, Collis and Parsons (1977) discovered that vocalizing was linked with looking behaviour in twenty-three to twenty-seven months old. In this study, the pattern of glances and the pattern of vocalizing supported each other in setting up a sequence of turn-taking/floor exchange similar to that observed in adult interaction (see Chapter 4). By the age of two then, the structure of conversational, symbolic interaction seems to be established.

From action sequences to symbolic interaction

Of course, turn-taking is not a prerequisite of symbolic interaction alone; even at the level of the conversation of gestures turn-taking is part of the structure. Thus the research reported above is in line with the idea that, in gestural interaction can be seen the formal precursors of symbolic interaction but without symbolic functioning.

Development from gesture to symbol appears to be facilitated by the action of adults, who frame gestural interaction with the child in such a way that it has a formal structure which is sufficiently similar to that of symbolic interaction to allow for the assimilation of, and accommodation to symbolic functioning when it emerges. No, indeed, more than this, there appears to develop within gestural interaction a formal structure that itself facilitates symbolic functioning (Bruner, 1977a). Such a view has been expressed by Newson (1977; also J. and E. Newson, 1975), writing that interaction is to be seen as 'an attempt by the mother to enter into a *meaningful* set of exchanges with her infant, despite the fact that she herself will often be aware that the semantic element in any resulting communication lies more in her own imagination than in the mental experience of her baby' (p. 47, his emphasis). Thus the mother organizes her own activity so as to impose an interactive framework on the behaviour of the child. However, as we have seen, the child is biologically primed to enter into such a structure with a relevant set of behaviours to contribute.

We now have to consider the evidence bearing on the processes by which gestural interaction elaborates into symbolic functioning. Schutz (1962, 1972; Ashworth, 1977) attempted to provide an account of the presuppositions which must be made by the participants if social interaction is to proceed. It can be argued that such understandings must either be already available to the infant, or emerge in gestural interaction, for symbolic interaction to emerge.

One root assumption is that the world including the world of social interaction is meaningful. The evidence on temporal and spatial expectations in the very young infant suggests that this assumption is part of the infant's basic endowment. Thus the mother's attempt to structure interaction with the infant so as to be meaningful, even if this is only effective in producing a certain orderliness in the experience of the child, does at least meet with a biological being for whom orderliness and chaos are different. Stern, Beebe,

Jaffe and Bennett (1977) have commented that the mother provides a highly ordered 'stimulus world' for the infant, and they (and Schaffer, 1977b) indicate some of the strategies of ordering which are used.

A further presupposition for interaction discussed by Schutz is intersubjectivity. The world is not experienced as private to the individual who is experiencing it, but rather as common to all of us. Thus the child must come to take it for granted that others are confronted with the same world as he is. Moreover, he must therefore understand that he and the other person can observe the same object, and have the same thing in mind. A cognate presupposition is the existence of other minds: the child must take it for granted that others are minded beings like himself. This Schutz terms the 'general thesis of the alter ego'.

Along with intersubjectivity and the general thesis of the alter ego, Schutz discusses 'reciprocity of perspectives'. Although the objects and events of the world are all part of our common world, it must be understood that each individual perceives then from his own point of view. Not only from his own spatial point of view, but also from his distinct mental vantage point, brought about by his unique experience. However, just as one assumes that a person can walk to the place where another stood and will see what is for all practical purposes the same scene, so reciprocity of mental perspectives is possible. There is interchangeability of standpoints. Actual interchange depends, of course, on interaction through shared typifications, particularly language. The assumption of reciprocity of perspectives is an essential prerequisite for interaction. This perhaps becomes clearer still when we see that reciprocity of perspectives entails the assumption that cooperative action can be accomplished. If it were not for the assumption of reciprocity of perspectives, playing roles in social situations would be inconceivable because each would be locked in his biographically-determined situation with his own incommunicable viewpoint, and could not therefore imagine the standpoint of the other (cf. Mead, 1934).

If the assumption of meaningfulness is to some extent available to the infant, it is less clear that intersubjectivity and reciprocity of perspectives are. The general thesis of the alter ego is possibly less problematic: it may be conjectured that the infant has no choice but to assume the alter-ego-ness of his adult caretakers who adopt the dominant role and take the initiative in so many aspects of his life.

Bearing in mind, then, not only Mead's characterization of symbolic interaction, but also Schutz's notions of intersubjectivity and reciprocity of perspectives, let us now consider the recent work dealing with the way the infant begins to participate in symbolic interaction. The infant has experience of sequences of gestural interaction, structured especially in terms of turn-taking.

Imitative behaviour (Pawlby, 1977) would seem to be an extension of gestural interaction, and it appears to be a very frequent occurrence. In interactions between mothers and infants of seventeen to forty-three weeks old, Pawlby found that it occupied 16% of interaction time on average. Initially, mothers tended to act the role of imitator, but infants increased in imitative skill during this age range. Imitation of sounds was more prevalent than imitation of facial gestures, but the latter did occur. Pawlby suggests that there is some evidence here for intersubjectivity (in that there seems to be a shared understanding of events which is recognized by the infant to be shared). Possibly the assumption of the alter ego and reciprocity of perspectives are involved in this behaviour as well.

Intersubjectivity is central to the work of Collis (1977; Collis and Schaffer, 1975). He points out that, although the very earliest interaction merely involves the two participants themselves, soon the objects of the environment constitute a source of interest for the child. The adult now must make use of, and participate in, the child's flow of attention amongst these objects. Collis and Schaffer showed that the mother monitors the direction of gaze of the infant, and interacts with the child in terms of their shared focus — thus intersubjective understanding is developed in the context of the mother continually showing the infant that she has the same thing in mind as he. At the same time the mother is likely to comment on, especially to name, the object of their joint attention. Note that at this stage what is for the child gestural interaction (if it can be even said to reach this level) is for the mother symbolic interaction — she is very directly concerned with taking the attitude of the other.

Later, the child begins to intentionally direct others' attention to the objects that concern him. This clearly depends on symbolic functioning. Prior to the development of this level of interaction, Murphy and Messer (1977) have indicated that the mother attempts to direct the infant's attention, rather than merely following his line of regard. The pointing gesture seems to be understood in the early months of the second year of life. By comparing the effectiveness of pointing by the mother when the angle between the finger and the object being indicated varies, Murphy and Messer found that infants of around nine months seem to look at the pointing finger because it arouses their interest in itself, rather than for its significance. If these children actually shift gaze from the finger to the intended object, this appears to be a shift of attention rather than an indication of understanding, and it occurs when the finger and the object are close together in the child's field of regard. To see the pointing finger as a *significant* gesture, and to infer from it the attitude of the other, is to be on the verge of symbolic interaction — certainly intersubjective understanding is being exercised to an extent.

The work of Bruner (1977a, b; Bruner and Sherwood, 1976) takes the study of the transition to symbolic interaction further, in that he has attempted to show in the process by which gestural interaction develops significance, the earliest roots of language (significant gestures providing the ground for significant symbols).

Like Mead, Bruner (1977a) considers language as developing in adult-child interaction as a means of coordinating interaction. He argues that it is an extension and transformation of the earlier, gestural modes of regulating joint activity. In discussing the development of language from this perspective, Bruner contends that there is a relation between the instrumental function of language in regulating interaction and its grammatical structure, and that this relationship is central to the way in which language is acquired. In short, language as a symbol system is held by Bruner to share formal characteristics with the structure of activity between gestural interactors.

For example, Bruner discusses the subject-predicate structure which is a universal feature of language. He reduces this notion to the idea that any utterance consists of the location of a topic plus some comment on that topic (The bus [subject/topic] is full [predicate/comment]). Now, he suggests, this structure is analagous to the structure of interaction in the situation where a mother notices the line of regard of her infant and comments on what he seems to be looking at (see our earlier reference to Collis and Schaffer, 1975). Routines of joint attending shared by mother and child become richer as pointing and other significant gestures are established. And the form of such interaction sets up the expectation of a topic-comment structure in language. This may be reflected in the importance of order in the early grammar of the child.

In pointing to an object, presumably the gesture locates a topic and naming the object constitutes a comment. One logical difficulty of Bruner's analysis is that, since subject-predicate structure is a universal of language, his descriptions of interaction (or of anything) will have this form. Nevertheless, enough evidence on the role of interaction in linguistic development has been amassed for us to be sure that Bruner is correct in his view that this problem is a central one.

Bruner has also discussed the possibility that a correspondence exists between the case structure of language and the characteristics of mother-infant interaction. Universally, language provides categories of agent, action, object of action, recipient of action, location, possession, etc. (Simply, the class containing 'mine' denotes possession, and so on.) Bruner claims in this context that 'What is universal is the structure of human action in infancy which corresponds to the structure of universal case-categories. It is the infant's success in achieving joint action (or the mother's success, for that matter) that virtually leads him into the language' (p. 93). Evidence on the acquisition of language in the earliest stage of language use suggests that the child is concerned to pursue or comment on action being undertaken jointly by himself and another (thus we have agent, action, object and possession); calling attention to the objects and people involved (naming, demonstrative marking, registering non-existence, greeting, location); and to the elements to be attended to (feature marking).

Bruner sees play as elaborating these rule structures (especially commenting on 'give and take' — Bruner, 1977b — and 'peekaboo' — Bruner and Sherwood, 1976). Playful activity draws the infant's attention to the communication itself, and to the structure of the interaction sequence within which communication is occurring. The rituals become the objects of attention, rather than being instrumental to something else.

The mother's interpretation of meanings is crucial: not only her attribution of intentions to the infant, but also her activity in setting up joint formats of action (Newson, 1977), and her activity in marking off the segments of action (e.g. by use of indications of completion: 'Good boy'). Within this context, the infant learns to make the conceptual distinctions embodied in case grammar through acquiring the rule structure of the play activity. Thus the categories of agent, action and so on occur as particular elements of the interaction and are confined to these ('privileges of occurrence'). Mastery of these privileges of occurrence constitute the acquisition of a 'grammar' or rule structure of interaction, in that 'agent' (for instance) has such and such a locus, yet there is a range of possible candidates for the role of agent. The flexibility of the play interaction allows the gradual experimental working through of the substitutions of elements within the rules, so that a game in which the mother (agent) pushes an object towards the child with appropriate vocalization, and to which the child originally responds with a smile only, later develops into give and take, in which the sequence is repeated with child as agent.

So we reach the stage of gestural interaction where significance in gesturing is realized, language as a decontextualized symbol system is being acquired, basic assumptions for symbolic interaction such as intersubjectivity, the possibility of taking the attitude of the other, reciprocity of perspectives are developed.

Mead would seem to suggest that we are now in the unambiguously social realm. Yet language development is not unambiguously social. There is universality in several aspects of the early acquisition of grammar (Brown, 1976), beside the case grammar mentioned by Bruner. The characteristic feedback which children receive from adults is generally to do with the truth-value of the utterance which the adult supposes was intended — not the grammatical correctness of the utterance (Brown, 1976 but cf. Slobin, 1975). Adult intervention in the language acquisition of children may well be relatively unimportant in their development of adequate performance in the structural form of the language. So it is not clear that this aspect of symbolic interaction is entirely an emergent from social interaction.

Of course the language used by adults to talk to infants is special. It may well be that two distinct but overlapping functions determine the nature of these utterances. Simplicity (Slobin, 1975; Snow, 1972) is attributed to 'motherese', and possibly this lightens the child's load in trying to acquire the language. At the same time, Ferguson's (1964, 1969) cross-cultural work indicates that 'baby talk' may have the social function of marking the status of the child as a child. It could be that these factors play a different role depending on the child's age. Other aspects of talk for children are treated by Nelson (1973) and Wells (1975).

Further discussion of language, and its role as a symbol system may be reserved for Chapter 3. This section has shown in some detail how recent research enables Mead's treatment of the transition from gesture to symbol to be elaborated and made more concrete.

DEFINING THE SITUATION

Some attempt has been made, in the section of Chapter 1, 'Mead: society and social roles', to indicate the way Mead's view of the individual/society relationship should be understood. However, some further dimensions of the debate over the interactionist standpoint must be taken up at this point, for there is indeed ambiguity (for instance, in the question of determinism); lack of depth in the perspective (especially when social, historical, structural topics are to be considered), and a resultant difficulty in framing research based on an interactionist conceptualisation of the area.

As a focus which throws these matters into relief, the notion of 'defining the situation' will serve effectively. It is usually regarded as owing its developed formulation to W.I. Thomas (1966) — though Merton (1957) cites predecessors. Thomas' epigrammatic statement of the notion is, 'If men define situations as real, they are real in their consequences'. Ball (1972) explicates this as pointing to the meanings of situations, as experienced by the actors within them, as the basis of social conduct. Situational definitions are 'constructions of reality' (Berger and Luckmann, 1967).

Of course, this idea is a thoroughly interactionist one, and concords with Blumer's (1962) statement already quoted: 'Human beings interpret or define each other's actions instead of merely reacting to each other's actions. Their response is not made directly to the actions of one another but instead is based on the *meaning* which they attach to such actions. Thus, human interaction is mediated by the use of symbols, by interpretation, or by ascertaining the meaning of one another's actions' (p. 180).

As Ball points out, the importance of the statement 'If men define situations as real, they are real in their consequences' is not in saying that the consequences of conduct are a function of situational definitions, but that the specification of the definition of the situation as a reason for action means that the perceptual activity of the person, the meaning that he sees in the situation, becomes the focus of interest for those who wish to study human social behaviour in an interactionist manner.

Let us now consider some aspects of the psychology of defining the situation. No doubt, 'taking the attitude of the other' is a fundamental process in defining the situation. This being so, the sort of preconditions for symbolic interaction mentioned in the previous section, associated with Schutz's work, are preconditions for achieving a definition of the situation. Again, if defining the situation is as integral a part of interaction as this suggests, there must be an element of interpersonal 'negotiation' which forms part of the flow of the interaction episode, and which stands open to the possibility of disruption — so that the mutuality between participants in their definition of the situation may break down. The 'physical' environment (say, the chairs and tables, their arrangement in the room, and so on) may be defined as relevant to the interaction, so that their social meaning forms part of the interactors' definition to the situation. Finally, the interactor's own selves — as presented in their taking of social roles — form part of the definition of the situation; part of the process of negotiation, and equally open to the possibility of a disruption of mutual acceptance of definition as any other aspect of the situation — one's presented self may be discredited.

Some of the essential, taken-for-granted presuppositions, which are preconditions of symbolic interaction and entailed in defining the situation, have been discussed in the previous section: meaning-attribution, intersubjectivity, 'general thesis of the alter ego', reciprocity of perspectives. Additionally, Schutz (1962, 1972) developed the idea of reciprocity of perspectives by pointing out that this entails the assumption that cooperative action can be accomplished.

If it were not for the assumption of reciprocity of perspectives, playing roles in social situations would be inconceivable because each would be unable to take the attitude of the other. However, this can be managed, and the participants' perspectives on their joint enterprise — whatever the details of the interaction may be — can be interlocked sufficiently well for their practical purposes. (There can be 'congruence between their systems of relevancy'.)

These basic assumptions are necessarily made in any interaction. In addition, taking the attitude of the other depends on the other acting in typical (i.e. 'typifiable', understandable) ways. The set of typifications of people and actions — categories of perception dealt with at length in Chapter 4 — is part of what Schutz terms the individual's 'stock of knowledge at hand'. Mutual understanding depends on interpretation of roles.

However, role does not mean for Schutz, and certainly not for Mead or Thomas, a definite category reflecting general social position. Rather the typifications employed in interaction are very flexible, reflecting the specific, momentary interests of the participants, every shift entailing a change in typification. Roles in this sense are the subject of an ongoing negotiation.

This delicate framework which supports interaction clearly allows the possibility of breakdown. The mutually-negotiated definition of the situation can suddenly lose reality as one of the partners acts contrary to expectation in a way that makes untenable the definition of the situation that had — it was assumed — been taken for granted (though whether it had or not now becomes problematic).

The breakdown of definitions of the situation has been investigated as a deliberate 'experimental' procedure by Garfinkel (1963, 1967). The purpose of these so-called 'breaching experiments' seems to be to demonstrate, by disrupting elements of the definition of the situation, how social interaction is normally achieved. Now presumably the essential characteristics of interaction — those which Schutz outlined — cannot be breached while the phenomenon remains an interaction. Thus Garfinkel's breaching experiments have only a surface layer of assumption as their focus. It may be suggested, then, that there are two levels at which defining the situation occurs. The first layer is the set of tacit, taken-for-granted assumptions which must be made for symbolic interaction to be possible at all. The second layer consists of the particular, continually negotiated, typifications which define *this* situation.

Consider this example, by one of Garfinkel's students:

> On Friday night my husband and I were watching television. My husband remarked that he was tired. I asked, 'How are you tired? Physically, mentally, or just bored?'
>
> (Husband:) I don't know, I guess physically, mainly.
>
> (Experimenter:) You mean that your muscles ache or your bones?
>
> (H:) I guess so. Don't be so technical.
>
> After more watching —
>
> (H:) All these old movies have the same kind of old iron bedstead in them.
>
> (E:) What do you mean? Do you mean all old movies, or some of them, or just the ones you have seen?
>
> (H:) What's the matter with you? You know what I mean.
>
> (E:) I wish you would be more specific.
>
> (H:) You know what I mean! Drop dead!   (Garfinkel, 1967, p.43)

This example of a breaching experiment is trivial — the student merely pretended not to understand a couple of the minor typifications in her husband's chatter. But it is instructive that she understood such tacit conventions as the form of a question, so the deeper understandings of the conversation were not 'breached'. And the sort of assumptions described by Schultz were not put in doubt at all.

An interesting feature of breaching experiments is that, despite the fact that they only disrupt interaction superficially, they appear to put great strain on the 'experimenters' who set up the breaching event. Gregory (1977) cites several examples of such experiments in which the people who carried them out specifically report the difficulty they had in screwing up their courage to the extent of breaching the definition of the situation. Gregory argues that this feeling is exacerbated by the fact that the experimenters were, by the rules of their game, restrained from giving the subject of the experiment an account of their own odd behaviour. For instance, the experimenter in the example cited could not tell her husband (at least not until the interaction was well and truly breached) that the whole thing was merely an experiment; she had not really misunderstood; a new definition of the situation could be negotiated.

Gregory's observations point to the fact that, when the definition of the situation is breached in the natural way in interaction — as is the case when an embarrassing incident flaws the mutual definitions which participants have arrived at (Goffman, 1956) — the conditions are ripe for motives to be demanded. As Chapter 7 details, motives are sought when a person acts in a way that cannot be construed within the other's definition of the situation. It seems that the discomfort felt in actually breaching these expectations is made worse by the knowledge that a patching up of the interaction by redefining the situation in terms of a motive for the untoward action will not be possible.

The maintenance of an agreed basis for interaction by means of ongoing definition of the situation seems then to be an activity of normative significance. It might be concluded that there is a social contract to construct and continually adapt to current circumstances a definition of the situation. Breaching the definition of the situation breaches that norm.

Definition of the situation obviously involves perception of people, but the physical setting has a meaning which is also very often of relevance in defining the situation. Goffman (1969) treats this matter in terms of 'region behaviour', although this only covers those aspects of physical setting which involve barriers to perception — obviously there are many aspects of physical setting that must be correctly perceived in order to define the situation besides the meanings attached to areas bounded by barriers to perception.

However, with this limitation, Goffman discusses various phenomena connected with region behaviour. For him, region is a relatively segregated area where particular roles are conventionally enacted — so the correct behaviour is guided by a definition of the situation which takes account of the setting. Goffman points out that some roles (or 'performances') are more public than others, and setting may have a social meaning reflecting this dimension. Goffman terms more public physical settings 'front regions' and private settings 'back regions'. He suggests various possible distinctions between these regions in the definitions of situation which reign in them: 'The performance of an individual in a front region may be seen as an effort to give the appearance that his activity in the region maintains and embodies certain standards' (p. 93) whereas 'A back region...may be defined as a place where the impression fostered by the performance is knowingly contradicted as a matter of course' (p. 97).

The importance of an outsider correctly defining the areas as public and private is clearly of utmost importance. The norm barring customers from repair workshops, and the ubiquitousness of 'staff only' areas in organizations where staff and clients use the same building, are formal embodiments of region behaviour.

Defining the situation clearly involves the formation of a general impression of the other and a continual updating of that impression, the most specific aspects of which fall under the rubric 'taking the attitude of the other'. Goffman (1969) shows that there is a mirror-image of forming an impression of the other: managing the impression one gives *to* the other. Defining the situation entails presenting oneself in the appropriate manner, and the other also managing the impression he gives. Blumstein (1975) states the axiom that an essential feature of social interaction is negotiation about the selves that each may present. Goffman tends to stress the fact that one is restricted in one's presentation of self by the situation. Blumstein shows that one may also define the situation in the light of one's self-concept, and in this way there is mutual influence between the negotiation as to definition of the situation between participants in an interaction and their negotiation as to presentations of self.

These then are some of the features of defining the situation. The notion has not gone without criticism, and it is to its limitations that we now turn.

Despite the interpretation of Mead which has been adopted in the section 'Mead: society and social roles' (in which we relied on Natanson's study of Mead's thought), it is at this level that much criticism of interactionist work has been deployed. Meltzer, Petras and Reynolds (1975) find that: 'The particular phenomena or specific problems selected for study are only rarely linked to their historical origins and development' (p. 97). Again, it has 'a limited view of the nature of social power' (p. 97), and social structure is lightly treated — there is inadequate concern with large-scale forms of social organization. Interactionists seem to be unaware of politics, although Meltzer, Petras and Reynolds merely state that 'whether or not symbolic interactionism is inherently apolitical is still an open question' (p. 91). (See also, for a Marxist account, Lichtman, 1970.)

These criticisms are serious if they are to be taken as indicating a general lack in the theoretical structure of interactionism. However, it may be that this lack is not essential to the nature of the theory, but rather that the actual studies carried out by interactionists, and the aspects of the theory which they have chosen to emphasize and elaborate, have been one-sided. I feel that this is in fact the case. Certainly the empirical studies carried out have been little concerned with history, social structure and power. And the theoretical developments since Mead have also lacked these interests.

Defining the situation is an instance of theoretical elaboration which may be criticized for lack of larger-scale concern. The idea of a 'negotiation' of a definition of the situation excludes from the picture the fact that many situations are entirely, and almost all are largely, 'predefined'. As Natanson (1973, p.17) writes in a statement already cited, 'Born into a world he did not create, destined to live and die under the shadow of institutions and social structures he did not order, and, finally, reared within the limitations of a language or of languages taught to him by elders, the individual cannot be held "responsible" for the objective situation in which he finds himself as a human being living among other human beings in societal reality'.

Other authors who are broadly within the interactionist tradition have made similar points. Chapter 4 of Schutz and Luckmann (1974), for instance, is concerned with 'Knowledge and society', and mentions the social relativity of knowledge; the importance of language to typifying; historical and social structural impacts on typification — all of which relate social interaction to the broader concerns mentioned by Meltzer and his colleagues.

Various authors have pointed out that an understanding of broad historical and social matters may be pursued without any recourse to the level of social interaction. Goffman, for instance, writes: 'This book is about the organization of experience...and not the organization of society. I make no claim whatsoever to be talking about the core matters of sociology — social organization and social structure. Those matters have been and can continue to be quite nicely studied without reference to frame [i.e. situational definition] at all' (1975, p. 13). While this is true, the reverse is not. Definitions of situation can only be ultimately understood in the context of the social world in which they are embedded.

Suffice it to say at this point that interactionism needs to be more centrally aware of the limitations that are placed on a person to determine his own reality (Schutz, 1964; Maloy, 1977). Defining the situation is a socially constrained activity.

Another aspect of social relationships which Thomas' notion of a negotiated definition of the situation tends to exclude is social power. 'Negotiation' implies perhaps that the participants in interaction have equal rights in defining the situation; their positions are balanced as far as power is concerned. This is frequently not the case. The class structure of the society predefines certain typifications so that there is little choice but to define the situation 'asymmetrically' — the standpoint of the participants who are prejudged more socially powerful will have more effect on the 'negotiation', and their definition will tend to frame the interaction.

The effect of such asymmetry in defining the situation attracts little attention amongst interactionists, although some discussion has recently begun to be heard. Scudder (1977) treats of sex role differences, Gallagher (1977) presents evidence on the doctor-patient relationship (arguing that some asymmetry is somehow essential to that interaction but not all the asymmetry usually observed is of this essential sort), and Pfohl and Bowman (1977) similarly tackle psychiatric diagnosing, a definition of the situation in which 'negotiation' is clearly one-sided.

The effect of social power, then, is another matter which has not been treated sufficiently earnestly by interactionists, and the use they make of the idea of defining the situation reflects this fact.

Several authors have commented on the ambiguity which is seen in Mead and in later interactionist writers over determinism. Gillin (1975), for instance, criticizes Mead for being a sociological determinist in the sense that he regards society as temporally prior to mind, and the cause of the development of mind in the child (in the 'conversation of gestures'). This being so, Gillin claims, Mead is guilty of attributing human action generally to the influence of society.

Certainly there is some evidence of this sort of thinking in Mead, particularly in his treatment of the self as arising from the perception and internalization of the attitudes of others to one, and eventually to an abstract, overall attitude of the 'generalized other'. This side of Mead's social psychology is discussed at length in Chapter 5 where the conclusion is that selves cannot be regarded as merely the sum of the social roles which they enact because Mead surely views role-playing as a constructive definition of the situation involving symbol-manipulation, language use. Thought is less constrained than Gillin would have us believe Mead suggests.

If Mead is criticized by Gillin for a tendency towards an over-socialized view of man (cf. Wrong, 1961), Gonos (1977) makes a criticism which finds Mead guilty of an opposite distortion. Thus, whereas Gillin sees in aspects of Mead's theory a view of human social interaction as the mechanical outcome of social structure, Gonos argues that interactionist concepts such as definition of the situation emphasize the precarious, negotiated, idiosyncratic nature of interaction. He contrasts this generally-held view of definition of the situation with Goffman's recent notion of 'frame' (Goffman, 1975), claiming that these concepts, similar though they may seem, in fact point to different perspectives on the process of interaction: 'For Goffman, everyday social encounters do not pose the problem of coordination, because they are examples of the ritualised reproduction of cultural objects according to preestablished formulae' (p. 865). If there is some truth in Gonos's interpretation of Goffman's work, there is also evidence for the opposite tendency, for instance in Goffman's understanding of embarrassment as arising from a breakdown in the web of interaction (Goffman, 1956, see Chapter 6).

To summarize the two poles of this debate: Mead is criticized by Gillin for seeing interaction as too bound by social convention, whereas Gonos takes exception to his and later interactionists treatment of interaction as a nicely-poised process of negotiation. Our conclusion is that Mead may best be interpreted as 'guilty' of the 'error' pointed out by Gonos — too fluid a view of the interaction. However, in the context of what has been already mentioned (the general lack in interactionism of a serious interest in social structure, power, and history), it may well be contended that the 'error' suggested by Gillin would not be too unfortunate!

Perhaps the most general statement that we can make in this matter is that interactionism as a school (in which we include Goffman, cf Meltzer, Petras and Reynolds, 1975) is ambivalent concerning determinism. There seems to be a 'tightrope' to walk between an over-socialized notion of man and social interaction (in which the negotiated nature of situation definition is underplayed), and an emphasis on interactions as precarious, negotiated activities (in which social predefinition of situations tends to be neglected). A view which combines these two opposite tendencies, with the process of definition of the situation being negotiated within socially provided structures of typification, would seem most true to the phenomena. If so, ambivalence concerning social determinism, in both Mead and Goffman might well be understood as accurately reflecting the nature of human social interaction.

Mead's concepts have been criticised as 'fuzzy', lacking in clarity. Kuhn (1964) has levelled this criticism against Mead's view of the self, which as we have seen involves the process of being aware of one's own actions and monitoring them, but (as Chapter 5 details) includes several other conceptions which make an overall grasp of Mead's meaning difficult. I regard this as a telling criticism of Mead's workmanship, but less important as a condemnation of interactionism as an approach.

However, taking this criticism together with the ambiguity of the interactionist standpoint on determinism makes for a further difficulty which has often been mentioned (e.g. Kuhn, 1964; Ball, 1972). Interactionist concepts are hard to operationalize and difficult to define in such a way that they can be used in empirical scientific research, involving operations of measurement and so on.

Defining the situation is a case in point. Ball suggests that a reason why Thomas' dictum 'If men define situations as real, they are real in their consequences' is rarely observed when it comes to actual research is because prediction of a consequence from a definition of the situation would be so fraught with difficulty. A cause of behaviour of this sort, which resides in the individual's interpretation of the meaning of the events with which he is confronted, is too elusive for most research techniques and is problematic for them all.

Forgas (1976) and a number of other authors (e.g. Bjerg, 1968; Magnusson, 1971; Frederiksen, 1972; Wish, 1976) have attempted to discover empirically the main types of situation which people perceive. Thus Forgas asked subjects to sort cards, which contained brief descriptions of 'social episodes' derived from an earlier open-ended questionnaire study, into sets of similar situations. Statistical analysis of the results of these card-sorts produced a taxonomy of situations.

Work of this kind can be regarded as indicating some very general tendencies in the social typification of situations, but of course cannot touch the negotiated, interpersonal nature of defining the situation. Bjerg's approach may allow for the emergency of this level of situation-definition. He provides an extensive list of perceptual categories, each one of which relates to the momentary social meaning of the utterances produces by members of the interacting group. For instance, person A may 'give' person B the 'agon' (social meaning category) of pleasing. Thus Bjerg requires that the observer analyse an utterance from the point of view of the person receiving the utterance, so that its social meaning may be shown.

Here, definitions of the situation are the subject of an ongoing negotiation which the observer attempts to divine by an analysis of the conversation.

A procedure such as Bjerg's, though on the face of it both a justifiable technique of data collection and one which allows the fluid, negotiated nature of interaction to emerge, is nevertheless subject to a further line of criticism — one which at least a large proportion of scientific techniques used in the study of interaction are exposed to. This is a general problem associated with all attempts to turn talk into data for analysis (and much research within the symbolic interactionist tradition of course attempts to do this).

Consider the situation which arises when the words that are said mean a certain thing if taken literally which obviously was not intended by the speaker. No-one listening does take it literally, indeed it may even be that they do not notice what is said but only register what is meant. For instance, in a recent radio phone-in programme on dressmaking a listener asked how she could alter her round-shouldered husband's jackets so that the collar at the back lay flat rather than standing up. The expert answered that it was a pity because 'if you were a lady' you could easily take darts in...Of course the expert did not intend to insult the listener, and merely meant to say that 'if you were making the alteration to a lady's jacket' darts could be taken in (but this is not conventional in men's jackets) — and indeed this is no doubt how everyone took her statement.

Examples of the context-bound nature of talk are by no means hard to find. The correct understanding of discourse depends on the realization that the categories of language are fluid, flexible structures that relate to situations in such a way that each depends on the other. Some sociologists of the ethnomethodologist school (Garfinkel, 1967) devote considerable attention to the methods by which 'glosses' (i.e. talk, whose meaning is never exhausted by the mere words uttered) are produced and heard (understood) as meaningful phenomena. Garfinkel and his school argue that utterances in ordinary language are *essentially* indexical glosses (glosses carrying a meaning embedded in the total definition of the situation). They explicate the characteristics of particular indexical glosses using a terminology including: 'ad-hocing', 'etcetera', 'unless', which refer to different methods by which participants in interactions themselves bring their knowledge of the situation to bear on the interpretation of discourse.

The point of mentioning the ethnomethodologists here is that, in taking talk and using it as data for understanding the interaction process, as Bjerg demands, the nature of talk as consisting in 'indexical glosses' means that the analysis cannot be based merely on the words used, but rather on their (context-bound) meaning. The result of this is that the observer must go through the same process of defining the situation as the social actors he is observing if he is to understand their talk. Which is somewhat unsatisfactory. (This argument is fully developed in a monograph by Wootton, 1975.)

The conclusion here is that, although the characteristics of defining the situation may be stated in general terms, the specific process of defining a particular interactional situation at a certain time by specific people is unique, and must be regarded as a single case — albeit with some features which are shared with other such cases.

Many of the studies reported in this book are based on the analysis of talk — either in natural language or in some form which limits the complexity of syntax and semantics (such as a closed-response questionnaire). Reports of such research rarely if ever specify the process of meaning-interpretation by which the social psychologists translated the indexical glosses into data relevant to their own purposes. Ethnomethodologists are correct to point out this systematic weakness in so much social science research.

Defining the situation, then, must be studied with an awareness of the impact of social structure, historical processes, and the reality of power. It is to be regarded as a delicate and subtle process of interpersonal negotiation as well. The fact that social constraint on defining the situation may seem to be at odds with the view of the process as an interpersonal negotiation must be regarded as correctly reflecting the actual phenomena, and both aspects must be given weight. The difficulty with which defining the situation meets when it is considered as a matter for empirical research (especially when discourse is used as a key to the process) is no reason for avoiding the area — for it is obviously a central concern if we are to adopt an interactionist understanding of social psychological matters.

MEAD AS A 'SOCIAL BEHAVIOURIST'

C.W. Morris, the editor of Mead's *Mind, Self and Society,* subtitled the work 'From the standpoint of a social behaviourist', and entitled the first part 'The point of view of social behaviourism'. But this characterization of Mead's approach is contentious. Natanson (1973) firmly disapproves, arguing that 'a close reading of Mead's works reveals a wealth of insights that by far transcends even the broadest conception of behaviourism' (p. 2).

Natanson uses evidence from the developments of Mead's thought in *The Philosophy of the Act* (1938) and *The Philosophy of the Present* (1932), which are not centrally concerned with social psychology, to demonstrate the transcendence of behaviourism achieved by Mead. But even within Mead's social psychology it is debatable whether interactionism can be allied to behaviourism. The first part of *Mind, Self and Society* makes a number of criticisms of the behaviourism of J. Watson, and in his introduction to that book, Morris lists several points of divergence between Mead and the behaviourist psychologists.

This debate is not merely of historical interest. Gillin (1975), in the paper mentioned earlier in connection with 'defining the situation', argues that Mead's 'social behaviourism logically impels him to make the self subservient to the social process...despite his intention to present a social psychology in which self and society are of equal importance' (p. 29) — and despite the conclusions of Ball (1972) and Gonos (1977) which contradict Gillin, it is clear that clarification of the position of interactionism with respect to behaviourism is needed.

It can be argued that the most rigorous contemporary equivalent to Watsonian behaviourism is that of B.F. Skinner. But the situation is confused by the fact that several authors (some of whom are important in social psychology) regard themselves as behaviourists yet diverge from the Skinnerian position. In this section, then, we shall briefly outline the main characteristics of Skinner's psychology, and then note aspects of the work of Bandura, a behaviourist with a somewhat distinct position. The standpoint of interactionism may then be compared to these authors, with a view to deciding whether a similarity exists to the extent that Mead, Skinner and Bandura ought to be considered together as representatives of a common school of thought.

Skinner (1975) assumes that a science of behaviour is part of biology. However, he does not think it necessary to await conclusive results from biology before setting out to investigate behaviour. Indeed, in certain respects looking 'inside' the individual for causes of behaviour is mistaken: behaviour finds its source in controlling forces in the environment.

For Skinner, then, the environment controls behaviour directly — he specifically contrasts this view with that of authors who argue that the control comes through environmental influence on conscious awareness. The reason for his concern to avoid invoking consciousness, introspection, and (at present at least) biology, is his positivism. This is the view that scientific accounts of any phenomena must be restricted to observables, and the demonstrable relationships between observables (Losee, 1972). Although it must be said that Skinner himself disclaims a basis in the philosophy of science for his viewpoint (Blanshard and Skinner, 1967), the positivistic assumptions are unmistakable (Harré and Secord, 1972). It could be argued that psychological positivism finds its most rigorous expression in Skinnerian behaviourism.

In describing behaviour, Skinner begins with identification of a certain movement of the 'organism' (no distinction is drawn amongst species); the movement is a *response* (Skinner, 1953, pp. 64-66). It might be, for example, an upward movement of a pigeon's head. Responses of the same type (e.g. all upward movements of the pigeon's head) are referred to as a class as 'operants'. A given response will occur at a certain moment when a particular set of *stimulus* conditions are in being. The response will be followed by a situation in which certain of the stimuli then existing are contingent on the response.

The stimulus conditions following on a response may lead to an increase or decrease in the observed likelihood that such a response will occur again in the presence of stimulus conditions similar to those which have already been observed to precede the response. When such an increase or decrease in the association of stimulus and response has been noted, Skinner regards this as an instance of 'operant conditioning'. The response is said to be under 'stimulus control', in that there is a likelihood that the response will occur again in the observed stimulus conditions. The condition of the environment which follows the response and which has had the effect of altering the probability of it occurring when the antecedent simuli are present is said to *reinforce* the association between stimulus and response.

Stimulus, response and reinforcing conditions are all observable. The idea of reinforcement refers to the observable relationship between stimulus and response and its association with the presence of certain conditions which are contingent on the response. Skinner has devoted considerable attention to the effect on stimulus-response association of different conditions of reinforcement, for example the effect of reinforcing each required response or reinforcing only some at particular intervals. Such 'schedules of reinforcement' are shown to be lawfully related to various characteristics of the relationship between stimulus and response.

Positivism demands that stimulus, response and reinforcement should be defined without reference to the mental state of the 'organism'. Others may attribute the effect of a reinforcing stimulus to the pleasure or pain which it means to the 'organism'. But for Skinner such internal matters are irrelevant: '...the only defining characteristic of a reinforcing stimulus is that it reinforces' (1953, p. 72) — not that it is desirable or repugnant.

Armed with such a definition, the only course to pursue is to discover, by experiment or other means, which stimuli actually act as reinforcers. Skinner (1953) finds that many phenomena of social interaction serve to reinforce responses. Thus, one may reinforce another's response by giving affection, being submissive, giving approval or attention to him, and so on. Skinner does not concede the need for any special model to cover human social interaction: operant conditioning is a sufficient framework. He writes, 'We may analyse a social episode by considering one organism at a time. Among the variables to be considered are those generated by the second organism. We then consider the behaviour of the second organism, assuming the first as a source of variables. By putting the analyses together we reconstruct the episode' (1953, p. 304). Thus an episode is a sequence of exchanges of stimuli, responses and reinforcement.

This brief sketch of the point of departure of Skinner's behaviourism does not do justice to the ramifications of his position (e.g. Skinner, 1957). However, it does indicate the nature of a developed form of positivism in social psychology, and it is Mead's alleged positivism which authors such as Natanson and Gillin debate.

Bandura's (1967, 1969, 1971; Bandura and Walters, 1963) theoretical position is anomalous. He regularly states his admiration for Skinner's work and claims a comparable, behaviourist stance, yet he argues that social behaviour demands an extended version of the operant conditioning model, and in responding to this requirement has, apparently, introduced concepts rather removed from strict positivism.

The empirical facts with which Bandura is concerned are indicated when he states (1971, p. 5): 'most of the behaviours that people display are learned, either deliberately or inadvertantly, through the influence of example'. He wishes to press the case for *imitation* as a basic phenomenon in learning. At the very least, learning by observing others shortens the time taken to acquire a new piece of behaviour.

The position on imitation which held a dominant situation prior to Bandura's work was that of Miller and Dollard (1941). Their view, and Skinner's, is that imitation is a special instance of operant conditioning in which the response of copying another's action, is reinforced. This would require that, in order to learn a behaviour just performed by another, one would have to imitate it straight away (to ensure that it is the act of *copying* and not merely the specific movement performed on this particular occasion that is conditioned) and this imitative response would have to be immediately reinforced. However, Bandura and his colleagues have been able to demonstrate many instances of behaviour acquired through the observation of the actions of others even when the observer does not imitate the model's behaviour during the process of learning and therefore does not receive reinforcement. Interestingly, they have been able to show, as a type of imitative learning, instances of 'vicarious reinforcement', where the behaviour of the observer is modified due to reinforcement given to the *model*.

Bandura has developed a 'mediational stimulus contiguity' theory to account for imitative learning. This argues that the observation of another's stimulus situation plus the response made to it, when such stimuli and responses are closely associated in time, will allow the observer to acquire mainly symbolic representations ('mediations') of the other's behaviour. The observer does not need to be reinforced or even to respond, in the process of learning — which contrasts with the operant conditioning view. Note that Bandura here separates the acquisition (or learning) of behaviour from its actual performance; there have indeed been numerous studies in which reinforcing consequences have served only to activate behaviour previously learned without reinforcement (cf. Shaw and Costanzo, 1970, p. 62).

Bandura's treatment of observational learning and imitation thus involves a point of view at variance with Skinner on such matters as the role of reinforcement, the importance of cognition, and the relationship between acquisition and performance of behaviour. Man is able to represent facts (such as the behaviour of another person) symbolically, especially through the use of language, and such information may be used to guide later action.

On reinforcement, Bandura has stressed the idea that the knowledge one gains from the results of one's actions, though not necessary for learning, enables an assessment to be made of the efficacy of behaviour — indeed people often monitor their own actions and thus arrange to give themselves feedback. In the Skinnerian view, reinforcement is not a cognitive matter, but is an automatic process by which stimulus-response associations are strengthened by their immediate consequences.

The possibility of self-monitoring and self-administered feedback is one aspect of Bandura's treatment of 'cognitive control' of behaviour. Bandura (1971, p. 35) writes, 'If human behaviour could be fully explained in terms of external stimulus conditions and response consequences' (which is surely what Skinner claims) 'there would be no need to postulate any additional regulatory mechanisms. Actions are not always predictable from these external sources of influence, however, because cognitive factors partly determine what one observes, feels and does at any given moment'.

In order to substantiate his claim that an important place must be given in behaviour theory to cognition, Bandura cites many experimental studies showing that awareness of what was happening affected operant conditioning. He regards as 'most striking', work in which the extinction (i.e. the gradual loss of strength of stimulus-response associations due to withdrawal of reinforcement) of emotional reactions in people who are informed that the stimuli are no longer going to be followed by a reinforcer (e.g. a small electric shock), is compared to the extinction of such responses when they are not told but the shock is merely withheld. As workers such as Grings and Lockhart (1963) and Wickens, Allen and Hill (1963) have shown, awareness promptly abolished the conditioned emotional response, as measured by galvanic skin response.

Bandura's theory certainly develops Skinner's behaviourism. One could well ask in what sense they are both behaviourisms. Indeed, if the school is broad enough to include these two authors, might it not include Mead as well? In the final pages of this chapter, Mead's view is compared, first, with Skinner's (and here we are able to draw on Mead's own criticisms of Watson), and secondly with that of Bandura.

Skinner's behaviourism shares with Watson's the central characteristic of eschewing reference to the cognitive processes. Since the earliest days of behaviourism this characteristic has been the subject of stern criticism (Beloff, 1973). 'Conditioning' is supposed to be automatic, irrespective of the awareness of the subject. Moreover, behaviourists view conditioning as the basic process responsible for behaviour — where there appears to be active involvement in action by the actor, this merely suggests that all the variables in the situation are not yet under full experimental control.

The denial of the importance of conscious awareness by Skinner is part of his positivist orientation. Watson also preferred to exclude private awareness from the realm of science, and Mead took him to task for this, in a most informative and interesting way: 'Even when we come to the discussion of...''inner'' experience, we can approach it from the point of view of the behaviourist, provided that we do not too narrowly conceive this point of view. What one must insist upon is that objectively observable behaviour finds expression within the individual, not in the sense of being in another world, a subjective world, but in the sense of being within his organism' (Mead, 1934, p. 5).

So the internal aspects of conduct are not closed, but are part of the range of phenomena of the science. The sense in which he wishes here to adopt a behaviourist approach is not positivist, but rather means the attempt to understand and describe the experience of the individual in its dynamic relationship with the environment (largely, the social environment). Further, as Natanson suggests, Mead's view of consciousness is revealed in such statements. Consciousness is not to be seen as equivalent to 'conscious states', but to 'awareness'. It is 'a set of characters that is dependent upon the relationship of a thing to an organism' (Mead, 1934, p. 329).

A behaviourist response to the demand that awareness be included in the arena of research is that awareness as such does not affect the observed facts: the conceptual frame of operant conditioning is sufficient to account for behaviour. Mead put forward several criticisms at this level of argument. In particular, he pointed to the fact that the activity of the individual is effective in determining to some degree environmental stimulation, so the stimulus is subject to a certain degree of cognitive activity (selective attention, for instance). Moreover, whereas Watson had in effect emptied 'experience' of all content not covered by 'response', Mead's notion of social experience certainly does not reduce to observed movements of the organism in responding. A response for Mead is an intended action. Clearly also the notions concerning symbolic functioning are ones which depend on a view of meaning which is rather different to the behaviourists' only approach to meaning, which is a stimulus-response connection.

However, the matters raised, more by implication than by explicit statement, by Mead which distinguish the interactionist viewpoint from that of positivist behaviourists, are much more rigorously treated by later writers. Chomsky (1959) marshalls a number of the arguments in favour of a cognitive stance.

On the concepts 'stimulus' and 'response', Chomsky points out that, for Skinner, any response of the person is to be taken as being under stimulus control. Thus any statement a person utters, whatever it might be, is dependent on the stimulus situation. But it is not clear that there is any limit to the number of things a person might say in a given setting. Presumably a behaviourist must confine his attention to the 'objective' physical characteristics of the actual environment, too. All that could be said by Skinner of this state of affairs is that each of the possible responses is under the control of some separate subtle property of the stimuli. However, what the person is aware of at a certain moment is not specifiable in advance. It depends on an active selection of stimuli. Some cognitive notions are inevitable here. (Definition of the situation, we might suggest, is at the correct level.)

As Fodor (1965) points out, a key feature of speech is the lack of specifiable external stimulus control. Language is relatively context-free, and much human behaviour takes on that characteristic, at least when the child has reached a degree of competence in symbolic interaction. Further, anyone with a command of the language can produce a limitless number of sentences, many of which may well never have been uttered before. Yet he can be understood by others. The idea of predictability which is the touchstone of behaviourism fails here.

Linguistic phenomena pose problems for reinforcement as well. But the work of Bandura is sufficient to indicate the poverty of this concept as formulated by Skinner.

The concepts of stimulus, response and reinforcement do not play a role in Mead's theory. The distance between Skinner and Mead is perhaps most clear in considering symbolic interaction. Behaving according to the individual's definition of the situation, including a process of taking the attitude of the other, is not responding to the stimulus situation. For instance, the other might utter an unusually-phrased sentence: the person's reaction is to its meaning, which is not specifiable in terms of the objective characteristics of the sounds (as has already been pointed out in connection with the treatment of talk as indexical).

Skinner's treatment of social interaction, in which analysis of the behaviour of each person taken separately is regarded as giving all the information which can actually be derived from the situation, is also far too simple a view to encompass Mead's approach. Recall that the 'behaviour' of the participants does not, for Skinner, refer to the meaning-attributions which each makes in the light of the other's actions. The interactionist understanding of interpersonal processes is clearly cognitive.

Mead's concern is with 'social experience' and with 'behaviour of the individual organism of self in its dependence on the social group to which it belongs...'(Mead, 1934, p. 1). However, Natanson points out that social experience, though the phrase is never discussed analytically by Mead, surely involves more than merely the relation of the individual to the collectivity. Indeed Mead uses the term to refer to an area which includes such clusters of ideas as 'organism, self, individual, person; society, group, environment, situation; interaction, process, activity; object, percept, phenomenon; cognition, intuition, understanding, awareness, and so on' (Natanson, 1973, pp. 6f). This field is not behaviourist.

Mead, then is in no sense behaviourist in the manner of Skinner or Watson. Perhaps he comes closer to the position of Bandura (though Bandura only conforms to a few of the characteristics of Skinnerian behaviourism)?

Bandura certainly feels that cognitive processes ought to have a place in psychological theory. But the exact nature of the theory he proposes is not quite clear. It may be that, like Skinner, his viewpoint is essentially positivist. In this case he is arguing that the observed relationship between stimulus and response is not entirely predicted by reinforcement contingencies, and other concepts must be invoked. If this is indeed Bandura's position, then his cognitive concepts have the status of intervening variables (MacCorquodale and Meehl, 1948). The new concepts are not hypothetical mental processes, but merely involve the attempt to improve the prediction of observable behaviour by introducing variables intervening between stimulus and response. Such concepts do not carry any meaning that is not reducible to the observed behaviour of individuals.

This theory would be of the sort exemplified by Osgood's (1952) behaviourism. Here, in order to avoid the problem which has already been mentioned, that Skinnerian behaviourism demands a specific stimulus and specific response which are causally connected, Osgood proposed that the 'meaning' of a word might be conditioned as a 'mediating response'. Mediating response is thus an intervening variable, so that a word evokes an internal response which may develop internal associations. However, Fodor (1965) has shown that this notion merely changes the locus of the problem, since the relationship between the stimulus and mediating response, and between whatever internal associative network might be postulated and the observed response, are direct mappings.

Bandura's 'mediational stimulus contiguity' theory may be of this type; on the other hand his cognitive variables may be regarded as having specific effect, not directly predictable from the observables. Probably this is the case. These would be hypothetical constructs, rather than merely intervening variables; there is 'surplus meaning' (MacCorquodale and Meehl, 1948) in the cognitive concepts over and above their function in linking observables in a lawful relationship. If this is the case, cognition for Bandura does not merely have a place in his theory which improves predictive power, it refers to a set of really existing processes. Cognition is not just a term in the formula, but a real fact (cf. Harré, 1970).

If Bandura's theory is comparable to Mead's, cognition must be regarded as a hypothetical construct rather than an intervening variable. Bandura might then be able to concur with Blumer's (1962, p. 180) statement, 'This mediation' — he is referring to the way human interaction depends on mutual interpretation by means of symbols — 'is equivalent to inserting a process of interpretation between stimulus and response'.

The nature of this problem of meaning-interpretation may be made clearer by reflecting on this imaginary exchange between a mother and son: 'Are all your toys packed away now, John?'/'I'm not coming shopping now, so there!' Accounting for behaviour exchanges such as this in terms of direct stimulus-response connections misses the point, since the focus of attention is on the physical sound (of the other's voice), whereas the important factor is the perceived situation. Much of this ground is covered in the debate on 'defining the situation'.

The implications of taking awareness as seriously as this, however, take us far from behaviourism. As Merleau-Ponty (1965) argues, behaviourists wrongly construe behaviour. Behaviour is a 'manner of existing'. In the symbolic forms of behaviour which human beings display, the 'response' to a given 'stimulus' is mediated by rules *which can be altered* by the person. His behaviour is manipulable by him. It is his action, not describable without reference to the human capacity to attribute meaning to events and consider them in various perspectives. Thus meaning-laden perception, rather than stimulus, and intentional action, rather than response, are central to the study of the conscious social actor.

The interactionist stance, then, demands that we take the point of view of the subject. The scientist must 'take the attitude of the other', the social actor. If this is a behaviourism, it is one in which perception, rather than stimulus is focal. As Rose writes (1962, p. x): 'All social objects of study... are interpreted by the individual and have a social meaning. That is, they are never seen as physical stimuli, but as definitions of the situation'. In a similar vein, Piaget (1972, p. 47) quotes the neurologist V. Weizsäcker: 'When I perceive a house I do not see an image which enters my eye; on the contrary, I see a solid object which I can enter!'

In these chapters we have attempted to describe a framework for the study of various phenomena which form part of the consciousness and social interaction nexus. The arguments of later chapters are, it is asserted, locatable within this general, symbolic interactionist perspective. But of course, the truth of this claim may only be judged in reading what follows.

CHAPTER 3

Language Use and Thinking

As the prime example of a system of significant symbols, language is both a means of communication and a means of representing situations to oneself and reflecting on them: mind and interaction are both symbolic processes. This basic argument is developed in several directions. Firstly the distinction between symbolic and non-symbolic interaction is made again (cf Chapters 1 and 2) — this time leading to an account of the intimate connection of language development, the development of interaction skills, and the development of mind. A second main area of debate in this context is linguistic relativity. Finally the question of species-specificity in symbolic functioning is raised.

Close attention to Chapters 1 and 2 will have left the reader with a clear impression of the centrality of symbolic functioning in interactionism, it being synonymous with mind, and the basis of adult human interaction. It is not merely that people use symbols as a means of communication with each other, but that — since mental activity is postulated to be internalized interaction — mind also consists in an internal 'conversation'.

Moreover, external and internal communication (i.e. interaction and mind) are of-a-piece: adult human interaction takes place against a continuous background of mental activity and is only possible because there is such mental activity. In interacting, we imagine the viewpoint of the other person ('take the role of the other') and frame our actions with this criterion in mind. Additionally, we do not only act in a way that is interpretable by the other, for our actions are also being continuously monitored and interpreted by ourselves.

For Mead, the fundamental distinction was between *gestural* interaction (in which the early stages of an action call out a relatively automatic response in the other) and *symbolic* interaction (in which the verbal or non-verbal symbol is perceived in terms of a meaning by the participants). But Mead did not go on to discuss the special characteristics of language — as a particularly developed symbol system — contrasted with significant symbols in general. Yet the discussion of the transition from the conversation of gestures to symbolic

45

interaction of Chapter 2 implied that this was at least partially accomplished *prior* to the acquisition of language, and that the internalization of significant gestures of a non-linguistic kind prepared the child for such characteristics of language as subject-predicate structure.

Mead's conflation of language and significant gestures is plain in the following statement: 'When...a gesture means this idea behind it and it arouses that idea in the other individual, then we have a significant symbol. In the case of the dog fight [see Chapter 1] we have a gesture which calls out appropriate response; in the present case we have a symbol which answers to a meaning in the experience of the first individual and which also calls out that meaning in the second individual. When the gesture reaches that situation it has become what we call "language". It is now a significant symbol and it signifies a certain meaning' (pp. 45f).

In line with the research discussed in the previous chapter, then, it is necessary to amend the interactionist view of the development of mind through interaction, in that cognitive capacity — though it can still be supposed to arise through social interaction — is a prerequisite for the acquisition of language proper.

This amendment does not actually change the centrality of language for symbolic interactionism. It is the prime system of significant symbols. The processes of mind and of social communication take place through the use of significant symbols. Thus the question of the relationships among language use, thought and interaction is of great importance.

Later in this chapter, the suggestion that language actually determines thought is discussed. Since mind is to be understood as involving the 'manipulation' of significant symbols, an individual may be unable to mean anything which is not a direct derivative of the words and structure of the language, which constitutes the major symbol system. But prior to this discussion, the relationship between language use and thinking is elucidated through a consideration of the views of Piaget (1926) and Vygotsky (1962) on the course of development of language use and thought, and the place of interaction in this development. Where relevant, Mead's approach to this matter is compared with these views.

LANGUAGE USE, THINKING AND SOCIAL INTERACTION

Piaget, in *The Language and thought of the Child* (1926), argued that the early style of interaction of the child is *egocentric*. He does not, for instance, bear in mind the requirements of others for information, but rather he attributes to them information that they could not possibly possess but which he possesses. Thus the conversation of a child is often hard to follow, even though he is quite fluent, because he assumes knowledge which you do not have. Possibly, new terminology he has invented is never defined; the child points imprecisely at objects he wants to indicate. Effective speech requires, as we know, that the point of view of the listener be imagined vividly. If the listener needs information that will enable him to understand the child's conversation, then the child would realize this and supply it if meaningful communication were to be established. But the child does not 'take the role of the other'. He formulates a thought and utters it irrespective of the other's viewpoint.

Piaget also observed that children at the egocentric stage in the development of the skills of communication will talk to themselves in non-social situations. He interpreted this to mean that egocentric speech is not speech-for-others. Such speech, he reasoned, develops later as *social speech,* and egocentric speech fades away. For him, egocentric speech is merely talking, without regard to whether one is understood, and this is replaced by speech that takes account of the point of view of the listeners.

Brown (1965) points out that the process may not actually be once-for-all. Of course one aspect of this is that everybody is capable of making errors about the attitude of the other so that his communication is inappropriate. But also we have many daily instances of 'adult egocentrism', such as the lecturer who is ostensibly talking to the students in his lecture-room, but who mentally is addressing fellow-experts. Errors like this are easy to fall into and do lead to what looks like egocentric speech. However Brown is wrong to argue that adult egocentrism is the same as child egocentrism. The mechanism is different. For the adult the egocentrism comes because he has taken a role but not that of his audience; the other whose attitude he has in mind is therefore inappropriate. For the child the egocentrism arises because he cannot take the role of the other at all. Early egocentrism is, as Flavell and colleagues (1968) point out, fundamentally an inability take roles.

Mead and Piaget agree that the process of acquiring the skills of role-taking is lengthy. Mead related it to the development of a sense of self (see Chapter 5). Piaget has studied the process as one amongst a family of related developments at the cognitive level, including the capacity to realise that a scene would appear differently when perceived by someone from a different point. He believes that at the age of 7-8 the child gradually rids himself of egocentricity, largely because his contacts with others (especially other children) give him abundant information which indicates that his egocentric speech is not communicating, and that the others all too clearly have different viewpoints. This diminution in egocentric speech is just one indicator of a general cognitive skill that is emerging in this age group: the ability to *decentre,* that is to be able to stand aside from the point of view one holds and to see the situation from a different standpoint. This is the skill involved in 'taking the attitude of the other'.

It seems likely that Piaget overestimates the age at which taking the attitude of the other is shown. For instance, Gelman and Shatz (1972) report experiments which indicated that four year olds take the attitude of the other to the extent of talking differently to two year olds and adults. Thus the capacities of the other may be being taken into account in formulating utterances. Yet evidence that information requirements of the other are not fully taken into account until a later age than this, is provided by Krauss and

Glucksberg (1969), and Robinson and Robinson (1978), as well as Flavell and his colleagues.

A possible response to this ambiguity over the extent of taking the attitude of the other in early years, is to suspect that egocentrism is not a unitary construct, and that therefore different degrees of awareness of the attitude of the other may be present in the same child in different social contexts, and indeed that several different types of skill are confused in the use of the one term. Despite the empirical support for Piaget's view that there is an underlying similarity in the various forms of child egocentrism provided by Rubin (1973), it does seem likely that such aspects of taking the attitude of the other as develop in very early mother-infant interaction (Chapter 2) will be rather different in their process of development from the sort of skills required in order to take the attitude of the other towards some specific social situation.

On the general question of the relationship between thought, language and interaction, then, Piaget is certainly of the opinion that language *reflects* thought. Particularly in his earliest research the method used to gather evidence for his model of cognitive development involved the questioning of children and listening to their replies. But for him cognition antedates language, and the talk of children is to be interpreted in terms of cognitive structures which direct thought.

To what extent this emphasis contradicts the amended version of Mead which has been described in the previous chapter is not entirely clear. Adopting the view of internalization of significant gestures which Bruner's work suggests, the priority of cognitive capacity may be accepted (while leaving the details of development aside). But an interactionist approach would insist on the place of social interaction in the formation of this initial cognitive capacity. Mind arises from the internalization of gestural interaction. Piaget appears to be less definite about this. Social interaction is certainly an important part of the child's environment, but not, for him, as central as Mead would contend. (For a review of research on language and Piaget's stages of cognition, see Herriot, 1970.)

A view which stresses more firmly the interdependence of thought and language, and which may therefore be considered nearer to Mead's concern that mind is to be seen as the use of significant symbols, is that of the Soviet psychologist Vygotsky.

The study of the relationship between speech, thought, and social interaction has been a stronghold of Soviet psychology — indeed psychology in the USSR has developed in a manner very similar to symbolic interactionism, although the terminology of Pavlovian conditioning is always scrupulously maintained (see Volosinov, 1976; Luria, 1969; Luria and Yudovich, 1959). Luria (1969) writes: 'The problem of speech and its role in the formation of mental processes occupies a special place in Soviet psychology. Soviet psychologists proceed from the position that even the most complex manifestations of mental life are formed in the process of active reflections of reality. Complex mental processes are formed during the child's association with adults. They are complex functional systems formed with the intimate participation of language. That is why the study of how social relations are developed in the child, how he masters language, how, with the aid of speech, he masters the experience of prior generations, and finally how speech aids the formation of higher, conscious mental activity — constitutes a fundamental part of psychology' (p. 122).

A member of this school, Vygotsky, published *Thought and Language* in 1934 (translation: 1962); in it he criticized a key feature of Piaget's study of this topic — the gradual 'socialization' of the child's speech from egocentricity to the form more fitted for social communication. The idea that, as soon as the child has mastered the ability to decentre, etc., necessary for social speech, the egocentric form begins to disappear, having been, as it were, superceded, misses the point of egocentric speech according to Vygotsky.

In Vygotsky's view, language has two functions. Unsurprisingly, these are: external communication and the internal processes of thinking. In very early life, thought goes on without language. Equally babbling is not controlled by thought'. However, at about the age of two a 'new kind of behaviour' emerges when 'thought becomes verbal and speech rational'. This new kind of behaviour is egocentric speech. Egocentric because, until about the age of seven, the child cannot distinguish between the two functions of monitoring his own behaviour and communicating with others. After the age of seven or so, the child fully masters the ability to keep his self-monitoring activity silent, and to therefore evolve *internal speech*.

Thus Piaget is making an error when he refers to egocentric speech as fading away to be replaced by socialized speech. Rather, egocentric speech is being internalized. Much evidence is paraded by Vygotsky and his colleagues in favour of their view. Egocentric speech becomes increasingly *unlike* social speech as it begins to disappear from the child's conversation. Vygotsky noted that egocentric speech, previously unusually loud and detailed, gradually becomes abrupt, incomplete and whispered. Again, egocentric speech becomes especially clear where the child is having difficulty in his activity: 'Artificially producing such a difficulty while the child is carrying out some kind of task (e.g. the child is asked to draw on a piece of paper; then a pin which supports the paper is removed or one of the colored crayons is inconspicuously taken away) always evoked an outburst of egocentric speech from the child' (Luria, 1969, p. 144).

Evidence such as this indicates the 'external-thinking' characteristic of egocentric speech. Internal speech is a development from this external conversation-with-oneself. The characteristics of egocentric speech discussed by Piaget, therefore, come from two sources: partly the child has not yet internalized the attitude of the other and therefore assumes too much about the information his hearers have, but partly also the talk is aimed at himself and parallels the situation of the child who slaps himself when tempted. (Other experimental work, e.g. by Luria and Yudovich, 1959, was aimed at showing that the process of the development of mental activity did depend on verbal interaction and not on general maturation.)

Vygotsky also describes the characteristics of inner speech. External speech always remains most importantly the channel of communication with others. Inner speech loses this function. For one thing, the topic of 'conversation' is well known to both parties! So the inner speech can be telegraphic, condensed — not necessarily comprehensible to anyone else. The aim of inner speech is often just to indicate elements that need further consideration — it fixes and regulates mental activity. Its grammar is 'folded', contracted. But it is always possible to develop this inner speech into a complete utterance.

The views of Piaget and Vygotsky, taken together with the empirical studies reviewed in Chapter 2, provide a significant body of work with which Mead's suggestions may be supplemented. Though this must be tentative, in that much still remains unclear, it seems justifiable to support Mead's insistence on the primacy of gestural interaction. Significant gestures are internalized by the infant, and thus mind emerges in that the capacity for representing meanings is present (albeit in a very restricted way, at this preverbal stage). Such internalization may be regarded as providing the child with those presuppositions which are necessary for the acquisition of language (see Chapter 2). Finally, with the development of language the process of mind is immensely enriched because of the new availability of significant symbols. Now thought and interaction may begin to be separated in the manner suggested by Vygotsky, and adult symbolic interaction develops the many facets which later chapters of this book discuss — various perceptual tendencies, attributions of motive and of emotion, and so on.

LANGUAGE AS A DETERMINANT OF THOUGHT

Though the details of their arguments may differ, and we would ourselves wish to enter a caveat that internalization of significant gestures is prior to the development of language, nevertheless Vygotsky and Mead agree that thought derives from the internalization of speech (as the major form of communication through significant symbols). Piaget places greater emphasis on purely cognitive operations which are independent of language. (See Cromer, 1974, for a detailed review of much of the evidence concerning the relationship between thought and language: he inclines to a weak version of the view that cognition is prior to language.)

The emphasis of Mead and Vygotsky — and of this book, as a symbolic interactionist account of consciousness and social interaction — would lead to tendency towards *linguistic relativity:* thought would be to some extent predetermined by language. Learning a new language would be a reorientation of thinking: 'A person learns a new language and, as we say, gets a new soul. He puts himself into the attitude of those who make use of that language. He cannot read its literature, cannot converse with those who belong to that community, without taking on its peculiar attitudes. He becomes in that sense a different individual' (Mead, 1934, p. 283).

Sapir put the point of view that thought is determined by language in this way: 'Human beings do not live in the objective world alone, nor alone in the world of social activity as ordinarily understood, but are very much at the mercy of the particular language which has become the medium of expression for their society. It is quite an illusion to imagine that one adjusts to reality essentially without the use of language and that language is merely an incidental means of solving specific problems of communication or reflection. The fact of the matter is that the 'real world' is to a large extent unconsciously built up on the language habits of the group. . . We see and hear and otherwise experience very largely as we do because the language habits of our community predispose certain choices of interpretation' (quoted in Slobin, 1971, p. 20). Sapir wanted to show the intimate relationship between the most taken-for-granted modes of thought we adopt and language. B.L. Whorf was a student of Sapir, and his work is perhaps the best known research on the topic of linguistic relativity. He wrote (1956) that the relationship between language and thought had struck him very clearly in his professional work before he studied with Sapir. Whorf had been a fire insurance company's inspector, and at one time he undertook the job of analysing the circumstances surrounding a large sample of fires. Although the analysis was aimed at purely physical factors such as faulty electrical wiring, the meaning of the situation for the people involved often took a hand, especially when the linguistic description of the situation indicated that all was safe when actually it was extremely hazardous. For example, 'empty' petrol drums are safe — at least the term empty conveys the notion that there is no danger. But actually empty drums are full of petrol vapour which is a great fire hazard.

Now, Whorf wants to say more than this. It's not just that the nouns and adjectives we apply to objects affect our thinking about them — but much more detailed facts about the language affect how we perceive and behave towards things in our environment. He argues that one cannot help suspecting a much more far-reaching effect arising from the patterning in the language of grammar. He refers to the pattern of grammatical categories such as plurality, gender, tenses (and other verb forms), 'parts of speech' and so on. Of course it is very difficult to guess what such patterns imply for one's own language and thinking. But the situation is easier to investigate when the linguist studies an exotic language, and draws conclusions, from its pattern of grammatical categories, about the habitual ways of thinking that speakers of that language have.

An example which Whorf deals with at length involves the comparison of Hopi American Indian language and the general form of language and thought in European cultures ('Standard Average European'), in the matter of numbering events in time — the varying treatment of sequences of cyclically-recurring periods of time. For instance, Whorf points out that in European languages we can say 'ten days' just as we can say 'ten bottles' or 'ten men'. But note that 'ten days' is a different sort of grouping to the others. One can actually collect ten men or ten bottles and stand them together as a perceptible group, whereas we only experience one day at a time — a grouping of ten days is imaginary. In Hopi, plurals are used only where the objects can form an objective, perceptible group. So expressions such as 'ten days' are not used. Such a statement as 'They stayed for ten days' would be rendered as 'They stayed until the eleventh day' or 'They left after the tenth day'. In other words, groups of time periods are dealt with in terms of the operation of counting days passing rather than groups of days. 'Ten days' is not regarded as a length of time, but as 'on the eleventh day', relating such and such a time to others in sequential position.

So, European language and thought can envisage 'artificial' groups of time-periods ('ten days') whereas in Hopi such groups are not treated like that, but rather single time-periods are compared to each other using the construct 'lateness'. What does this grammatical difference say about the ways of thought of the two cultures? Whorf says that European language is more 'objectified' — more independent of particular experiences — whereas Hopi language reflects a more subjective outlook. 'Ten days' (the European phrase) is an imaginary grouping, yet it construes days like bottles standing in a quite perceivable row. This is independent of subjective experience — days are construed as existing objectively. 'Until the tenth day' (the Hopi phrase) construes days as being lived through — subjectively experienced.

This difference in language concerning how periods of time are to be construed is paralleled by differences in tenses. European languages have a basic structuring of three tenses for verbs — past, present and future — whereas Hopi has a system that orders events according to whether one reported event is earlier, later or simultaneous with another. Time here is not *absolute* past, present and future, but *relative* lateness.

So Whorf shows differences in language that have to do with the perception of time. He goes on to discuss the relation of these language differences to the habitual patterns of thought of the language-speakers, and also to the cultures in general. He writes of European culture that the 'objectified' view of time favours everything to do with keeping record of events — 'collecting time' as it were. Time is visualized as a ribbon marked off into equal spaces, and with such a view (which no doubt has been influenced by writing), European culture allows the development of interest in exact sequence and thus the invention of clocks and calendars; the general interest in past events, archaeology, history, concern with the labelling of past periods such as geological periods and cultural tendencies such as classicism and romanticism; and diaries, book-keeping and accounting. And European interest in the collecting of time extends to the future, producing schedules, budgets and timetables.

Hopi culture is unfavourable to such phenomena, because the view of time is too loose and fluid. There is, for instance, no ready-made answer to the problem of the boundaries of an event — when it begins and ends. Everything that happened is not to be regarded as completely dismissed but as still existant, though in a different form from that remembered or recorded.

Whorf is very convincing in drawing attention to instances of the relationship between our habitual thought and perception of objects and events, and the language. But how strong is this relationship? Are we entirely 'at the mercy' of the language we use?

One question is whether we perceive things differently or whether we merely talk about them differently. Does the fact that the Eskimos have many different words for different types of snow mean snow is perceived differently by them? Consider the fact that in attempting to learn to identify such things as butterflies with the help of a book one finds the major difficulty is deciding on key features to concentrate on. One can perceive the features of the butterfly, but in matching them with the two or three apparently similar pictures in the book there is a problem of selecting those particular things which differentiate, say, red admiral and small tortoiseshell. Perhaps this is a process of perceptual learning which is then fixed by the use of a name. Greene (1975) argues that 'everyone *can* see the world in the same way, and insofar as we can read and understand what Whorf says about the Hopi, it is possible to understand other people's categories. On the other hand, how we conceive of things depends on categorisations which draw attention to particular aspects of the environment' (p. 72). However, evidence on this is discussed in the next chapter.

We must therefore not go so far as to say that we can only think those things *immediately* available in the language. No — language is very flexible, and although no doubt it is true that habitually we use the most straightforward categories of our language to enable thought, nevertheless thinking is not entirely constrained by the categories of the language. For instance, English was sufficiently flexible to allow us to discuss Hopi thinking and language.

R. Brown (1965) has discussed the matter in terms of *codability*, that is the ease with which a concept can be expressed in a language. He cites work by Lantz on the ease with which people could remember and talk about colours, which showed that (a) colours that could be memorized efficiently were also those that could be named relatively easily, and (b) colours that could be communicated effectively to others were also those which are easily coded. Codability within the language is the key factor — and this depends on the vocabulary being adequate to the objects requiring to be distinguished. In some languages it may be easier for people to form constructs about certain things because their language makes it easier for them to do so. In some languages certain words, for instance, have additional ranges of meaning to their nearest equivalents in other languages. In French the one term *conscience* is used for the two English words conscience and consciousness (Slobin, 1971). On one hand this means the French do not have readily available a distinction that is readily codable in English. However, on the other hand it means they are more open to the partial identity of the two terms — which requires explanation in English. Some authors think that the French fusion of two English terms can partly account for a tendency to a fusion of the concepts in some French writers. Our usual language codes easily those categories we habitually use. So our thought is habitually confined to things easily coded in the language. More strenuous thought using less straightforward use of language is nevertheless possible. And we could suppose that early on in the history of wheeled transport, thinking about wheels, etc., was strenuous — there were not straightforward linguistic categories for coding the things needed to consider wheels — but soon categories such as hub, rim, axle, diameter would no doubt have emerged, making thought easier.

What viewpoint ought, then, to be adopted towards the language and thought relationship? Thought in the sense of Mead's 'mind' depends on symbolic activity for its very existence, and to that extent it is true that the internalized structure of gestural interaction must be expected to determine the nature of thinking as an activity. But this leaves open the question of what is actually thought. The further assertion is that the acquisition of language as a system of significant symbols provides the stuff with which thinking and interpersonal communication is carried out. From this it must be deduced that the words and grammar of the language must have a strong influence on thought.

How determinative is language? Slobin (1971) favours a form of the hypothesis of linguistic relativity which distinguishes between *habitual* and *potential* thought. In the case of colour discrimination, for instance, Slobin suggests that most poeple use only a few colour terms in everyday speech, although he supposes that they can potentially discriminate a very large number. This idea requires further debate in the light of the relationship between perception and symbol use, and the earlier pages of Chapter 4 provide this. But the general viewpoint is a useful one.

The distinction between habitual and potential thought reminds us that thought is *occasioned*. It is almost undeniable that for a large part of the time the situations with which one is confronted are unproblematical. The language provides easy access to relevant definitions of the situation. Codability is quite high. In such conditions, our life in a 'symbolic universe' actually requires little thought in the sense of effortful cogitation. The meanings, with which perception of events is supplied through symbol use, are entirely adequate. Language now appears transparent: obviously it is a bucket which one sees — the idea that such a percept is attained through the unreflective application of a linguistic term does not arise. Habitual thought, in which definitions of the situation are unproblematic, may be regarded as relating directly to readily available linguistic categories.

However, in acknowledging that language use is occasioned by the situation, the implication is that — since situations are not limited to a range of entirely predictable events into which the categories of the language may immediately map — the individual may well find that the habitual definitions of situation which the language most readily supplies are on occasion discredited. The perception of an event, whose meaning was provided by a symbolic operation which was an indissoluable part of the act of perceiving, is negated by the consequences of acting on that percept. In negotiation of a definition of the situation with another person, for instance, one's original view is found inadequate.

In such circumstances, new meanings must be discovered through symbolic activity aimed at reconstruing the event. Now we are faced with non-habitual use of language. Yet there is sufficient plasticity in this symbol system to allow such use. The grammar of the language allows operations which seem to coincide with the actual structure of the world — time, for instance, can be thought linguistically. The words may be redefined to fit the situation, or new terms coined to fit this or similar future events.

Thus language may determine habitual thought, and there are no doubt constraints to do with codability on the possibility of original thought. But if language is to be viewed as determinate, it is an extremely liberating form of determinism! It is not an inflexible, closed system, since it allows the perception of events in terms of situational definitions, attitudes, desires etc., and when these are found unsatisfactory in the face of the refractoriness of the world, it is the very same symbol system which enables a redefinition to be formulated.

This is a point at which a notion strongly-related to the hypothesis of linguistic relativity may be mentioned. This is B. Bernstein's view on the relationship between social class and language use. He relies on the evidence of a 'fundamental linkage of symbolic systems, social structure, and the shaping of experience' (Bernstein, 1970, p. 164), i.e. a hypothesis of linguistic relativity that is not merely aimed at showing differences in language, and therefore thought, between widely different cultures such as 'average European' culture and that of the Hopi Indians, but also between subcultures. Moreover he wants to invoke a very strong form of the linguistic relativity hypothesis: 'I shall argue that forms of socialisation orient the child towards speech codes which *control access* to relatively context-tied or relatively context-independent meanings' (Bernstein, 1970, p. 164, my emphasis).

Bernstein differentiates social structure into a middle class and a working class — defined in terms of educational attainment and other criteria. He goes on to argue that these two classes are typified by different patterns of social relationship. The working class relates in terms of the need to maintain rapport and solidarity, which results in a context-tied language ('restricted code'). The middle class is individualistic, and expresses individual differences and long-term goals in its mode of interaction. This generates a context-free language ('elaborated code').

Herriot (1970) reviews empirical work which aims to test the theory and concludes that this shows 'differences in language behaviour correlated with social class' (p. 153). However, it 'has so far failed to show convincingly that these differences are the cause of cognitive differences' (p. 155).

Herriot's review does not include the work of Labov (1969) who argues cogently that non-standard language (i.e. non-middle class language) is not to be regarded as inferior. Complex ideas can be transmitted; complex structure is discernable. When assessment of working class cognitive and linguistic styles are undertaken it is likely that these styles will be shown to disadvantage because the standpoint of the assessor is within middle class linguistic assumptions; indeed the idea of assessment is middle class.

LANGUAGE AS SPECIES-SPECIFIC

Mead continually drew the distinction between symbolic and gestural interaction by comparing animals and man. His position appears to be that only man has the neurological make-up necessary for the development of the significant symbol (cf. Mead, 1934, pp. 242-244). This is not an important point as far as interactionism is concerned, although of course it is only recently that scientists have been released from the obligation to treat opinions on the similarities between man and animals as if they were of confessional significance.

The conflation by Mead of language with significant gestures makes elucidation of the matter more difficult. It may be that animals are able to communicate using significant gestures without having anything approaching a developed language.

Lenneberg (1964) also has argued that language is a phenomenon specific to humans, who have certain biological propensities for the acquisition of language. Among these Lenneberg discusses the fact that man has anatomical and physiological peculiarities which facilitate verbal behaviour, and that there seems to be a clear schedule of development through which children pass at roughly the same age (cf. Brown, 1976), which indicates a biological mechanism since it does not appear to be affected by cultural and linguistic variations. Again, it is not a skill that requires careful teaching; on the contrary, it is difficult to prevent language acquisition even in the face of dramatic handicaps such as parental deafness. Lenneberg also points to the fact that language has not been taught to a non-human animal. This was true enough in 1964 but has been challenged since, as we shall see. Finally, he argues, with N. Chomsky, that there are 'universals' of language. All human languages have the triple structure of syntax, semantics and phonology. Chomsky has argued further, that syntax has universal features, and if this is so it is added evidence for a biological basis to language. (Another author who writes in this vein is C. Hockett, 1963, who has described sixteen 'design features' which describe aspects of the nature of language. Similarly, Miller, 1965, has listed characteristics of language and language use which are to be regarded as essential features which must be considered in any theory of language.)

The view of Lenneberg, then, is that language is species-specific, with a large biological component. Since the publication of his paper, however, a great deal of research involving the teaching of language to chimpanzees has been carried out, with a degree of success. The methodological breakthrough was by Gardner and Gardner (1969), who noted the lack of success met by attempts to teach chimpanzees to speak, and reasoned that this might not be due to a lack of capacity to acquire language but rather a lack of the physical apparatus necessary for controlled vocalization. They therefore proceeded to teach the chimpanzee Washoe a language intended for the deaf: American sign language (Ameslan).

Washoe has acquired a vocabulary of at least 160 signs (Gardner and Gardner, 1969; Linden, 1976; Brown and Herrnstein, 1975). The Gardners report that from the time that Washoe had about ten signs in her vocabulary, she used them in strings of two or more, and, although some such strings were probably imitated, a number were inventions of her own in the sense that her trainers had not signed such strings to her. Thus 'open feed drink' refers to refrigerator.

Brown and Herrnstein (1975) and Greene (1975) are of the opinion that Washoe and other chimpanzees that have since been taught Ameslan (see Linden, 1976) are capable of the level of communication ability of an eighteen-month to two-year-old child 'able to express immediate needs and feelings' but not to deal 'with the past or future nor to express abstract ideas' (Greene, 1975, p. 78). It may be, as Greene suggests, that Ameslan is itself a cumbersome medium for dealing with abstract matters since it lacks subtle grammatical inflections and consists mainly of single signs for nouns, adjectives, verbs and adverbs.

Another line of research involves the training of the chimpanzee Sarah to respond to and use coloured plastic shapes that refer both to objects and actions, and also symbolize logical relationships such as 'same as', 'different' (Premack, 1971). It appears that the shapes are treated as referring to the objects by Sarah, for instance she acquired the concept 'brown' by being informed via the shapes 'brown colour of chocolate'.

The fact that Sarah is able to treat 'apple is red' and 'red colour of apple' as equivalent seems to bear out the view that the coloured shapes are functioning as significant symbols. However most of her activity appears to be a complex form of problem solving rather than the use of the shape 'language' to aid thought or communication. This contrasts with Washoe's behaviour — and may well relate to the fact that Sarah lived in a cage, with a regime of formal and lengthy training sessions whereas Washoe's life consists of interaction in a relatively free setting.

Washoe's performance has been particularly hotly debated. It has been argued that she has an extensive vocabulary; is able to sign about objects not present; uses signs that are concepts (e.g. 'sorry') and invents meaningful combinations of signs. However Bronowski and Bellugi (1970) have suggested that some key aspects of language use are not present (Bellugi has since revoked her opinion as expressed in that paper). They agreed that Washoe's behaviour might be taken as demonstrating these four criteria (which are supposed to reflect the evolution of language in man): (1) A delay between stimulus and response; (2) The separation of emotion from the actual content of the message; (3) The ability to refer backwards and forwards in time and therefore to exchange messages about future action; (4) The internalization of signs so that they cease to be just a means of social communication and become also means of refection, and formulation and choice of alternative messages before communicating.

Bronowski and Bellugi are not willing to concede that an animal has been able to show a fifth linguistic capacity, which is the structural activity of reconstitution, consisting of both a procedure of analysis (whereby messages are not treated as inviolate wholes but are broken down into smaller parts) and also a procedure of synthesis (whereby these parts are rearranged to form other messages).

It is clear that the debate as to whether chimpanzees such as Washoe have language rests to a large extent on a continual refinement of definitions of language in the face of the evidence the chimpanzees are providing. This in itself is valuable. For our present purposes, the matter may be allowed to rest with the observation that there certainly seems to be evidence of the use of signs as significant gestures (and studies of animals in the wild show evidence of significant gestures — e.g. Goodall, 1971). But the question of whether full linguistic ability can be shown is still moot.

CHAPTER 4

Perceiving Physical Objects and People

In discussing the perception of physical objects, it is argued that the idea of a perceptual process in which passive reception of stimulation at the senses is later interpreted is misleading. Rather, objects are already perceived as meaningful — awareness of objects is awareness of them 'as symbolized'.

This approach is continued in treatment of the perception of people. Others' 'physical' characteristics are perceived as reflecting their mental states — here emotional expression is discussed at length. Moreover in the perception of others, tendencies of the perceiver can often be seen as a source of bias (although they are an essential part of the process even when it is assumed to be taking place in an unbiased manner) thus discussion of stereotyping and the action of 'implicit personality theories' is necessary. Finally, the characteristics of the impression formed are delineated (after D. Bromley), and the general outline of the development of the capacity to perceive others suggested.

Perceiving is not to be regarded as distinct from thought, or from any of the topics that are used to organize discussion in later chapters — emotion, motivation and attitudes. Indeed, all these are largely labels of convenience, chosen merely to pinpoint a given focus of interest. After all, we perceive others' emotions, motives and attitudes, in some sense; motives lie behind our emotions and attitudes and so on. The linkages between these topics are so strong that they are best regarded in the way which reflects the truth of the matter: as aspects of one interaction/awareness nexus. Nevertheless, for purposes of exposition, topics must be isolated for comment. In this chapter and the next, perception is so isolated.

Triandis (1964), in an important review of research on the relationship between cognition and culture, introduced the topic of perception with an attempt at a definition: 'Physical energies impinge on the organism and are processed in such a way as to acquire meaning. The activation of the organism, in response to such energies, is called *sensation;* when meaning is added to sensation, the process is called *perception*' (pp. 12f). This passage is a concise and accurate account of the traditional treatment, in psychology and social psychology, of perception: the organism is regarded as stimulated at eyes and ears by various physical energies (which are best described in terms of physical science: light and sound waves of various frequencies and intensities). The resulting sensations of the eyes and ears (etc.) are uninterpreted, meaningless. At this stage physiological processes are activated that begin to process the sensations, and eventually conscious recognition and interpretation — i.e. perception — occurs.

It may be that as far as the physiology of perception is concerned this traditional view is adequate (though contrary evidence is given in Merleau-Ponty, 1962). However that may be, the social psychological understanding of perception must be quite different. We are, after all, entirely unaware of sensations. As J.J. Gibson (1968) pointed out, 'When the senses are considered as channels of sensation...one is thinking of the passive receptors and the energies that stimulate them...A great deal is known about the receptors...but all this exact knowledge of sensation is vaguely unsatisfactory since it does not explain how animals and men accomplish sense perception' (p. 3).

Accomplish perception? For Gibson perception is an active process, obviously. Not active in that the person somehow adds meaning to the raw sensations he has received, but rather the process of gleaning information from the environment is in itself active. Gibson goes on to describe the way in which the structuring of light is perceived in itself as meaningful, giving immediate information about surface textures, our own position and movement, and so on. For a conscious being, perception is not usefully regarded as a process by which sensation is interpreted, but it is more in keeping with the truth of the matter to regard environmental information as inherently meaningful: the categories of interpretation are presupposed in the act of surveying the environment. Meaning is simultaneous with sensory stimulation.

Merleau-Ponty (1947) refused to accept the usual model of perception, whereby one is assumed to take sensations and from them construct an interpretation which is the perceived object. 'I perceive before me a road or a house, and I perceive them as having a certain dimension: the road may be a country road or a national highway; the house may be a shanty or a manor. These identifications presuppose that I recognize the true size of the object, quite different from that which appears to me from the point which I am standing.' Do I, then, take the sensations and 'restore the true size on the basis of the apparent size by analysis and conjecture'? No, in fact I never *see* the 'apparent size'! 'It is a remarkable fact that the uninstructed have no awareness of perspective and that it took a long time and much reflection for men to become aware of a perspectural deformation of objects. Thus there is no deciphering, no mediate inference from the sign to what is signified, because the alleged signs are not given to me separately from what they signify' (pp. 198f). So, for the purposes with which we are concerned, what we see and hear is already meaningful and does not have to be interpreted by us in order to attain the status of percepts. This is not to deny that further thought might reveal new meanings in the sights and sounds, of course.

Some insight into what this point of view on perception entails is given by this research reported by R. Brown (1956). At the turn of the century, Rivers conducted a test amongst natives in the Torres Straits in which standard Holmgren colour yarns were to be sorted into categories. Rivers found that they consistently made certain 'odd' groupings which corresponded to verbal categories for them. Rivers decided that these colours did not really look alike but were put together because of a common name. But Brown argues that Rivers was being culture-bound here: 'One naturally hesitates on the threshold of believing that the categorization of physical reality is culturally relative.' Brown comments: 'But what ground can there be for denying that these colour groupings were perceptual categories? The subjects grouped the yarns with both linguistic and nonlinguistic class responses. What more do we do with our red, green and blue?' (Brown, 1956, pp. 306f).

To give another example of cultural variations in colour perception, Conklin (1955) reports that he was at a loss to understand the colour classifications of the Hanunóo of the Philippines until he asked his informants to *contrast* specimens rather than attempt to define isolated examples. In this way it was possible for him to discover that their system was organized in terms of different dimensions from our own.

Even colours then, which are open to fairly unproblematic specification in physical terms, and which are often regarded as being transduced at the receptors into some form of neural equivalent; even such examples of 'pure sensation' are not perceived as such. Colours are perceived as already meaningful. And the considerations of the effect of symbols on thought which were the subject-matter of Chapter 3 are as relevant in the field of perception.

PERCEIVING OBJECTS

Many authors, in the context of discussion of perception, have attempted to elucidate the notion of 'meaningfulness', and the common conclusion is that, if an entity had meaning, then the person would be able to categorize it in some way. Thus Bruner (1957) wrote 'Perception involves an act of categorization' (p. 123) and that perception 'depends upon the construction of a set of organized categories in terms of which stimulus inputs may be sorted, given identity, and given more elaborated, connotative meaning' (p. 148). Unfortunately, Bruner here appears to be reverting to the traditional view of perception as a process of interpreting stimulus data. However I feel that in his case the objection is merely to the form of words he adopts: the approach he is actually advocating concords with our view. (For other authors who have approached perception along similar lines to Bruner, see Shaw and Costanzo, 1970).

G.A. Kelly (1955), in his book *The Psychology of Personal Constructs* (see also Bannister and Fransella, 1971) puts forward a general view of human psychology that bears a resemblance to symbolic interactionism. He also views perception as inherently meaningful and moreover he arrived independently at a notion akin to Bruner's 'categorization': 'construing'. For Kelly: 'A person's processes are psychologically channellised by the ways in which he anticipates events' and 'a person anticipates events by construing their replications' (Kelly, 1955, p. 103). Although Kelly's work is marred in this way by odd language, what he means in these slogans is, partly, that perception (among other psychological processes) involves, not merely categorization of events after they have occurred, but an anticipation of probable events and the erection of a system of interpretative categories, in terms of which perception is accomplished, and is of inherently meaningful events. (By 'events' Kelly means all occasions for perception.)

Finally, to round off this short list of authors who have adopted views of perception which take full account of man's existence as a being that cannot but interpret his environment as meaningful, P. Kelvin (1970) takes the view that man's psychological processes are largely used to 'project' orderliness onto the environment. His view will be dealt with at greater length in Chapter 8. Its relevance here is that such an emphasis again demands that we reject the physiologist's sensation-based notion of perceiving. As Meltzer (1964) points out, we cannot view the environment as having a fixed character for everyone. Each has his own system of personal constructs or categories in terms of which his experience is ordered. More than this, his experience *really does* appear to him as he categorizes it, since objects and events are perceived as inherently meaningful.

A large number of different lines of empirical research have a bearing on the question of the extent to which individuals actualy differ in their perception of the world. Perhaps the most direct approach is again through cross-cultural studies.

Berry and Dasen (1974), in a collection of articles on *Culture and Cognition,* cite the work of such early psychological anthropologists as Rivers. Rivers and his team carried out a large number of experiments on memory and perception amongst the Torres Straits Islanders. For instance, he reported that visual acuity, for these 'savage and half-civilised people, though superior to that of the normal European is not markedly so'. On the other hand 'by long continued practice...in attending to minute details in surroundings with which he becomes extremely familiar, the savage is able to see and recognize distant objects in a way that appears almost miraculous, but it is doubtful whether his visual powers excell those of the European who has trained his vision to any special end' (see Berry and Dasen, 1974, p. 4).

Perhaps this conservative view of Rivers betrays the same culture-bound prejudice that Brown has detected in him (as we saw earlier). For there is evidence that measured visual acuity and other basic sensory capacities may vary with culture. Berry (1971) has argued convincingly that the skills which are particularly highly developed amongst a certain people relate to the demands imposed by their environment, and that the general culture and the language of the people can also be seen to be part of the response to environmental demands. He showed that hunting peoples possess good visual discrimination and spatial ability in comparison with peoples less dependent on hunting, and that similarly cultures differ in their support of the development of these skills through a vocabulary rich in 'geometrical spatial' concepts, a highly developed and widely shared concern with the production of craft goods, and socialization practices emphasizing independence and self-reliance — these differences being positively correlated with dependence on hunting.

In another study, Doob (1964) has shown a high incidence of 'eidetic imagery' (that is, the ability to retain an image of a perceived scene for a length of time with great clarity, so that it may be scanned and new information noticed in it) amongst the Ibos of Nigeria. Unlike Berry, he is unable to suggest a reason for the skill, although he believes it may be associated with the non-literate culture of this society.

Such research indicates the possibility of a general effect of the style of life and culture of a society on very general perceptual skills. However of more interest in the context of this book is evidence concerning the relationship between culture and more specific perceptual tendencies of a group. Here we are clearly back in the area of language and thought (Chapter 3) and the problem of linguistic, and perceptual relativity. Recall the viewpoint which this problem brings to the fore: 'Symbolization constitutes objects not constituted before, objects which would not exist except for the context of social relationships wherein symbolization occurs. Language does not simply symbolize a situation or object which is already there in advance; it makes possible the existence or the appearance of that situation or object, for it is part of the mechanism whereby that situation or object is created' (Mead, 1934, p. 78). Anyone who has spent long periods of time painstakingly comparing flowers or butterflies to the illustrations in their field guide, and who is later able to make instantaneous identifications as 'second nature' will understand something of what is meant by Mead's statement. And if they further reflect that their perception of this flower as a pyramidal orchid and that butterfly as a purple hairstreak brings into play a whole set of tacit understandings about the structure of natural reality, they will thereby be led to realize the social basis of their perceptions.

In this context, consider Sapir's view of the relationship between language, perception and culture: 'The 'real world' is to a large extent unconsciously built up on the language habits of the group. The worlds in which different societies live are *distinct* worlds, not merely the same world with different labels attached. We see and hear and otherwise experience very largely as we do because the language habits of our community predispose certain choices of interpretation' (cited in Fishman, 1960, p. 64).

Let us recall the theoretical basis for the view that the perceptual worlds of different societies are, in a sense, distinct worlds. It is that perception is a process of categorization, we perceive things already essentially meaningful, already interpreted. Since language provides us with preformed categories, then we will tend to perceive the world as coded through linguistic categories. Thus language will dictate perception. Certainly there is some evidence for such a view. Luria (1969) reviews Soviet work which shows the effect of verbal labelling as a means of enhancing discrimination and in aiding the person focus voluntary attention on particular aspects of objects with which he is confronted. This is in line with that view of linguistic relativity which regards a language as providing a means by which some perceptions are easy to make since they are 'easily coded' (Brown, 1965) or provided with readily-accessible categories (Triandis, 1964). However, the view that language *dictates* perception is too strong. For one thing, new objects can give rise to new perceptual categories and new words. Also it is possible to translate some notion of the Hopi perception of time, as shown in the language, so that English readers grasp some elements (Whorf, 1956).

Perhaps the strongest argument against the view that language and perception are 'container and thing contained', is, as Malinowski (1927) showed, that language itself is not self-contained. It depends on the situation and a large number of tacit conventions for its meaning. This fact points to a danger, incidentally, in the current dominant approach to ethnoscience. Ethnoscience, Goodenough is quoted as writing, takes as its starting point the view that: 'A society's culture consists of whatever it is one has to know or believe in order to operate in a manner acceptable to its members, and to do so in any role that they accept for any one of themselves' (Sturtevant, 1964, p.41). The dominant mode of research in ethnoscience aims to clarify this knowledge or belief by attempting to elucidate classifications of objects etc. as reflected by native terminology. This is an attempt to discover how people perceive and think about the world by means of the vocabulary they use to talk about it. This is all very well, but any approach to thought and perception through vocabulary and grammar assumes that language is self-contained and integral.

So Malinowski's warning is that the theory of linguistic relativity does *not* mean that we can discover the habitual constructs people use for perceiving things and situations just by looking at a dictionary of their language and a grammar. No — contructs people use for perceiving are largely coded by language-as-used; lived categories, not dictionary language. This is not surprising, after all Mead argued that the capacity to construe is developed by internalizing the process of interacting so that one has an internal conversation. This internal conversation is made possible by having symbols to represent things, people and events — and these symbols are largely linguistic.

Now if Mead's view is right it is language-as-used that supplies the symbols by which we can construe, not dictionary language. Language-as-used is intertwined inextricably with the situations in which it is used. We see now that language is not social merely because it is a product of our cultural group; it is not just that society gives us words which we can then use to refer to objects and events. Language is social in a broader sense than this: it is social situations that give us occasions for using the language, and the meaning of the words depend on the social setting in which they are uttered or employed to construe. This argument has already been aired to some extent in Chapter 2 in the context of the discussion of the interactionist notion of the definition of the situation, where the idea of verbal expressions as being 'indexical', and the notion of 'ad-hocing' in the categories of experience, both foreshadowed the understanding established in this section.

PERCEIVING OTHER PEOPLE

An initial consideration in treating the matter of perceiving other people is whether there is any fundamental difference between the accomplishment of object perceptions and the perception of people. Tagiuri (1969) argues for a basic similarity, and Heider (1958) agrees with earlier authors in concluding that, at least as a framework for discussion, it is valid to assume that 'the objects of social and non-social perception are similar in regard to their formal characteristics as well as in regard to the processes by which they are perceived' (p.21).

The perception of objects and persons is indeed similar, but it must be understood by this that both are perceived as inherently meaningful entities. The argument outlined in our discussion of perceiving objects applies equally to the perception of people. We are not conscious of meaning-free sensation; our perceptions are of already meaningful — already categorized or construed — people. To give an example, we do not interpret a stimulus (which I will come to know is a person) as of a certain configuration of face and body and then perceive that the person is categorizable as downcast and must be sad. No, in perceiving the person, his posture *is* sad — if I want to analyse what makes him look sad I do not run back through a process of inference to discover at what point I interpreted the stimulus as sad; the attempt at a process of analysis is a very different matter, not a mere reversal of the process of perception.

An effort of abstraction is required for one to see a person's facial expression, not as 'smiling' but as a particular configuration of muscular states. It is of course possible, but it is not a more basic, less elaborate percept — rather the reverse. Moreover, to reach this percept is by no means to get nearer to some primary configuration of stimuli, but is itself a meaning construction in every bit as complete a way as perception of a smiling face. The argument is the same were I to perceive the face, not as a smiling face nor as a set of muscular states, but as a pattern of colours, brightnesses and shades, and textures (cf.Gibson, 1968).

Another implication of the notion that perception is of meanings is that the enterprise of analysing person perception into contributory components is seen as of limited value. It is certainly not to be regarded out of hand as mistaken to study the part played by, for example, the various modes of non-verbal communication to the impression formed of another person. Yet there is an element of accuracy in Birdwhistell's dictum that 'non-verbal behaviour' is an area that is as sensible to delineate as such as 'non-cardiac physiology'. The total Gestalt is what is perceived by the observer. A person wearing a blank mask who moves angrily is seen as angry, and the face is also angry.

Shantz (1975), in a review of research on the development of person perception in childhood, states as a reason for using the term social cognition in preference to person perception: 'The suitability of "perception" has often been questioned because the characteristics, qualities, and covert experiences attributed to another person are not immediately given as observables' (p.265). This is an argument which opposes the view we have stated. However, it may be countered by the observation that 'mental states' are immediately understood as part of the meaning of the perceived facial expression or speech or movement. If perceiving a physical object as a 'red traffic light = stop' is regarded as a genuine percept, then perceiving a person's face as 'frowning = thoughtful' is no less genuine a percept. Of course room for error exists in both; and both percepts are bound by total context.

Secord and Backman (1964) err in picturing the process of person-perception as an interpretation of stimulus information, through the application of the perceiver's personal set of assumptions, stereotypes etc., to arrive at impressions of the person perceived including ideas about his personality, motives, likeability, etc. The error is not in recognizing that the various factors that Secord and Backman list are important, but rather in viewing the process as a sequential one, from stimulus through a process of interpretation to perception.

When the attempt is made to describe expressive behaviour, for instance, as if it were meaningless in itself — pure sensation — the attempt fails: one reason is that such and such a set of movements are selected from many as worthy of discussion only because of their meanings. Other reasons for the failure are clear from what has been said about perception as inherently meaningful.

Heider (1958) has pointed out that, because of people's meaning for us, we see them as distinguished from objects particularly in view of our immediate assumption that they 'can benefit or harm us intentionally, and we can benefit or harm them. Persons have abilities, wishes and sentiments; they can act purposefully, and can perceive or watch us. They are systems having an awareness of their surroundings and their conduct refers to this environment, an environment that sometimes includes ourselves' (p.21). These things we are already aware of when we perceive a person.

Thus, the perception of objects and people is similar in that in both cases perception is of inherently meaningful entities. But therefore there are differences between perceptions of objects and things because of the very different meanings involved.

What has been said thus far will indicate that our concern here is not with the physiology of the process of perception, nor with any attempt to uncover a process of inference whereby somehow a stimulus becomes a meaningful percept. Rather the concern is with what Heider differentiated as 'phenomenal': describing the direct experience of the person in perceiving others.

Cook (1971), in a review of the literature on person perception, argues against a version of the phenomenal approach. He differentiates between inferential (causal) views of person perception and 'intuitive' views — which emphasize the immediate meaningfulness of perceptions. Intuitive views, he believes, involve three propositions. Firstly, perception is *innate*. Here Cook cites the eighteenth-century philosopher Thomas Reid, who said, 'Nature is so constituted that certain empirical facts are signs of certain metaphysical facts and human nature is so constituted as to be able to interpret these signs intuitively' (Cook, 1971, p. 28). Inasmuch as this statement expresses the view that perception is immediately meaningful it concords with our view. However Cook argues cogently against the notion that any particular percept is innate, and indeed this view cannot be seriously held. Immediacy of meaning in perception does not require this. There is no limitation, implied by the idea that perception is inherently meaningful, on the human capacity to cogitate upon percepts and to invest them with further significance. Neonate perception is doubtless minimally structured — the meanings will be as limited as is the capacity for symbolic functioning.

Secondly, person perception is *global*, i.e. the perception of others is not a matter of piecemeal inference, but an immediate general impression. Again this concords with our view. Cook merely points out that people *can* judge isolated aspects of personality, when asked. This is true, but not relevant to the question, since it either demands an analysis of a perception already achieved, or is dependent on judgment situations that are quite artificial (e.g. Asch, 1946). Finally, person perception is *immediate*. Cook believes this implies perception is infallible. I do not see why this should be an implication — and of course it is certainly not true.

As Cook indicates, our approach to perception involves the view that perceiving 'does not require any identification or description of the physical appearance of the subject' (p.29). No pure stimulus is registered, later to be turned into a percept by a process of interpretation. I do not see a hat and coat moving along, and infer a person is there; still less do I base my interpretation on registering sensations of meaningless colour!

Perceiving others: appearance and expressive behaviour

Secord and Backman's (1964) presentation of the 'process' of person perception has been criticized earlier, on the grounds that it suggests a sequential train of events whereby meaningless stimuli (physical appearance; expressive and other motor behaviour; verbal behaviour) are, as it were, operated on by a number of 'perceiver variables' (including previous attitudes to the stimulus person, and implicit personality theory and stereotypes), to produce a finished perception of the person (including attributions of personality, motive and so on). This implication of their scheme must be resisted. Nevertheless, the factors they list are undoubtedly relevant to the study of person perception — though not as 'variables which determine the process' but rather as descriptive categories which the observer may abstract from the total perceptual realm for separate consideration. To repeat what has become a leitmotif, treatment of what Secord and Backman call 'stimulus information' should not be divorced from 'perceiver variables' and 'resultant impressions' other than for ease of exposition; skin colour is already categorized as good or bad in the very fact of being perceived by a person holding certain stereotypes.

Physical appearance

Let us consider clothing as an example. Stone (1962), in a paper entitled *Appearance and the self,* was partly concerned to criticize and remedy an overemphasis on verbal language in symbolic interactionist social psychology. Of course words are very important in social psychology because they allow us to construe situations, role expectations and so on. But Stone argues that words have been overemphasized, and it can be argued that clothing can form a symbol-system. We make statements about ourselves by means of clothing. In his paper, Stone points out that clothing changes during childhood reflecting the culturally significant process of 'growing up'. He quotes, as a graphic example, a postal clerk in the Southern states of the USA who recalled his childhood sequence of clothing like this: 'I can remember back in the South, 45 years ago, the . . . boys always wore dresses up to the time they were 3 or 4 years old. When I was about 5, 6, 7 or 8 (I) wore those little Fauntleroy suits. God damn! I hated those. Then knickers came. I wore those until I was about 15 years old . . . when I had my first long pants suit' (p.107).

This sequence (Stone says) reflects culturally defined stages in childhood. So clothing helps others form an impression of the age of the child — and puts him in a role-category. Stone also argues that the child's clothing is a prop that helps him gain a self-concept. Stone's paper contains a lot more than this. But perhaps this is sufficient to indicate the importance that clothing and appearance have. The details of the nature of the symbol-system of clothing are far from clearly worked out yet. All that really can be said is that there surely is a meaning to be read from the clothing people wear. As Argyle (1975) points out, some elements of clothing are quite overtly intended to convey a meaning. Badges, uniforms, special ties, wedding and engagement rings and so on. Membership of age, sex and class categories is conveyed by clothing. On the relationship between class and clothing, Veblen (1899) argued that high social status was signalled by the wearing of clothes that were unsuitable for manual work and involved conspicuous consumption.

Hair is a part of one's physical appearance which can be treated as clothing. One 'wears' one's hair in a certain way. Possibly the meaning of hair style is to assign the wearer to some very broad category. Hallpike (1969) has put forward the view that many societies have a similar interpretation of long hair, which is taken to indicate being beyond social normative control, and is worn by outcasts, intellectuals, religious ascetics and anyone, in short, who wishes to signal that others are not to regard them as necessarily conforming to usual attitudes and behaviour. However, as Leach (1976) points out, in another context, almost all such cultural signs are capable of reversal: 'The indices in non-verbal communication systems . . . do not have meaning as isolates but only as members of sets. A sign or symbol only acquires meaning when it is discriminated from some other contrary sign or symbol' (p.49). Thus long hair is categorized and perceived as meaning non-conforming in contrast to 'normal hair length', and it is entirely possible (as in the 'skinhead' phenomenon in the UK in the late 1960s and early 1970s) for the sign to be reversed. Similarly, a sign of wealth can be the adoption of poor clothing.

Expressive motor behaviour

This area is usually referred to as non-verbal communication. Under this heading, research has been carried out, in particular, on the following matters: (1) Bodily contact, physical proximity and orientation of the body with respect to the other person (an area of research sometimes called 'proxemics', Hall, 1966); (2) Gestures, and small-scale body movements (which is an area included in what Birdwhistell, 1968, has termed 'kinesics'); and (3) The special area of the study of eye movements and patterns of gaze. These three divisions of non-verbal behaviour merely order the research, they have no other status — they are not even mutually exclusive.

1. *Bodily contact, proximity and orientation* An indication of the meaning of proximity is seen in findings by Jourard (1963), who has shown the relationship between bodily contact and intimacy. In general, the meaning of the spatial relationship between one person and other appears to be that closeness signals intimacy, distance — indeed, the word can be the same: we say a person who signals lack of intimacy is 'distant'. The spatial metaphor in the verbal expression of intimacy directly reflects a nonverbal sign.

    The meaning of spatial proximity as intimacy is only a very general tendency. Other meanings are also present, depending on other features of the situation of interaction (non-verbal signals always are in context, and their meaning relates to the 'definition of the situation'). For instance, Henley (1973) found that men touched women more frequently than women touched men — a result she viewed as showing that status or power was a factor, not just intimacy. Although this interpretation is contentious, it is certainly the case that, as Argyle (1975) details, status and power are reflected in spactial behaviours in a large number of contexts, perhaps because authority and intimacy are, in some contexts, at opposite poles of a dimension of meaning — authority is cold and distant and sits behind the desk rather than on the same side as a person of lower status.

E.T. Hall (1966) coined the term 'proxemics' to cover the study of human spatial behaviour. He devised eight operational categories for assessing proxemic phenomena, each category being intended to assess a particular aspect of spatial relationship:

(a) Postural-sex identifiers — a category which classifies people as to sex, and whether standing, sitting or lying down.

(b) Sociofugal-sociopetal axis — which scores people according to the relationship of the axis of one person's shoulders to those of the other.

(c) Kinesthetic factors — a ranking of people in terms of closeness to each other.

(d) Touch code — categorizing people in the degree of contact during interaction.

(e) Visual code — scoring the degree of visual contact, from mutual gaze to complete avoidance of catching sight of the other person.

(f) Thermal code — provides for the possibility of detecting the other's body heat.

(g) Olfaction code — gives a score if the smell of the other is detected.

(h) Voice-loudness scale — a measure of the actual physical intensity of sound produced, a loud manner of speech being regarded by Hall as proxemically 'close' behaviour.

Work within the framework of proxemics has been carried out cross-culturally. Hall himself has described, for instance, the varying definitions of 'personal space' amongst Germans, French and English — illustrating cultural differences in matters related to what Goffman terms 'front' and 'back' regions. Watson and Graves (1966), using Hall's operational categories, studied differences between students in the USA who came from various parts of the United States and those who came from Arab countries. They found consistent differences between those from these cultural backgrounds: the Arab students faced each other more directly than the Americans, were closer together, more likely to touch each other while talking, looked each other in the eye more frequently, and talked louder. However, Watson and Graves' work was entirely at the behavioural level, and they confess that no information was gleaned about the meaning of the behaviour. Mehrabian (1968), on the other hand, has attempted to relate behaviour to the attitude it embodies. For instance, he reports that greater relaxation, a forward lean of the body, and a close proximity to the person one is interacting with communicate a positive attitude.

2. *Gestures and small-scale body movements* Gestures have been studied by Birdwhistell as 'kinesics — the science of body behavioural communication' (Birdwhistell, 1968, p.379). He is not concerned with the meaning of the movements, but merely with behavioural description. In particular, he has attempted to classify kinesic phenomena in a quasi-

linguistic manner, claiming that there is a 'language' of movement comparable to a spoken language.

Perhaps the most interesting part of the question of whether non-verbal stimuli form a language comparable with verbal language is the part that deals with structure. Can there be said to be a grammar of gestures? Can kinesic research discover structural units like the linguists' phonemes (approximately: sounds), morphemes (approximately: words) and sentences. Birdwhistell claims it can. He calls the least perceptible unit of body movement a *kine* (comparable perhaps with a phoneme). The eyebrow lift and return is regarded as an example (transcribed vv V). Larger units (e.g. the whole face when deadpan: O) are *kinemes* (=morphemes). Thus a conversation of gestures and facial expressions can be recorded by Birdwhistell in terms of what he regards as their constituent parts.

Birdwhistell has reported 33 positions of face and body, including four positions of the eyebrow, four of the eyelid and seven of the mouth. Argyle (1969) reports that the Indian Nandikesvara theatre uses 28 eye-positions and six formalized positions of the eyebrow — so there is a wide range of discriminable facial expressions. As far as the question of the analogy between language and gesture is concerned, the criterion must be Mead's. If gestures are intended to convey a meaning to another, whose attitude is imagined in the formulation of the gesture, then the gesture is significant, and is communicative whether verbal or not.

3.   *Eye movements and pattern of gaze* The study of eye gestures is part of kinesics, but a part that has received special attention (cf.Argyle, 1975, Chapter 12). Apart from gaze as an aspect of intimacy-signalling, eye movements are said to play a part in the regulation of verbal interaction. Kendon (1967) showed that, in conversation, looking indicates attention to the speaker. Listeners look, but speakers only glance. The end of a stretch of talk by the one is signalled by, for example, the speaker glancing to signify he is ending. Kendon has suggested that the typical pattern of speaker/hearer glances serves to regulate 'floor apportionment' such that a hearer is aware that he may now take the role of speaker because the current speaker gives him a 'sustained' gaze. However, this function of gaze has been questioned by Beattie (1978) and by Rutter and colleagues (1978), and Kendon (1978) concurs with the argument that gaze pattern is not inevitably associated with the regulation of floor apportionment, and suggests that there might be an overwhelming effect of the specifics of the situation. Apart from this very specific hypothesized function of gaze, Steer (see Argyle, 1975) has suggested that any change in activity is the occasion for increased gaze, and particularly the special transition point of beginning and ending an encounter. Less problematic than the function of regulating conversation are the function of gathering information about the interlocutor, and the expressive function of communicating feelings and attitudes. It is to the facial expression of emotion that we now turn.

Facial expression of emotion

Plainly a great deal of non-verbal behaviour is perceived as carrying emotional meanings. Eye movements are interpreted, in context, as indicative of the other's feelings as we have seen. Indeed, Exline (1972) mentions the widespread belief in the evil eye, among other evidence of the importance of gaze in signalling feelings. Mutual gaze has been regarded as either establishing bonds of unity of feeling (Simmel, 1969) or as a channel mediating the robbery by the one of the personal autonomy of the other (Sartre, 1958). Exline suggests that gaze is ambiguous: it can be occasioned both by love and by a relationship of dominance/submissiveness. (This particular ambiguity is not unusual in interpersonal relations, as Laing, 1970, has persuasively argued.)

Yet, 'it seems clear that eye engagement alone is not sufficient to indicate the nature of the relationship' (Exline, p. 200). The total context is perceived in terms of such meanings. Part of the total context is facial expression, and — although the fact that it is only part of the situation makes the study of facial expression a limited enterprise as we shall see — a great deal of valuable work has been done on the perception of facial expression as emotional.

Dimensions of emotional expression Darwin (1872) postulated that emotional expressions are universal: the physical movement of face and body (and the experience of which it forms a part) are innate: they are the vestiges of reactions which were, in earlier stages of the evolution of man, effective in the service of survival. If this universality of emotional expression were actually found, it would necessarily imply that cultural differences were not operative in this behaviour, and it would also suggest that a search for an orderly way of categorizing, or otherwise regularizing, the description of emotional expressions could sensibly be undertaken, with the expectation that a biological basis to the description might be found.

The question of the universality or cultural relativity of emotions is taken up below. Work on the orderly description of the very varied facial expressions of emotion began by a consideration of confusability between different expressions. The stimuli often, but not always, being posed photographs.

Woodworth (1938) attempted to find some regularity in the errors made by subjects in recognizing facial expressions. Six categories of expression were used (love, mirth, happiness; surprise; fear; anger, determination; disgust; contempt), and Woodworth showed that confusion is generally between neighbouring categories in that list. Thus a fearful expression, if not correctly perceived, might be judged as angry/determined, or as surprised. Judgments of loving/mirthful/happy or disgusted were less frequent when the intended emotion was fear. Woodworth viewed this finding as indicating that emotions could be arranged in order along a single continuum from love to contempt. As Stringer (1973) points out, Woodworth's contribution was the idea that accuracy in perceiving expressions might be less interesting than the pattern of errors.

Schlosberg (1952) observed that, since errors occurred in judgments of facial expression across the ends of Woodworth's continuum (such that happiness could be confused with contempt), the ordering of expressions was better represented as a circle. Furthermore, since a circular surface can be defined in terms of two axes, Schlosberg hypothesized that facial expressions can be located on a circular surface when subjects judged them according to the degree of pleasantness/unpleasantness and attention/rejection the expressions exhibit. Thus fear would tend to be located in the 'high attention, high unpleasantness' part of the surface.

In a later paper, Schlosberg (1954) proposed that facial expressions could be ordered in a three dimensional space, which accounted for almost all the variation in the expressions. These three dimensions were: pleasant *vs.* unpleasant; sleep *vs.* tension, and attention *vs.* rejection — the last one being least well substantiated in subsequent work. Osgood (1966) conducted an experiment in which subjects had to label, from a list of forty emotions, a number of live, but motionlessly posed, expressions. These were analysed adequately in terms of three underlying dimensions: pleasant *vs.* unpleasant; intensity (comparable with Schloserg's tension *vs.* sleep), and control — the last being a dimension which originated with Osgood. Finally, Frijda (1970) asked subjects to rate 68 photographs of an actor and 62 of an actress on forty bipolar adjectival scales. Analysed separately for the two 'stimulus' figures, five dimensions emerged: pleasant *vs.* unpleasant; emotional intensity *vs.* control or indifference; self assertiveness *vs.* dependence; natural *vs.* artificial; attention *vs.* disinterest. Dissatisfied with such results because the dimensional model did not seem to Frijda to allow the emergence of a sufficiently differentiated picture of emotional expression, he turned to the analysis of the data in terms of clusters, which reproduced the dimensions already discovered, but with the addition of finer differentiations. He argues for a 'hierarchical' view of the relationships between emotional expressions, each emotion having 'amongst its defining attributes some that represent...more or less general variables...Other attributes are specific for that group of emotions' (pp. 246f). In this way eighteen different emotions appear in Frijda's results. In another paper, he confesses that 'the question of the number of expressive dimensions, or aspects, or categories, has yet to be decided' (Frijda, 1969, p. 217).

The process of sorting photographs or posed, motionless expressions of emotion, is clearly an artificial one. In a review of this field of research, Stringer (1973) suggests that it has much to offer, yet he argues that it should be linked to studies of emotional change, and studies of social interaction in emotional situations. Certainly many authors express some dissatisfaction with the approach — largely because the 'emotions' are 'expressed' out of any emotional context and free from movement (see, for instance, Frijda, 1969, 1973). The total context is fragmented, and thus the perception is of an unreal event.

Universality or cultural relativity in emotional expression Darwin postulated universality in emotional expressions. Labarre (1947), on the other hand, cited example after example of cultural variation in the signalling of emotion.

Consider, first, some of Labarre's examples. He points out that anthropologists must be sensitive to cultural divergences in expressing emotions if only because their safety in fieldwork could well depend on a correct interpretation. Thus even so apparently basic an expression of emotion as smiling 'may almost be mapped after the fashion of any other culture trait' (p. 52). The Japanese smile is not necessarily a spontaneous signal of amusement but a social duty, a rule of behaviour adopted in certain circumstances so as to avoid inflicting sorrow on another. Cultures vary a great deal, according to Labarre, in the readiness with which laughter and smiling are displayed; he contrasts Papuan hilarity and Dobuan dourness, for example, in the South Pacific.

Putting out the tongue is merely a childish sign of contempt and provocation in European culture; Bengali statues of the mother goddess Kali show the tongue protruded as a signal of rage and shock; South Chinese use the same expression, very briefly, to show embarrassment.

Such examples as these are marshalled as evidence for Labarre's view that emotional expressions are culturally relative. Darwin and he are perhaps at the most extremely opposed points in this debate. The position of Klineberg (1938), though relativist, is less dogmatic.

Klineberg (1938) studied similarities and differences between Western non-verbal expressions of emotion and Chinese emotional behaviour. He did this by reading a number of Chinese novels, and noting all the instances where emotional behaviour was described. There is a clear danger in this method — the literature of a society may reflect the characteristics of one social class, or there might be a stylized, literary convention about emotional behaviour that is remote from real life — e.g. 'holding up one's hands in horror' is a literary phrase that may or may not reflect what actual, horrified people do.

Bearing these dangers in mind, then, here are some of Klineberg's discoveries from Chinese literature: 'Everyone trembled with a face the colour of clay' expressed fear, as did 'Every one of his hairs stood on end'. Fear appears to be expressed in these cases in ways that Europeans would recognize. But 'They stretched out their tongues' represented surprise in the Chinese books Klineberg read, and 'Her eyes grew open and wide' indicated anger, not surprise or fear. 'The pimples came out on the skin all over his body' and 'It was as though her two feet were nailed to the ground and she would fain have shrieked, but her mouth was like a mute's' are both expressions of fear which a European would have recognized. 'He looked at them and smiled and cursed them' reminds one of the smile or sneer of contempt that occurs in our culture, but it seems that in China a smile of anger is a more frequent occurrence than in Europe. 'He was so angry that several times he fainted from his anger' introduces a convention surrounding the action of fainting that we would not recognize. Fainting as a way of expressing emotions seems to vary in its meaning in different cultures. Chinese faint in anger. Mid-Victorian, delicately nurtured young ladies fainted elegantly as an expression of surprise.

Some expressions of emotion are specific to the Chinese culture — others seem more universal. Perhaps we can guess that some of the globally-shared non-verbal behaviour is built into the structure of the human nervous system, and is a product of human evolution. However this may be, Klineberg's theory involves two types of non-verbal behaviour: universal and culture-specific. Klineberg himself gives more weight to culture-specific expressions of emotion. So he is a cultural relativist in general — though he does acknowledge *some* universals.

Ekman (1971; Ekman and Friesen, 1971) has adopted a somewhat more rigorous methodology in an attempt to reconcile the universalist and cultural relativist views.

How can the debate between the universalists and the cultural relativists be settled? What is required is some unquestionable piece of evidence that strongly supports one view and cannot be explained at all by those who hold the other view. Ekman argued that if people from culture A could correctly recognize emotional expressions produced by members of culture B this would be strong evidence for universality, since the cultural relativist would only be able to explain it by suggesting that, by chance, the two cultures had developed the same signal for the same emotion. Such an explanation would hardly convince. Ekman also saw that the more cultures were studied, and the more emotional expressions were correctly interpreted by the members of these cultures, the greater the weight of evidence for the universalist position would be produced.

In the first of his cross-cultural studies of the recognition of emotion, then, Ekman chose thirty-two photographs of facial expressions of emotion. These were chosen from over 3000 pictures — some posed and other spontaneous. And they were chosen as clearcut, definite examples of single emotions (that is, unmixed — so that in the case of happiness, any pictures showing also an element of surprise were rejected, as were any other mixed emotions).

The photographs were shown one at a time to individuals who were asked to judge whether the picture represented happiness, fear, disgust, anger, surprise or sadness. Participants were 99 Americans, 40 Brazilians, 119 Chileans, 168 Argentinians and 29 Japanese.

The result of this study was that agreement was very high. In 30 of the 32 pictures there was little dissent from the intended judgment. In two of them, however, the Japanese judges were more likely to see the pictures as indicating disgust than, in the one case happiness and in the other case anger.

Ekman took this result as heavily supporting universal expressions of emotion — five cultural groups are generally agreed about the meanings of facial expressions of six emotions. But of course criticisms can be raised — and have been. All the cultures were literate and exposed to the influences of mass media, which are largely western influences. All the pictures were of white, western people. So, even if a facial expression means something else in Japan, a Japanese participant in Ekman's study might well realize that, since the pictures are of westerners, western rules of facial expression apply, so he uses the knowledge he has from the mass media and other contacts with western culture to judge the photographs. A critic of Ekman could therefore argue that this is not evidence of universality, but merely shows that members of culture A can pick up the rules of facial expression used by culture B without too much difficulty. This study, then, does not force us to reject cultural relativity in the expression of emotions.

Ekman conceded the validity of these criticisms of his study and thereupon designed a second piece of research which was intended to overcome the problems we have discussed. This time the cultures were remote, non-literate tribal groups in New Guinea. The Fore people were one group, and participants were chosen who had seen no movie films, neither spoke nor understood English or Pidgin, had not lived in any western or westernalized settlements and had never worked for a westerner. Ekman argued that such people would not have had the opportunity to learn western emotional expressions. A second group, the Dani people lived some 500 miles from the Fore. These also had nothing but casual and incidental contact with westerners.

Now the method had to be adapted quite a lot, because non-literate cultures do not merely differ from literate ones in that they do not have writing: this difference brings with it quite marked differences in ways of thinking. So presenting the New Guineans with photos and asking what emotion they represent would be a very foreign task for them. Instead the individual Fore or Dani participant would be shown two or three photographs together, and he would be given a short description of some emotional situation. Now which of these pictures shows the emotion fitting that situation?

The situations were chosen as reflecting emotional events for the Dani or Fore — they would not necessarily be emotion-provoking for westerners. The test was whether the New Guineans would pick pictures of, say, what westerners would regard as happy expressions when they had heard a description of what would be for New Guineans a happy situation. If so, the universalist view would be upheld. When New Guineans are happy, they express the emotion in the same way as westerners. This was indeed what happened. So this is good evidence for the universalist view. For happiness, sadness, disgust, anger, fear and surprise the Dani and Fore recognized the faces which westerners, too, would associate with those emotions.

Ekman's work might suggest that the universalist view is entirely vindicated and that all cultures share the same set of emotional expressions. But what about Klineberg's evidence of cultural relativity — was he mistaken in thinking that the Chinese have some unique emotional expressions? Ekman himself has provided evidence that Klineberg is, paradoxically, correct. There is universality, but there is specificity as well.

Ekman (1971) reports a study comparing American and Japanese expressions of emotion. He arranged for participants to view a short film containing both non-emotional material and fairly horrific sequences (of body mutilation). The two cultural groups were studied in their own countries. During the showing of the film, unbeknown to the participants, their reactions were videotaped so that a comparison between the cultures could be made. In this situation the facial expression of horror were similar.

So far, this is in line with Ekman's other research in supporting the idea that emotional expressions are universal. But after the film had been shown, participants discussed it with a fellow-countryman who had not been with them seeing it. Now the facial expressions were *not* the same for Americans and Japanese. The Americans still made horror faces when talking about the film whereas the Japanese discussed it with polite smiles. Here we have an example of the sort of cultural relativity Klineberg showed in Chinese literature.

It appears, then, that the immediate emotional reaction is universal, so we could expect to interpret the feelings of another person correctly, whatever their culture, if we saw their immediate reaction. However cultures differ in their conventional emotional displays, and we might misunderstand the expressions of other cultural groups when members are describing an emotional situation or reacting after the event.

Moreover, a certain expression which is universally the immediate reaction to a given situation, may also be attached by a culture to a quite different situation as its conventional emotional display. Leach (1976) writes, 'Nearly all such automatic reactions may be used to convey culturally recognised messages. For example, in English convention weeping "means" sorrow, laughter "means" joy, a kiss "means" love. But these conscious associations are not human universals. . . For example, formalised weeping very frequently forms part of the correct behaviour of mourners at a funeral. But the official mourners are not necessarily the individuals one might expect to be emotionally affected. Indeed, in some cases, "those who weep" are simply hired professionals quite unrelated to the deceased' (p. 47).

It may be worthwhile to consider immediate reactions as being at the level of Mead's conversation of gestures whereas the culturally-determined emotional expression is a significant symbol. It is also possible to view the immediate reaction as linked to emotional expression by 'display rules' (e.g. 'stiff upper lip' or 'when in sorrow, smile').

The suppression of immediate reaction in favour of conventional expressions guided by display rules does not eliminate immediate reactions. Ekman and Friesen (1969) have argued that those who can sensitise themselves to attend to these responses have a means of discovering the true attitude of the person to the interaction.

Finally, in comment on this cross-cultural work on emotions, I would like to point out that the cultural relativity of emotional reactions does not put into doubt the immediacy with which perception of emotional reactions occurs. Even these culturally relative expressions, such as the Chinese plucking of a sleeve to indicate frustration and dissatisfaction with the situation experienced, are perceived as categorized — immediately meaningful.

To put this matter of cultural relativity of emotional expression in context, Triandis (1964) has reviewed the evidence and concludes that in general people universally agree in the categorization of facial expressions of emotion. The cultural differences 'must be considered in the same class as customs, rather than as fundamental differences in cognitive functioning' (p. 17).

Implicit personality theory and stereotypes

Generally, implicit personality theory is taken to refer to the idea that everyone has a set of beliefs about people, including an informal set of notions concerning personality, which they bring to each interaction and in terms of which they perceive others. Early experimental research on this was carried out by Thurstone (1934) who asked sixty people to underline on a checklist every adjective which referred to a person who they knew well. The data from all subjects was used to compute the regularity with which each adjective was used in conjunction with each other adjective, and by this process Thurstone showed the relationship between adjectives — and therefore the likelihood that, in forming an impression of a person, evidence that *one* adjective is correctly used to describe him, will be taken as evidence also that other descriptions are correct. (We know Jim is systematic, and we also infer that he is hardworking and persevering, although we have no evidence except that he is systematic — the other descriptions are projections of our implicit theory of personality.) Other key researches akin to Thurstone's have been carried out by Asch (1946), and — as a correction and extension to Asch's work — Wishner (1960).

There are quite a number of methodological problems with this approach. Bromley (1977) and Mischel (1968) have argued that the claim of Thurstone and the others to have shown that traits of personality form clusters when individuals rate others using these traits, may not indicate a mental fact but a linguistic one: 'Studies of so-called "implicit theories of personality" have shown that, in the mind of a judge or a rater, the possession by a stimulus person of one trait tends to imply the presence or absence of other traits, with some measurable degree of probability. We have already seen, however, that in natural language certain words tend to go together or to be related, as synonyms or autonyms, for example, or in other collocations and associative networks' (Bromley, 1977, p. 69).

There is no solution to this paradox in a symbolic interactionist approach to mind and language: mind is to be regarded as a process of symbol-use, and language is the main system of symbols. The one will mirror the other. So what Bromley says is correct, but the apparent problem posed is perhaps best regarded as illusory.

A further criticism made by Bromley of the type of approach to research on personality description exemplified by the work on implicit personality theory is more weighty. It is the very idea of using checklists of traitnames as research instruments. He reviews the approach as it appears in work of Allport and Odbert (1936), who published a list of 17,953 trait terms: 'individualised ways of behaving due to psychological dispositions'. Allport and Odbert are taken to task on three grounds in particular. They seem to make the mistake of believing that words are equivalent to meanings. But 'words do not carry a fixed quantum of meaning, but are capable of a wide range of meanings depending on their linguistic context and the surrounding circumstances' (Bromley, p. 72). If it is words-in-action that are meaningful, rather than dictionary entries, then Allport and Odbert hide an indefinitely large number of descriptive meanings behind their 17,953 items. And the enterprise of using traitnames as the bases for rating scales makes the same mistake. Bromley suggests that the error is made plain in Allport and Odbert when they exclude from their treatment the whole area of idioms and circumlocutions', yet acknowledge that 'There appears to be no limit to the possible making of phrases' (Allport and Odbert, 1936, p. 30).

A second complaint of Bromley concerning the Allport and Odbert study which may also be applied to studies of implicit personality theories, is that personality description ought not to be analysed merely in terms of personality traits. Moods, motives, intentions, habits, personal circumstances, and so on, are also of the utmost importance in our perception of others. Bromley's own work in the treatment of these varied aspects of personality description will be reviewed below.

Finally, Bromley is dubious about the constraint on language-use which checklists impose. The richness of structure of ordinary language, in which people may be described with real precision using not only 'and' and 'but', but also qualifying the traits described by citing evidence, stating limitations on the appropriateness of a particular term, hesitating about the representativeness of a particular behaviour for inferring a trait, etc. All in all, Bromley argues very convincingly for the superiority of free descriptions of persons.

Perhaps rather more impressive evidence on the effect of implicit theories of personality then, is found in the work of Dornbusch and his colleagues, reported in a paper entitled *The perceiver and perceived: their relative influence on categories of interpersonal perception* (1965). Children's *free* (cf Bromley, 1977) descriptions of other children were collected in interviews. Children were aged between 9 and 11, and were taking part in summer camps for the underprivileged. A category system for content analysis of the descriptions was devised so as to stay as near to the children's own reports as possible, and 69 categories were used (for a comparable attempt for adult personality descriptions, see the next section of this chapter). The reliability of the coding, when coders were compared in analysing the same reports, was high (in more than 86% of the elements of description, coding was identical.

Analyses were made of the descriptions in three ways: (a) Individual children's descriptions of two other campers were compared; (b) Pairs of children were compared in their descriptions of the same camper; (c) Pairs of children were compared in their descriptions of two different campers (A's description of X being compared with B's description of Y).

These analyses were used to test whether a person's implicit theory of personality so determines his description of others that his descriptions of two others (analysis a) are more alike than his description and another's description of the same camper (analysis b). Dornbusch and his colleagues found that indeed this was the case: there was the highest overlap of categories where the same person was doing the describing; descriptions in which the person being described was the same but different people supplied the reports were next in degree of overlap of categories. Those descriptions which merely shared language and setting, where different children described separate other campers (c) were least similar in the categories used — though there was still a degree of overlap which the investigators found surprising. In toto, the overlap in analysis (a) was 57%, in analysis (b) 45%, in analysis (c) 38%.

The degree of category overlap where two campers are described by two separate children (c) indicates the restricted vocabulary of person-descriptive categories being employed: the children only had access to a limited range of terms — and, as we shall see, the capacity to describe people develops during childhood and adolescence (Shantz, 1975).

Two children describing the same person seem to view him in rather different perspectives, so that the category overlap is only 7% greater than if they were describing quite different people. And when one child describes two different people the effect of the describer's perspective is seen: there is quite a lot more overlap (12% more) than in two children's descriptions of the same fellow-camper.

Dornbusch and his colleagues argue that this indicates the importance of the cognitive structure of the perceiver in describing others: the implicit personality theory is an aspect of this structure. It is erroneous, in our view, to interpret this notion as meaning that the 'true stimulus' and the 'perceiver factor of implicit personality theory' can be separated. Perception is inevitably 'owned' by a perceiver — were it not meaningful within his cognitive structure it would not be perception. The work of Dornbusch and the other authors in this field is rather to be taken as demonstrating the fact that the perception arrived at by a person is to be located within his mental framework, and ultimately to his biographical experiences, his language, culture and so on.

Stereotyping is a parallel phenomenon to the use of implicit personality theory in perceiving others. However, where a person is perceived as stereotyped, there is an implication, in describing the perception as stereotyped, that the description would be widely shared. An implicit personality theory would structure the way the perceiver described another person in such a way that the description of him would conform to certain empirically determined rules: certain personality traits would be mentioned, others thereby being excluded from the description — and the implicit personality theory might well contain rules of description which are relatively idiosyncratic. Other perceivers might have rather different implicit personality theories (cf. Dornbusch's analysis (a) compared with his analysis (b) shows that the perceiver may be different from other perceivers in aspects of his description of others). In stereotyping, different perceivers will tend to share a system of categories for perceiving others, because of some overriding characteristic that the person being perceived is seen as having.

In stereotyping, then, there is wide agreement among perceivers about the description of a person (Dornbusch's analysis (b) might have tapped some stereotyped perceptions, whereby two perceivers tend to agree on the description of another). But note that the agreement obtained through stereotyping is not due to 'accurate' reading of characteristics of the perceived person. Rather, stereotyping involves the assignment of a person to a category because of perceived group membership (e.g. dark skin pigmentation → a Black). With such categorization is invoked an assumption that the person has a set of predetermined personal characteristics. Thus the agreement between perceivers is not due to an assessment of the characteristics of the individual being considered but is due to a shared set of assumptions about the characteristics expected of all individuals of that category.

Stereotyping, therefore, allocates an individual, not just to a category, but to one which is 'constellatory' (Kelly, 1955; Bannister and Fransella, 1971): as a constellation is a cluster of stars perceived as a unit, so stereotyping involves the assumption that 'Black', for instance, involves a cluster of associated characteristics. Moreover, stereotyping is 'pre-emptive': the individual is regarded as nothing but an exemplar of the category. His personal characteristics as an individual are unconsidered.

Finally, in stereotyping it is usually thought that we find very stable perceptions; ones that are not liable to easy change (Allport, 1954a). The reasons for this will be apparent in reading Chapter 8 on attitude structures, but briefly the fact of the constellatoriness of stereotypes assists stability since the interrelated attitudes are mutually supportive. Again, their pre-emptiveness helps avoid the disrupting effect of dissonant attitudes. Stereotypes serve personal functions for the perceiver (Katz, 1960) such as ego-defence, which may be expected to lead to a desire to preserve them. But the functions of stereotypes are not merely personal, there are also bases in wider social and historical processes for the stereotypes which make up ideologies (Brown, 1973).

Stereotyping can, of course, have a very strong effect, as Zillig (1928) showed in an experiment in which two groups of children, one well liked and the other disliked performed physical exercises in front of their fellow-pupils. The liked pupils intentionally made errors, and the other children performed accurately and well — yet the audience recalled later that the liked group had performed better than the disliked group.

Although the tendency in our account of stereotyping has been to emphasize its negative aspects, there is no doubt that some such mechanism is essential to social action. On the basis of slight knowledge (occupation, sex, age, etc.) wide predictions of behaviour may be made that are often accurate, and without which quite unattainable demands would be made on our capacity to acquire relatively certain knowledge of others.

Much research on stereotyping has involved the use of rating-scale techniques similar to those often used in studies of implicit personality theory (Katz and Braly, 1933; Gilbert, 1951). The same objections can be made to this approach. However by no means all the evidence on stereotyping comes from such research.

An example of a possible instance of a person 'activating' an unfortunate stereotyped perception is provided in a paper by Rosenhan (1973). The nub of the paper is this: eight sane people (i.e. people who had no prior experience of anything describable as a mental illness), including Rosenhan himself, arranged to get admitted to twelve mental hospitals — some visiting more than one. They gained admittance by complaining that they had been hearing voices. When asked what the voices said, the 'pseudo-patients' would reply that the voices seemed to say: 'empty', 'hollow' and 'thud'.

Besides complaining of phoney symptoms, and giving false names and (where the investigators were in mental health jobs) giving false occupations, the pseudo-patients told the truth about their circumstances and personal history. Relationships with members of their family and so on were stated accurately — and since these and other aspects of the pseudo-patients' biographies were boringly normal, this should have led the psychiatrists to detect the sanity of the pseudo-patients. But they didn't.

Once having gained admittance to the hospital, it was up to the pseudo-patients to get themselves discharged by acting with exemplary sanity. They did not complain of further symptoms. When asked, they said they were feeling fine and had not experienced voices since entering the hospital. The stresses within the hospital were quite marked, so the pseudo-patients were generally paragons of cooperation, wanting to get out as soon as possible. However, the hospital staff did not detect their sanity as such. Each was eventually discharged, not as a sane person, but with a diagnosis of 'schizophrenia in remission'. Nor were there any indications in the various hospital records (which Rosenhan inspected) that the status of the pseudo-patients as mentally ill people was ever questioned. It seems that once labelled schizophrenic, the pseudo-patient was stuck with that label.

The false claim to have heard voices led to the people being labelled schizophrenic. But surely their normal 'case histories' should have told against such a diagnosis. Rosenhan comments: 'As far as I can determine, diagnoses were in no way affected by the circumstances of a pseudo-patient's life. Rather, the reverse occurred: the perception of his circumstances was shaped entirely by the diagnosis' (Rosenhan, 1973, p. 253).

An example of such translation is the case of a pseudo-patient whose relationships with his parents altered from a childhood experience of closeness to his mother but distance from his father, to a later closeness with his father and cooling of his relationship with his mother. Rosenhan conjectures that there is nothing particularly pathological about such a history, which also involved a close and warm relationship with his wife. But a psychiatrist recorded it as follows: 'This white, 39 year old male...manifests a long history of considerable ambivalence in close relationships, which begins in early childhood. A warm relationship with his mother cools during his adolescence. A distant relationship with his father is described as becoming very intense. Affective stability is absent...' (Rosenhan, 1973, p. 253).

Rosenhan argues that the facts of the case were perceived within the categories provided by a popular theory of schizophrenia. The observations were viewed theoretically. The very fact of being categorized as mentally ill led to symptoms being detected.

An aspect of stereotyping that will be apparent, yet one which must await treatment until the next chapter is the effect it has on the person being stereotyped. The question of the effect of social relations on self-perception is, of course, wider than the specific effect of stereotyping. Yet, through so-called 'labelling theory, symbolic interactionists have been quite active in studying that effect, as Chapter 5 indicates.

The impression formed of another and personality description

Secord and Backman (1964) mention the following three characteristics which are present in our impression of another person: (a) Attribution of personality traits; (b) Feelings toward the person being considered, arising out of our impression, and (c) Perceptions of the causes, intentions, justifications underlying his behaviour. (The third characteristic is a major consideration in Chapter 7 of this book, and Chapter 8 is very germane to a treatment of (b) because it has to do with attitude structure and dynamics.) Certainly these are important aspects of the impression formed of another person. In this section we attempt to relate the perception of another — the mental impression made — to the description of the other that the perceiver is able to write or say. In this we rely heavily on Bromley's *Personality Description in Ordinary Language* (1977).

Bromley himself contrasts person perception with personality description, writing that 'The term "person perception" refers to the perceptual and cognitive processes that occur when our interest is directed towards a person and the circumstances he is in' whereas 'The term "personality description" refers to any set of statements which purports to offer a sensible answer to questions like, "What sort of person is he (she)?", "What do you think of him (her)?" "What information can be given in the way of a personality appraisal?". A personality description, therefore, is simply a verbal account of the impression formed of a person' (p. 1). Now, this distinction tends to disappear when we take what has been termed a phenomenal view of person perception. The meaning-laden percept of the person that the perceiver has in mind and the verbal account of that impression converge.

If we consider the research that is accorded the title of studies of 'person perception', it normally relies on verbal reports (e.g. the 'implicit personality theory' work, and that on stereotyping). Indeed, it would be difficult for it to be other than of this form, unless the methodology was very indirect, and the implications of the work for the study of person perception merely inferred.

Since thought is taken by interactionists to be rooted in symbolic functioning (even allowing Vygotsky's (1962) valid point discussed in Chapter 3, that adult thought is likely to be 'telegraphic', condensed and characterized by inferential leaps which are hardly registered) there is unlikely to be such a divergence between perception and speech that personality description is irreconcilable with person perception. But this assumes that the technique whereby the personality description is obtained allows as rich a statement as possible to be made. Bromley criticizes earlier work on this basis.

For example, Allport and Odbert's (1936) work on trait names was criticized, as we have seen, because actual personality description does not confine itself to remarks on traits: 'Allport and Odbert never reach the point of discovering that the language of personality descriptions is a working language with lexical, syntactical, semantic and pragmatic aspects. Instead, they think of it as a long list of trait names with relatively fixed meanings, from which a number can be selected to describe and interpret observations about individual behaviour' (pp. 67f). At best, a personality description can marshall all the subtlety of the language, and be composed of arguments as sophisticated in their informal logical structure as the structure detailed by Toulmin (1958) in his essay on the 'layout of arguments'. (Toulmin mentions elements of informal arguments such as stating a claim, offering evidence, showing how the evidence upholds the claim, stating qualifications limiting the claim, stating other limitations such as assumptions underlying the relationship between evidence and claim.)

Few pieces of research on person perception have utilized ordinary language descriptions of personality, however. Dornbusch and colleagues (1965) used free accounts in their study of children's implicit personality theories as we have seen, and other studies of the development of person perception have also been concerned with wider matters than the use of trait names.

Anderson and Lopes (1974) point out that much of our information about other people is conveyed by words, and these words affect our perceptions and opinions about them. Thus psycholinguistic considerations are relevant to the field of person perception. However, unlike Bromley, Anderson and Lopes are still concerned with very limited syntactic structures (adjective/noun combinations).

Jones and Rosenberg (1974) were again not interested in complex grammatical structure, but asked people to write descriptions of five people they knew, the descriptions being lists of short phrases or single words (that is, free choice of traits). The most frequently occurring traits were taken and co-occurrence was measured — this being the regularity with which two traits are used together in describing the same person. Descriptive categories of these traits were arrived at by hierarchical clustering and by multidimensional scaling, which are statistical procedures which show relationships between traits (such-and-such a set of traits go together with a certain probability).

Table 1 Summary of Bromley's (1977) Coding Categories

1.	'Internal' aspects of personality (Bromley, Chapter 5)	
	General trait	Object of an attitude
	Specific trait or habit	Expressive behaviour
	Ability and attainment	Principles and moral values
	Motivation and arousal	Self concept
	Orientation and feeling (attitude)	
2.	'External' aspects of personality (Bromley, Chapter 6)	
	Identity (i.e. name, nationality, etc.)	Prospects
	Physical appearance	Routine activities
	Physical and mental health	Material circumstances and
	Life history	possessions
	Contemporary situation	Actual incidents
3.	'Social' and other aspects of personality (Bromley, Chapter 7)	
(a)	Social relationships	
	Social position	'His' response to others
	Family and kin	Others' response to 'him'
	Friendships and loyalties	Comparison with others
(b)	Relationships with the subject (i.e. the describer)	
	'His' response to subject	Joint action with the subject
	Subject's response to 'him'	Comparison with the subject
(c)	Evaluative statements and residual category	
	Evaluation	Collateral or irrelevant information

Jones and Rosenberg argue that clusters derived in this way tap the cognitive world of the individual — and in another paper (Rosenberg and Jones, 1972) they used the coincidence method to describe the perceptual categories of T. Dreiser, the author of a book of personality descriptions. This is an approach to implicit personality theories.

Beach and Wertheimer (1961) argue that to ask for ratings on fixed trait scales produces results which are hard to interpret because, in particular, there is no certainty that the traits will be regarded as the most meaningful ones to use in describing the particular persons being rated. The method they adopt is also that used by Bromley. Unrestricted descriptions were collected and subjected to content analysis. Thirteen categories were found adequate to the analysis of the descriptions (they overlap very significantly with those used by Bromley — see Table 1). The content analysis was reliable in that judges agreed in large measure in their allocation of items of description to the categories. It was found that subjects varied in category use (an evidence of implicit personality theories), and of course the person being perceived had an effect on the resulting description.

Bromley used the categories of Table 1 for the description of personality descriptions. His main aim appears to be to demonstrate the variety of material used in perceiving and describing others, and in this the categories speak for themselves. The range of possible descriptions becomes indefinitely high when, for example, the argument about the flexibility of ordinary language in enabling the construction of descriptions of general traits is taken into account.

We do not wish to criticize Bromley's valuable approach to the study of personality description. A few points must be made, however, concerning difficulties in translating free descriptions into data for the construction and test of hypotheses. Notice, firstly, that the researcher does not code the content of descriptions merely by referring to the particular words used. Rather, the descriptions are read for their *meaning*. And it is notoriously difficult (perhaps in principle impossible) to specify how a particular piece of text is to be interpreted. The fact that there is agreement between judges in coding a description is of course helpful. But this does not show how the judgment is made. The working of a scientific technique ought to be specified.

On a related point, Bromley allows that there is a certain arbitrariness in the particular categories used in the content analysis: the descriptions could be read in another way. The categories used in a study are chosen in the light of the practical purposes of the analysis, given the aims of the study. Wootton (1975) has shown that such problems are intractable, and are not limited to content analysis. All the work in the human sciences in which, somewhere, the talk or writing of subjects has to be interpreted and its meaning related to a hypothesis, has the same difficulty. This is not the place to debate the matter, but this is surely a sign that social psychological research is a process of interaction with subjects, and so the unresolved problems of human communication are not merely a topic of research, they also present a methodological difficulty.

Development in the capacity to perceive others

The discussion in this section is limited to development after some level of symbolic functioning is established; the rudimentary perception of others before this, in which the other/self distinction begins to be made and other precursors to perception of others are developed, is outside the scope of this chapter (but see Chapter 2 for a treatment of some of these early developments).

It is the theoretical viewpoint of interactionism that the development of sophistication in the perception of others, and in the perception of self, are intimately related to the growth of competence in interaction. These various elements are aspects of the same phenomenon: self- and other-perception arise from interaction, and at the same time each is a prerequisite for developed symbolic interaction. There are various ramifications of this view, some of which are discussed in Chapters 1, 2 and 3 (where symbolic functioning is related to interaction), and aspects of the development of the self concept are treated in the next chapter.

Shantz (1975) has reviewed the literature on the development of person perception, and Livesley and Bromley (1973) have also reviewed work on the development of the capacity to describe others. Weinstein (1969) has provided an overview on the much smaller body of research on 'interpersonal competence'. All these fields plainly overlap.

In her review, Shantz points out that role-taking has been emphasized as a major process by which understanding of others is developed: taking the attitude of the other is forced upon the child in interaction (Mead, 1934). As Selman (1971) argues, this capacity may be contrasted with the phenomenon of egocentrism to which Piaget has drawn attention. Arising from this perspective, Selman (1971; Selman and Byrne, 1974), has produced a model of a sequence of structural forms of roletaking skill. Although the ages at which the 'stages' appear is subject to dispute, the general sequence appears to concord with other workers' results (e.g. Feffer, 1970).

Prior to the age of six, Selman regards the child as egocentric in that no distinction is drawn between his viewpoint and possible alternatives. It may be that the child knows that the other is able to see things differently, but he cannot specify their viewpoint; or he may merely assume concordance between his thoughts and those of the other (Selman, 1971). (But note the caveat on egocentricity in the first part of Chapter 3.)

In middle childhood (six to twelve years) three stages occur in sequence. Firstly, between about six and eight a period of 'social-informational role-taking' occurs, in which the child understands that the other may have different amounts of information about a social situation and therefore adopt a different viewpoint. So he sees people as interpreters of situations. Moreover he understands that he and the other can draw the distinction between intended and accidental actions.

In a second stage (nine or ten years), 'self-reflective role-taking' appears. Here the child is aware that he and his thoughts and feelings can be the object of another's thinking. 'He can figuratively step outside himself and reflect on his own and other's thinking and the other's thinking about him' (Shantz, 1975, p. 287). But he cannot *simultaneously* think and bear in mind the other's view of that thought. This awaits stage three. In this stage of 'mutual role-taking' (ten to twelve years), the child understands that he can take his own perspective and the other's simultaneously.

At adolescence, role-taking extends beyond the dyad to taking the attitude of the 'generalized other' (Mead, 1934): the viewpoint of some set of people can be taken into account. Furthermore, the adolescent recognizes the possibility of both he and the other distancing themselves from mutual role-taking and reflecting on the interaction.

Byrne (Selman and Byrne, 1974) has added another, post-adolescent stage, in which the relativity of perspective held by both self and social group is understood.

The model of Selman and Byrne indicates the relationship between interactional skill and person perception. In the last section of Chapter 5,

Mead's treatment of this in the context of the development of the self-concept will be discussed. Selman and Byrne's stages also indicate limitations on the child's capacity to perceive and describe others. It is to research on this that we now turn.

In their study of children's personality descriptions, Livesley and Bromley (1973) obtained one self-description and eight descriptions of others from 320 children. The eight others to be described were limited in the instructions to the children so as to comprise one person with each combination of each of the dichotomies adult/child, male/female, like/disliked. There were eight age groups of subjects ranging from seven to nearly 16 year olds, and two intelligence levels were separated for purposes of analysis. Descriptions were written on separate pages, each headed with the characteristics of the person to be described, thus 'A boy I know very well and like is...'. Children were asked not to describe physical characteristics, but to say 'what sort of person' the object of consideration was.

The proportion of psychological statements rose significantly only between $7\frac{1}{2}$ and $8\frac{1}{2}$ years of age (22% at $7\frac{1}{2}$, 43% at $8\frac{1}{2}$). The greatest increase in the number of categories used (category-use being judged according to a content analysis similar to that of Bromley, 1977, see Table 1) was between 7 and 8 years. Livesley and Bromley suggest that this stage is somehow critical in the development of person perception, since the growth here is often greater than the difference between 8 and 15 year olds.

There was a move from overt qualities mentioned by 7 year olds to more inferential concepts (values, dispositional traits) in 8 year olds and older. Generally, trait vocabularies grew especially between 7 and 10 years. Older children used more abstract, precise terms, and referred more often to the impact of the perceived person on others.

In summary of these and parallel findings (Gollin, 1958; Yarrow and Campbell, 1963; Scarlett, Press and Crockett, 1971; Flapan, 1968), Bromley (1977) characterizes the process of development in personality description as a move from simple, brief, unorganized, egocentric and concrete descriptions to longer, complex, organized, socially-shared descriptions which include abstract, covert characteristics and tendencies in social relationships, and which allow for context-specific as well as stable, context-free behaviour tendencies. Older children have a larger trait vocabulary and use the resources of the grammar of the language to modify meanings.

A final piece of research which underlines Bromley's account is that of Peevers and Secord (1973), who collected free descriptions in tape-recorded interviews from eighty subjects at five age levels from kindergarten to college. The descriptions were of three friends and one disliked peer.

A content analysis was undertaken, and the results were coded for descriptiveness, personal involvement, evaluative consistency and depth. There were striking age differences in each category. 'Kindergarten children scarcely recognized a person as such, and described him in terms that failed to differentiate him from his environment or his possessions' (Peevers and

Secord, 1973, p. 126). During development, complexity of description increased and egocentrism decreased.

Peevers and Secord suggest that the gradual growth of precision and cognitive content in interaction, reflected in personality description, is in keeping with Mead's views. Bromley also relates his understanding of the development of person perception through interaction (where there is a regular verbal commentary) to Mead. We shall see in the next chapter that Mead's theory also has much to contribute to the study of self-perception.

CHAPTER 5

Perceiving Oneself

In continuing the discussion of perceiving, we consider perception of the self. The starting point is the recognition of a distinction between the self concept, and the self as a continual tacit 'presence' at the horizon of all perception (a distinction drawn in various ways by Mead, James, and Duval and Wicklund). This distinction draws attention to some characteristics of perception generally. Mead's account of the development of the child's self concept as a product of social interaction is outlined, and the chapter concludes with a discussion of the extent to which the self concept is determined by others' perceptions of one.

The theme of 'the self' has been very variously treated by psychological and other writers. The interactionist emphasis has been on the idea that we only become aware of ourselves as persons, with such-and-such a set of characteristics, in interaction with others, and this is a view to which the bulk of the chapter is devoted. But first some clarification needs to be performed on the woolly and confused notion of the self.

TWO ASPECTS OF THE SELF

In a paper on *The ego in contemporary psychology,* G.W. Allport (1943) mentioned eight main uses to which the concept of ego or self had been put. The confusion has not diminished in the intervening years. Allport listed the following meanings: the self is that entity which does the thinking, perceiving, etc. — the self here is 'the knower'; equally the self is an object of knowledge, as in the idea of a self concept; the term 'self interest' implies three sorts of meaning — selfishness, a drive for dominance over others, and a 'value' or interest in achieving certain ends; a sixth application of the notion of self relates to the psychoanalytic concept of ego, which functions as a mechanism for organizing and rationalizing phenomena; some writers treat the self as one source of behaviour patterns amongst others; finally the self is often viewed in social psychology as the amalgam at the individual level of many cultural values — the self is composed of name, various roles, and a subjective commitment to certain norms, all of which emanate from the society in which the individual is immersed.

The idea of the self as labelling various motivational tendencies in the individual accounts for many of Allport's list of uses (cf. Bertocci, 1945). We may argue that this is a secondary phenomenon, dependent on the person's self concept: given a perception of himself, this functions as a basis for much of his behaviour and attitudes. These matters are taken up in Chapter 8. The final use of the self — as an amalgam of culturally-determined processes — raises the question of whether the concept of self is merely a social product, e.g. is it dependent on how others view you? This matter will be reserved for later debate, since it merely attempts to fill in the content of the 'self as known'.

It appears to me that the two fundamental meanings of self, on which the others in Allport's list depend, are the self as *knower* and as *known*. The distinction can be seen clearly when one considers that I have a self-concept (this is the self I am aware of, the self as known), but also — who is it that has this self concept? I myself have it (this is the self as knower). This, incidentally, is not a distinction which originated with Allport. William James (1892) also differentiated the being who knows from the actual knowledge of himself that he has, and pointed out that much of ourselves is not known by ourselves; all that we do know is what makes up our self concept.

The distinction we have outlined is a central one for Mead as well, though both Kuhn (1964) and Kolb (1944) have pointed out that his treatment is somewhat unclear. Within Mead's discussion of self, however, most lines of thought are recognizable attempts to develop the distinction between the self as knower, and the self concept. For instance he writes: 'The self has a character which is different from that of the physiological organism proper. The self is something which has a development; it is not initially there, at birth, but arises in the process of social experience and activity, that is, develops in the given individual as a result of his relations to that process as a whole and to other individuals within that process' (Mead, 1934, p. 135). By 'self' here Mead appears to be pointing to the self concept and contrasting it with the biological individual, and also we have here an indication of the line that Mead will take on the basis of the self concept. The idea of the self as 'object to itself', or the notion of the self as known, like any other object, by the self as knower occurs again: 'The individual enters as such into his own experience only as an object, not as a subject' — and Mead continues by drawing out the point that 'he can enter as an object only on the basis of social relations and interactions with other individuals in an organised social environment' (p. 225).

Although not in accord with the whole of Mead's treatment of the self, Duval and Wicklund (1972) draw a distinction which parallels those of James and Mead. 'Objective self awareness' is their term for the consciousness or perception of self obtained by turning one's attention to one's own actions, personal history, body, etc., 'but, in contrast, the same person in subjective self awareness will be aware of himself only as the source of forces that are exerted on the environment' (Duval and Wicklund, 1972, p.14).

This distinction appears to be in terms of focus of attention. In the act of doing something or attending to external events one is aware of oneself only tacitly. One is not actively considering oneself: attention is fully attuned to other matters. Yet one is still 'present' to the perceptual field, at the 'horizon', so to speak. This is subjective self awareness, in Duval and Wicklund's terminology. Objective self awareness involves a moment of reflection in which the focus of attention is turned to oneself — the self is an 'object' to oneself. Now, even in this reflective perceptual state, subjective self awareness occurs. All perception has, as a tacit presence, oneself as perceiver.

It seems clear that subjective self awareness is the perceptual version of self as knower, and that objective self awareness is comparable to the idea of self as known. If so, Duval and Wicklund are correct to criticize Mead for arguing that the self is not present in the earliest days of infancy. This assertion must be limited to objective self awareness and its parallel, the self concept. Moreover, one does enter one's own experience as a subject (contradicting Mead) but not at the focus, rather at the horizon; as an assumption which is taken for granted in the meanings perceived in the objects seen. They are objects at a certain distance from *me*, for instance.

Before returning to our treatment of Mead, the line of thought being developed is worth pursuing because it has a bearing on the reiterated emphasis of the previous chapter that all perception is of meanings, and the rejection there of the attempt to trace a mental process moving from sensation to perception. Such an attempt would be unable to comprehend the awareness one has of oneself in perception of external objects. Yet the meaning of such objects clearly involves the self. 'I' have a perceptual presence even when entirely 'un-self-consciously' absorbed in an intricate task.

It is not only the self which is implicated in the meaning of a perceived object. The object is not merely 'objective' in the way that might be specified by a set of physical measurements — it is not just a 'stimulus'. As we saw in Chapter 2, it is a contextualized system of meanings — part of a definition of the situation. The tendency to seek the source of perceptions in data from sense organs would miss this insight (cf. MacLeod, 1947; Merleau-Ponty, 1962).

To return to Mead. He elaborates on the distinction between self as knower and the self concept with the view that it is only because we are members of society that we are able to develop a self concept: 'The self, as that which can be an object to itself, is essentially a social structure and it arises in social experience' (p.140). What does this mean, that one's self concept — one's knowledge of oneself — is a social product? It has been taken to refer to various things, in particular: (a) That one's self concept develops by one internalizing the attitudes of others to one's actions; (b) That one is able to appraise one's own actions mentally because one has developed, through interaction, the capacity for internal reflection which Mead calls 'mind' (see

Chapter 1), and so one's self concept results from a skill which social interaction provides; (c) That the self concept is an abstraction refering to aspects of the process of mind, and that self is really a process which parallels mind. All these possibilities are explicit in Mead, and attempts to unite them in a general approach to the self (e.g. Meltzer, 1964) are only partially successful.

The view that the self concept results from internalizing the attitudes of others to oneself is found in other writers to whom interactionists look as historical sources, such as C.H. Cooley (1902), and the bulk of this chapter is devoted to a critique of this perspective. It is sometimes referred to as the theory of the 'looking glass self', because of Cooley's use of the image of the looking glass to indicate the manner in which our self concepts 'reflect' the standpoints of others. Mead expresses it as follows: 'The individual experiences himself as such, not directly, but only indirectly, from the particular standpoints of other individual members of the same social group, or from the generalised standpoint of the social group as a whole to which he belongs. For he enters his own experience as a self or individual, not directly or immediately . . . but only insofar as he first becomes an object to himself just as other individuals are objects to him or in his experience; and he becomes an object to himself only by taking the attitudes of other individuals toward himself within a social environment or context of experience and behaviour in which both he and they are involved' (p.138).

However, the view of Mead is not limited to the 'looking glass self' theory (a fact overlooked by Duval and Wicklund, 1972). It is also possible to view the self as a process of appraising one's actions made possible through development in interaction of the capacity for reflective thought. One may act unreflectively and see the responses of others to that action, or one may formulate an action mentally and reflect on it oneself prior to any overt behaviour. In this latter case mind is the process involved, and Mead argues that when it is concerned with reflecting in this way, a concept of oneself (as known) necessarily emerges. A complexity is introduced into this model by Mead when he refers to the action that is formulated, prior to reflection, as a function of the 'I', and the reflective function which modifies the action, as the 'me'. On this matter, he writes: 'The self is not so much a substance as a process in which the conversation of gestures has been internalised . . .' (p.178). So the self is seen (and it is open to the individual to reflect on his self) in the process of thought. Although it is not Mead's view that the self is divided, he analyses the internal conversation of significant gestures into two stages, the one — reflecting the 'I' — is the initial impulse to act, the unorganized tendency of the person; the other — a function of the 'me' — is the 'incorporated other within the individual. Thus, it comprises the organized sets of attitudes and definitions, understandings and expectations — or simply meanings — common to the group' (Meltzer, 1964, p.10). The process of reflection is a 'dialogue' between the 'I' and the 'me'. In this way one can reflect on oneself, one's conclusion being the result of the 'I' and 'me' interchange. Thus one is able to appraise one's actions — and this self concept is a social product because it results from the dialogue of mind which is internalized interaction.

A confusion comes from this model because it is not clear what the two phases of mind (the 'I' and 'me') really represent. Inasmuch as an internal conversation requires participants the model seems understandable. But it might be that the self (as knower) is represented by the 'I' and the self concept by the 'me'. This is a third possible theory in Mead. For instance, he writes as follows: 'Now in so far as the individual arouses in himself the attitudes of the others there arises an organised group of responses. And it is due to the individual's ability to take the attitudes of these others in so far as they can be organised that he gets self-consciousness. The taking of all of these organised sets of attitudes gives him his "me"; that is the self he is aware of... Now, it is the presence of those organised sets of attitudes that constitutes that "me" to which he as an "I" is responding. But what that response will be he does not know and nobody else knows . . . The response to that situation as it appears in his immediate experience is uncertain, and it is that which constitutes the "I"' (p.175).

Part of the confusion of these three models seems to be due to Mead's desire to show that mind and the possibility of a concept of self are social products (inasmuch as they result from internalized interaction), yet he does not wish to postulate a completely socialized being. The two functions of 'I' and 'me' enable him to avoid total social determinism, since the 'I' is an impulsive, biological, individual tendency. It might be a possible solution to argue that, while mind and, therefore, the possibility of a self concept are social products, the actual thoughts developed by the individual — including his thoughts concerning himself are open to innovation, particularly due to the agency of language. The concepts of 'I' and 'me' seem to this writer redundant.

I would favour the view of the self as known which sees it as a result of the capacity — developed through interaction — for reflective thought, and would regard it as a matter for empirical research to discover the extent to which the self concept actually depends on others' appraisals of one's actions. On the first of these views, Mead has elaborated the details of a theory of how mind develops in parallel with an increasing capacity to perceive the attitudes of others to one's actions. On the second, empirical research will be paraded in a later part of this chapter.

DEVELOPMENT OF MIND AND
THE PERCEPTION OF OTHERS AND ONESELF

Mead argues that mind develops, not only from the internalization of the process of interaction using significant symbols (discussed in Chapters 1 — 3), but also from detailed aspects of playing social roles. Roles are played in childhood in a sequence of increasing complexity, which requires and encourages the development of more abstract forms of 'taking the role of the other' and also enables the child to view himself from the viewpoint of, real and imaginary, other people.

The first stage (which Meltzer regards as implicit in Mead but which is nowhere clearly differentiated) is *preparatory*. This stage is one of meaningless imitation by the infant (for example 'reading' the newspaper when an adult in the room is doing that). The child does things that others near it do without any understanding of what he is doing. Such imitation, however, suggests that the child is beginning to take the roles of others around him in preparation for being able to act genuine social roles with them through the ability to understand their role expectations. Imitation is a process on the verge of putting oneself mentally in the place of others and acting towards them on the basis of understanding their situation. As far as self-perception goes, at the preparatory stage the child has no coherent sense of self in the meaning (c) referred to earlier: no clear self concept. Its imitative behaviour merely demands identification with the actions of the other person.

In the *play stage* (characterized by taking imagined roles), the child plays at being father, engine driver, postman, nurse or whatever. What Mead considers of central importance in such play-acting is that it places the child in a position of being able to act back toward itself in such roles as 'father' or 'teacher' etc. That is, in the pretend role of teacher, let's say, the child can refer to himself — the actual child — from the imagined external vantage point of that pretend role. He has momentarily stopped being John and become teacher — and he can (as teacher) talk about John, reprove John, wish John were not such a bad boy, and so on. In this play stage, then, the child first begins to form a self concept, and it does so by taking on in imagination the roles of others, so that it can see (as it were) its self from their viewpoint. This is indicated by the way in which children at this stage use the third person in referring to themselves rather than the first person: 'John wants bricks', 'John is a good boy'.

At the play stage, the child flits from one other role to another other's role, from teacher to parent, to postman, and views himself differently from these different vantage points. He has as yet no unitary, fixed standpoint from which to view himself. He has no unified self concept. And so he has not yet developed the sort of perception to himself that in adults we would accept as a self concept: an adult views himself as unified, albeit with many facets and aspects, not different selves viewed from different vantage points. A further development in the sense of self or, capacity for holding a self concept, is seen in stage three, the game stage.

The *game stage* is the final stage in the acquisition of the capacity for having a self concept or self as known. The child begins to find himself in, and to be able to cope with, situations in which he has to imagine the responses of a number of other people to his actions simultaneously, and he must respond to their expectations at the same time. Mead uses the image of the game. In games (but not only in games) each player must construe the intentions and expectations of a number of people at the same time. The child, then, must become able to construe the attitudes of groups of people to his actions, rather than (as in the play stage) only particular individual role-players. Mead claims that the child is able to do this by abstracting a 'composite' role out of the actual roles of particular people.

Thus the team is perceived as having an attitude towards him. So, in the process of acting roles with groups of others, the child begins to be able to conceive of himself as viewed from the vantage point of *generalized others* — not specific people but groups with common expectations of him. The generalized other represents, then, the set of standpoints that are common to the group.

From this abilty to view oneself from a generalized viewpoint rather than from some particular role, the person is enabled to adopt an overall, general image of himself: a self concept that is not dependent on the particular vantage point from which he wishes to see himself. He can then act with a degree of consistency in the face of the peculiarities of the particular situation, because he acts in accordance with a generalized set of expectations and views of himself that he has internalized.

Thus the person is finally able to form a view of himself that is general, fairly consistent and yet arises out of specific roles he has had to play. And just as mind is not an unchanging set of constructs or categories which the person is saddled with, but rather is a process which allows reconstruing in new situations throughout life, so a sense of self is not fixed. The three stages of preparation, play and game are stages during which the ability to gain a self concept, through reflecting on the attitude of the abstracted 'generalized other' to your behaviour, is acquired. Once the capacity for a stable, consistent self concept is acquired, the the self concept may of course be modified as one, as it were, gains more information about oneself during life by discovering the reactions of different people to the roles one plays.

Some doubt may be cast on the generality of Mead's account, on the grounds that it presents a picture of the adult self concept as an integrated, unitary awareness; a picture which does not concord with the facts. In the next chapter evidence is given of a broad distinction between *guilt* and *shame* cultures, and it is likely that different 'styles' of social control have an effect on the self concept, in that behaviour out of keeping with the person's 'ideal self' gives rise to guilt (and this presupposes a unitary self concept) whereas inadequate role performance is the source of shame (and here the self concept may be conceived as a fairly fragmented structure, each element relating to a different social role).

Arguably, then, the degree of integration demanded of the self-concept depends on the nature of the culture in which the person finds himself. It may be that Mead overlooks this possibility (though his scheme of self concept development allows it) because the self as knower does seem to have a certain unity, which is apparent in my awareness of a personal continuity in time, for instance. Whether this unity forms as central a part of the self concept amongst members of other cultures as it probably does in our own is an empirical question, on which I know no evidence.

Mead's sketch of the development of self- and other- perception in the process of interaction has only recently begun to gather empirical support. As we saw, in Chapter 4, in the work of Selman and Byrne (1974), aspects of Mead's account appear to be substantiated by the evidence (see also Feffer, 1970). The course of development is certainly more complex than Mead's model suggests, and Shantz (1975) has suggested that role-taking may well not involve just one skill but a large number which each have their own dynamics of development. Nevertheless, the notion that Mead holds to be fundamental is that self-perception and the perception of others grow in the course of social interaction, and that the demands made on the child's capacity to interact in a sophisticated manner in more and more complex situations become more heavy in direct relationship to his ability to perceive self and others. Thus the various elements of symbolic interaction develop in a concerted manner. This basic understanding of the process is by no means disputed in the current empirical research (although Duval and Wicklund, 1972, differ from Mead in emphasizing the child's growing awareness of conflicts in viewpoint between self and other as a source of 'objective self awareness').

DO OTHERS' PERCEPTIONS OF ME DETERMINE MY SELF CONCEPT?

Jersild (1951), in a paper arguing that the subject of self-understanding was worthy of treatment in school curricula, mentioned an unpublished study in which compositions were gathered from a large sample of schoolchildren (from 4th grade upwards) on themes to do with self-description or self-evaluation. Many children mentioned physical characteristics; a 'very large proportion of children at all ages' described themselves in terms of social criteria — relations with, attitudes, feelings about others and others' (especially parents') attitudes to them; moral/religious commitments and attitudes to personal mental powers and behaviour tendencies also mentioned.

There appears to be a substantial amount of social comparison in self-concept statements. Social group membership is also to the fore, and statements bearing on others' attitudes to oneself are often prominent. This again indicates the need to consider the impact of others' perceptions of one on the self concept that is developed.

One line of research, bearing on the social determination of the concept of self a person has, takes as a general approach the study of how the social role relates to the self concept. Consider these quotes from jazz musicians recounted by Becker (1951): 'I'm telling you, musicians are different than other people. They talk different, they act different, they look different. They're just not like other people, that's all...You know it's hard to get out of the music business because you feel so different from others' (p. 136). And, in discussing the audience: 'It doesn't make any difference what we play, the way we do it. It's so simple that anyone who's been playing longer than a month could handle it. Jack plays a chorus on piano or something, then saxes or something, all unison. It's very easy. But the people don't care. As long as they can hear the drum they're all right. They hear the drum, then they know to put their right foot in front of their left foot and their left foot in front of their right foot. Then if they can hear the melody to whistle to, they're happy. What more could they want?' (p. 139).

In the work of Becker we are shown that self concept may indeed be related to the role a person engages in, but in a complex way. In this example jazz musicians clearly conceive themselves in terms of that role, but — perhaps as Becker argues because of certain pressures which are typical of service industries generally — this does not mean that the audience's perception moulds one's self concept. The 'others' who are referred to in order to arrive at a self as known are other musicians.

Becker and Strauss (1956) suggest that 'central to any account of adult identity is the relation of change in identity to change in social position' (p. 263). It is possibly true that the effect of social interaction on adult self concept is most clearly seen in situations in which roles are in process of change. For instance, Becker and colleagues (1961) and Merton and colleagues (1957) have both published lengthy pieces of research on the reactions of students to medical training in which investigations were carried out on the question of whether the students identified with the student role or whether they regarded themselves as doctors rather than students. The contradictory results appear in Table 2. Merton found that during the course the students became more and more willing to concede that they regarded themselves as doctors more than students. Towards the end of the course almost all students regarded themselves as doctors. Becker found that students regarded themselves as students until the time when they had actually graduated. Why this conflict in the results? A key is in the attitudes of the tutors (the research was carried out on two different sites). By and large the tutors of Merton's students regarded them as younger colleagues, competent to do some jobs — whereas the tutors of Becker's students regarded them as trainees, not to be regarded as competent until fully qualified. This difference in the general attitudes of tutors, and in the roles the students were viewed as performing, was reflected in the self concepts of the students (cf. Bloom, 1965).

In this case, then, self concept is strongly related to the attitude of others. But note again that the others are *relevant,* not people who the students could regard as of no importance in developing a conception of themselves in that setting. The concepts of 'reference group' (Kelley, 1952) and 'anticipatory socialisation' (Merton, 1957) are important in this context. In the formation of a self concept, others' views are taken into account, not automatically, but as a result of a process of selection in which their relevance is accepted. This group of people is taken as a gauge of one's behaviour. For the medical students, tutors formed a reference group, and the process was one of anticipatory socialization into a future role, where this was encouraged (see, for other work on this topic, Lieberman, 1956; Videbeck, 1960).

Turner's (1976) recent views on the self concept are relevant here. He points out that only some actions carried out by a person are regarded by him as

Table 2 A comparison of studies on the development of a medical self concept

Research	Self concept	Site	Attitude of tutors
Becker	Student until actual graduation	Kansas	Students 'incompetent trainees'
Merton	Doctor-identification increases throughout course	Columbia	Students 'younger colleagues'

'really me'. Becker's jazz musicians played corny numbers merely at the behest of squares. 'Some emanations I recognize as expressions of my real self; others seem foreign to the real me' (Turner, 1976, p. 989). Credit and blame are only accepted for actions which concord with the self concept, in general. Thus there are actions which do not contribute to the 'me'.

Having made this analysis, Turner points out that it is quite feasible to investigate what is accepted by a person as 'really me' and what rejected (work along these lines is reported by Bannister and Fransella, 1971). More than this, it is possible to look for general tendencies within a culture, such that people share a view that it is more appropriate to locate one's sense of real self in such-and-such an area of life rather than others. Turner argues that two locations are especially central in contemporary culture in the USA: people either regard their true selves as revealed in action within institutions, so that work achievement is relevant, or adhering to a high standard under temptation, etc., or they regard impulsive actions as revealing their true selves: the true self is something to be discovered, 'A young person drops out of school or out of the labour force in order to reflect upon and discover who he really is' (p. 992). Thus there is a dichotomy between true self as attained, striven for in institutional activity, and revealed most clearly when one is in control of one's skills and faculties — and true self as discovered in circumstances of lowered inhibitions, openness, etc.

Armed with this distinction, Turner suggests that there has been a long-term shift in American culture from the institutional to the impulsive location of true self. He relates this to notions of social control: for the institutional perception of self, 'Concern with the prestige of one's role and the esteem that goes with high role adequacy buttresses the institutional structure' (p. 1011). Social control maintained through a perception of self as impulsive is less clearly formulated by Turner. He suggests that unrecognized social processes produce impulsive actions, and perception of self as located in this area of life will in this way be a vehicle of social control.

Another tradition of research on the relationship between self concept and social interaction is spearheaded by the interactionist M. Kuhn (e.g. Kuhn and McPartland, 1954). In an effort to make the idea of self concept open to empirical investigation, he developed the so-called Twenty Statements Test, in which people are asked to provide twenty brief answers to the question 'Who am I?' The results are expected to indicate the nature of the person's self concept (but there are methodological problems — see Tucker, 1966). The general finding of research using this measure is that, overwhelmingly, the statements refer to social roles, such as occupation, religious membership, family role. This is taken as further evidence of the social basis to the self concept.

The research outlined does have some bearing on the question of the extent to which we view ourselves according to our perceptions of others' attitudes to us, but only in very general terms: we conceive ourselves within the context of the social roles that are assigned to us. For a 'tougher' version of the association between these two factors, an orientation known as 'labelling theory' provides some material.

The central idea of labelling theory is akin to the notion of stereotyping, but whereas stereotyping in itself does not imply that the person being perceived in a stereotyped fashion is necessarily affected in any way, labelling theory does suppose that the fact that others (or 'society') stereotypes a person necessarily leads to an effect on the labelled individual (Becker, 1963).

In our consideration of stereotyping in the previous chapter, we looked in some detail at the particular work of Rosenhan (1973). This is an example of the perception of others in a stereotyped manner. However it also furnishes evidence of phenomena of relevance to labelling theory.

In Rosenhan's study people incorrectly diagnosed as schizophrenic were perceived in a stereotyped way by the psychiatrists and nurses involved as a result of that label. However, note the further effect of the label: it led to institutional consequences, such as difficulty in being discharged from the hospital. Labelling theory points beyond the act of perceiving a person as an exemplar of a stereotype to the fact that such *perceptual* categories often imply institutional categories: institutions are set up so as to cope with people according to such categories, which means that the people are hard put to it to find any way of behaving other than 'as labelled'. Goffman, in his book *Asylums* (1961) discusses, under the rubric of 'moral career', constraints imposed by the fact of being socially categorized. One's way of life, in many cases of labelling, may be forced by the institution to conform to a certain pattern — one's moral career. A mental patient has a typical sequence of experiences, Goffman argues, which might appear to have their cause in the individual, but which in reality can hardly be other than what they are because the institution's structure seems geared to such moral career and deviation from it — acting contrary to label — would not be met by the members of the institution with a suitable framework of explanation. It might, as Rosenhan seems to show, just not be perceived as action 'out of label'.

Not only in closed institutions, but in other settings, one's label often triggers a predetermined set of social categories for one, and thus a given sequence of experiences. The category of housewife has been shown to tend in this direction. But here we have a problem with labelling theory: often labels gain their force in determining the moral career of a person, not just because social categories are available which force certain experiences to occur in sequence with or without the will of the person labelled, but also because the labelled person *has accepted that label for himself.* Housewives acquiesce in their customary life and see it as normal and necessary. If they had a wider view of their own potential careers (meaning ways of life here — not necessarily jobs) they might well wish to adopt alternative self-descriptions.

So stereotypes can be of a sort that necessarily result in the individual experiencing a certain moral career, but where the social environment is relatively unconstrained a label may only gain effectiveness if it is accepted for himself by the labelled person. Rotenberg (1974) has suggested various ways in which a label might be accepted: it might concord with some pre-existing view one holds about oneself; it might be that some 'rite of transformation' weans the individual from his old identity and confirms him in a new one (Becker's medical students seem to have experienced graduation in this way) — this may require the adoption of a new role with the likely result that people are seen to perceive the individual in his labelled identity, which leads to his perception of himself by 'taking the role of the other' in accordance with the label. The third and fourth ways in which self-labelling may occur according to Rotenberg relate to this second mechanism since they involve taking the attitude of the other to one's behaviour and adopting the label that they attach to it. 'Transmutive labelling' refers to the special case of cultures where names are 'powerful' so that renaming a person is accepted without question by him as necessarily requiring a given, new self concept: 'indicative labelling' is a term used by Rotenberg to refer to situations where both labeller and labellee share a stereotype, and they both accept evidence indicating the appropriateness of the stereotype to the labellee. In some of these cases it is not irrelevant to view the situation in the light of the Whorfian hypothesis of linguistic relativity which would predict that labelling occurs (or, in the weaker version, is more likely) where the culture has a language which predisposed individuals to see others and themselves in certain categories.

Labelling theory thus presents a viewpoint which regards the perception one attains of oneself as — at least in certain situations — as socially determined, depending on factors such as the presence of relevant other people who view one as such-and-such a type of person, and the general acceptance of certain perceptual categories. However, note that the labellee must find these people relevant; he must share these categories. The determinism is not cause and effect but rather due to the sharing of certain cultural codes and it *could be otherwise in any individual case.*

Another side of the same phenomenon is sometimes termed 'identity search', where a person wishes to have a category available to him which he can accept as descriptive of himself. Active steps may be taken to acquire a self concept. For example, consider the work of Triseliotis (1973) in his book *In Search of Origins,* subtitled 'the experiences of adopted people'. It is widely regarded as relevant to the description of a person to locate their background of parentage, etc. Many adopted people feel unable to attain an adequate self concept because they are unable to state who their blood relations are. In

Scotland (and, with the coming into force at the time of writing of an Act of 1975, also in England and Wales) it is possible for adopted people to trace their blood parents through the public records. In fact only an average of 0.15% of those eligible do so, so possibly most adopted people do not feel this need very strongly or at all. But Triseliotis interviewed in depth those who did during one year — and their experiences are instructive in the present context because one of the book's main concerns is the reactions of people to the news that they were not — as they had previously thought — the blood-related children of the people who were acting the role of parents to them, but were adopted. Of course this might not change their perception of their selves in an at all significant manner — they may be so settled in a sympathetic, easy relation with their adoptive parents that the news is merely interesting, but hardly disruptive. But for other adopted children the information can be shattering. Their perception of themselves as children depends on the assumption of a blood tie — and if so central a role as child-of-one's-parents is disrupted, then it is likely that this will affect the self-concept generally. The reaction to the news of adoption depends on the total relationship betwen the children and adoptive parents.

Consider these quotes: 'I was made to feel I belonged and never thought of them as adoptive parents, but as parents. I never felt the lack of a blood-tie and I think of myself as having had a good home life. My parents' relatives are my relatives, and when I think of parents and family I don't think of birth-parents. But *learning more about my forebears should help me to complete myself*' (p. 71, my emphasis). And another respondent of Triseliotis's — this time someone who felt the fact of adoption more keenly (she was told the news, two years after she was married, by her husband): the age of the person and the manner in which they are told are key factors according to Triseliotis: 'I was shocked when my husband told me. I was 20 then and was beginning to suspect something fishy going on. . .it was a terrible burden for my mother to put on him. He more or less promised her not to tell me, as he too believed that it was not nice to know that you are adopted. I was just lost when he told me. . .I just had the feeling that who I had thought I was, suddenly was stripped away and I felt. . .I had no idea who I was. . .' (pp. 27f). And so on. Triseliotis's sample was, of course, biased — they were all people who were seeking to know who their birth parents were; 99.85% don't seek this information. Nevertheless it is instructive because of the fact that the motive is hardly ever idle curiosity. If people are concerned enough about their adoptive status to seek information about the circumstances of their birth, then it seems certain that they see this as an important fact about themselves.

Phenomena like this suggest that the self concept is not just socially derived, but rather that mind (which involves the potential of a self-concept) is a social product and that forming a self concept involves socially-available categories as one of the sources of information available for consideration. This view is supported by those who stress the fact that man is capable of monitoring his own behaviour and drawing conclusions about himself from such self-monitoring (Harré and Secord, 1972; Bem, 1972). If one were totally dependent on others' views for the attainment of a self concept, then such human possibilities as 'role distancing' (Goffman, 1972) would not be possible. Role distance is the deliberate introduction into one's actions which subtly mock the role one is enacting: 'I am not really like this'. To try and inform others that one is not a typical player of a certain role implies the capacity to consider one's activities from the viewpoint of one's self concept and to attempt to alter one's behaviour so that it concords more clearly with it. One 'presents oneself' (Goffman, 1969) in accordance with the features of one's self which it is hoped others will favour, a point which relates self to definition of the situation (Chapter 2). Similarly people differ in the degree to which they present evidence at all which others will take as bearing on their selves (Chaikin and Derlega, 1974) — there is no necessity to 'disclose' one's self concept.

The tentative conclusion of this debate on the degree to which one's self concept depends on the attitude of the other to your behaviour is that the *possibility* of forming a self concept is developed in tandem with mind partly through internalizing the conversation of significant gestures — and this involves the internalizing of the process of reacting to others' appraisals. However the actual self concept formed is not merely an internalization of others' labels, though such labels are evidence available for an attitude to oneself to be built upon. After the development of mind the individual is able to present himself in accordance with his self concept — or equally to conceal his perception of himself. He may search for information bearing on his identity, and he may thereby label himself.

CHAPTER 6

Experiencing Emotions

An account of the debate over the part played by physiological changes in the experience of emotion (James, Cannon) leads to a consideration of those authors who argue that physiological aspects of emotion and consciousness of emotion must be related to the person's perception of the social situation (Schachter, Valins). Conceptual matters to do with the relationship between emotion and social interaction are discussed. The question of the cultural relativity of emotional experience is raised, touching on the distinction between 'shame cultures' and 'guilt cultures'. Finally, some specific emotional experiences are considered: Happiness and sadness; guilt and shame; empathy and sympathy; anxiety and poise; embarrassment.

A study of the literature on emotion conveys the immediate impression of confusion and lack of an agreed view of how emotion is to be conceptualized. Part of the confusion results from the fact that, as Davitz (1970) has pointed out, emotions are thought of in everyday usage as mental states — which are not readily approached by the methods used by the generality of psychologists, who are wary of the 'subjective'. A common reaction of experimental psychologists is to consign the emotions to a category of physiological phenomena, thereby allowing them to be investigated using undoubtedly objective techniques such as galvanic skin response measurement or the assessment of heartrate changes. The early viewpoints of William James (1884) and W.B. Cannon (1927) seemed to sanction, and were taken to provide theoretical bases for this physiological emphasis. The poverty of such a view will emerge in this chapter, and we shall see that considerations of the symbolic nature of man and his 'embeddedness' in his society are as inescapable in the study of emotion as they are in the investigation of perception and — to look ahead — motivation. So I believe some of the confusion of the emotion literature may be resolved by putting the person who experiences the emotion not only 'in' a physical body which has certain physiological processes, but also in a situation of interaction with others.

A further source of confusion is terminological. P.T. Young (1961) points out that there is often a failure to distinguish emotions from other, kindred phenomena which have an affective (i.e. feeling-tinged) element. Young defines emotions as 'acutely disturbed affective processes which originate in a psychological situation and which are revealed by marked bodily changes ... ' (Young, 1961, p. 352). He goes on to list such emotions as rage, horror, terror, excitement, shame, embarrassment and joy as examples of the brief and intense affective processes indicated. Apart from the fact that his definition avoids reference to emotions as conscious experiences, it does cover the phenomena to be treated here. Emotions are to be distinguished from longer-term moods; from questions of personal temperament; from interests and aversions; from pathological moods known in psychiatry as affects; from persistent organic feelings such as hunger or thirst, or pain resulting from injuries, and from simply sensory feelings like sweet tastes, warm contacts, aches.

Recent reviews covering many of the aspects of emotion include those by Arnold (1968, 1970); Black (1970), and Strongman (1973). Bindra (1970) has presented research on the matter as falling into four categories: the study of the conscious experience of emotion; the investigation of physiological changes in emotion; the study of overt behavioural responses indicative of emotion; and the investigation of those aspects of the physical or social environment which produce conscious, physiological or behavioural indications of emotion. For our purposes the division will be different from that of Bindra, since here the concern is to show that it is insufficient to regard emotions as a private, individual matter — they are a product of the process of social interaction. Thus we will begin with the earliest writers who viewed the matter at a quite individual level and debated the relationship between body and consciousness in the development of emotional experiences and responses. Then the question of emotional experience and social interaction will be treated.

EMOTIONS AS PHYSIOLOGICAL DISTURBANCES

How should one view the relationship between physiology and our experience of an emotion? An early viewpoint was put forward independently by William James (1884) and a Danish physician C.G. Lange, and it generally goes under the name of the *James-Lange theory* of emotion (although Wenger, 1950, points to certain differences between James and Lange).

James' opinion was that '... bodily changes follow directly the perception of the exciting fact, and that our feeling of the same changes as they occur is the emotion' (p. 13). This certainly challenges the commonsense view that you first perceive something, immediately experience a relevant emotion and then bodily changes follow as a result of the experience of emotion (Fig. 1). James argued that, rather than catching sight of a bear, being frightened and as a result running away, the sequence is: first you register the presence of a bear, then the muscles tense and the glands begin secreting the hormones of escape, and only as a result of perceiving these physiological reactions does one experience fear.

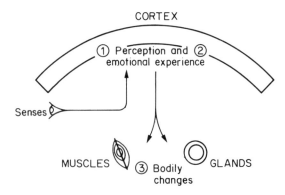

Fig. 1. 'Commonsense' view of emotional experience.

James suggested an introspective test of his theory. If you imagine a strong emotion such as anger or fear, and then try to expunge from your awareness all the feelings of bodily changes that accompany the emotion, then, to the degree that the eradication of these bodily feelings has been successful, the emotion will also have disappeared. Emotion is no more than our experience of bodily changes. We feel unhappy as a result of crying, angry because we strike out. (See Fig. 2.)

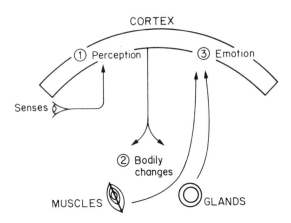

Fig. 2. James-Lange theory.

The James-Lange theory went without direct challenge for some years. But, as Deutsch and Deutsch (1973) point out, if it were correct then a person who had no information as to the state of the bodily apparatus of emotional response would have no emotional feeling. However, there are cases where the individual is deprived of such information through the lack of nervous connection due to injury. The patient nevertheless reports emotional feelings.

W.B. Cannon (1927) marshalled such evidence as this to undermine the James-Lange theory. Since much of the relevant experimental work was carried out independently by P.A. Bard, the hypothesis which was proposed to replace James' is known as the *Cannon-Bard theory*.

The several specific flaws in James' view include the following. It cannot be, Cannon argued, that physiological changes in glands and muscle tissue are the cause of emotional experience because, even when surgery separates these from the nervous system, emotional feeling is still present. Also, the bodily changes do not differ sufficiently from one emotion to another to account for the differences we feel between different emotions (for instance both fear and anxiety are accompanied by an inhibition of gastric juices being produced). Again, the brain is supplied with little information from the bodily organs — our experience of stomach, heart, and so on is vague and undifferentiated. Surely insufficient data on which to construct awareness of emotional changes, especially when the emotions are relatively mild ones. Another objection to James and Lange: changes in the body occur fairly slowly (of the order of two seconds after they are triggered off) — yet our emotions can switch quickly under some circumstances. For instance, if someone were to pop a balloon unexpectedly, one would immediately undergo a reflex shock, then adjust and either laugh in relief or be impatient and somewhat offended at the encroachment on one's dignity. Can such rapid changes in behaviour and experience be due to the action of sluggish glands? Cannon and Bard argued not. And a final argument (a very telling one) is that, when the body is artificially made to act as if in an emotionally-induced state by the administration of drugs, emotional changes associated with the artificial state do not occur. The body is in the emotional state: the person does not experience the emotion.

As Schachter (1964), Mandler (1975) and Fehr and Stern (1970) have noted, new data have weakened the strength of some of Cannon's criticisms of James' view of emotions. Wenger queried in 1950 whether it might be that, although patients who are unable to sense visceral changes due to surgery still experience emotion, an intact nervous system is necessary for the *acquisition* of emotions. Since Wenger posed this problem, there has been some evidence from experiments on animal avoidance learning that the acquisition of the response of avoiding noxious situations (supposedly a fear response) requires that the capacity to sense visceral changes be present, but the maintenance of such avoidance responses does not require that this part of the nervous system be intact. It might be, then, that the child's learning of emotional experience is dependent on relating the situation to the bodily change. However, the work of Schachter and later authors may lead us to reject a straightforward causal link between bodily change and emotion.

The definite rejection of James' theory is further complicated by the work of Hohmann (1966), who interviewed patients with lesions of the spinal cord about their emotional experiences before compared with after injury. He did find support for the notion that disruption of the nervous system in this manner was related to significant changes in emotional experience — and possibly that the greater the injury the greater the changes. In particular feelings of anger, sexual excitement and fear seemed to have decreased.

Interpretation of Hohmann's findings as favourable to the James view is not clearcut despite the apparent effect of injury on these particular emotions. The patients also reported a significant *increase* in feelings of sentimentality. From this finding, it seems that not all emotional experience is affected in the same way. Indeed it is possible that the lesion was not the causal factor at all — the style of life of the patients will clearly have changed as a result of injury, thus changing the range of emotional situations experienced, and their meaning for the individual patient.

James' theory of emotional experience as following bodily changes demands a certain distinction between the changes attributable to each emotion. Fear and elation, for instance, should be sufficiently different in their physiological symptoms for the person to be able to be aware of what emotion is present. Such authors as Lacey and Lacey (1970) have been able to show some such patterning which might distinguish various emotions from each other. However, the evidence of such research is not clearcut overall, and the conclusion from such reviews as Strongman (1973) and Mandler (1975) is that physiological differentiation of the emotions has not been convincingly shown.

The debate on the strength of Cannon's criticisms is reviewed by Fehr and Stern (1970), who conclude that the part of peripheral bodily reactions in emotion should not be dismissed out of hand, although the James hypothesis requires elaboration in the light of new evidence. Perhaps it could be allowed that bodily reactions provide further information that allows us to be more certain that, indeed, we are experiencing an emotion. But bodily reactions alone are not sufficient conditions for the experience of emotion.

The Cannon-Bard theory which was proposed as a replacement of James' view set aside the notion that emotional experience results from bodily changes. But the new hypothesis was not a return to the commonsense notion, rather a brain structure (but one unconnected with conscious awareness) was regarded by Cannon and Bard as the seat of the emotions. This was treated as a sort of switching station. The chain of events ran as follows: sensory stimulation from the external environment initiated a flow of nervous impulses towards the cortex, the seat of conscious awareness. These nervous impulses might reach the cortex via the thalamus (which is the brain structure Cannon invoked in his new theory). In this case the perception of the external event at the cortex would be accompanied by emotional experience. The emotional tinge is regarded as a product of thalamic excitation. Alternatively the nervous impulses from the senses might not immediately excite the thalamus but rather reach the cortex first and thus give rise to perception free of emotional feeling, but on being perceived give rise to a mental reaction which itself results in thalamic stimulation. (For these two alternative paths, see Fig. 3 and Fig. 4).

In both cases, awareness of emotion is regarded as only possible after the

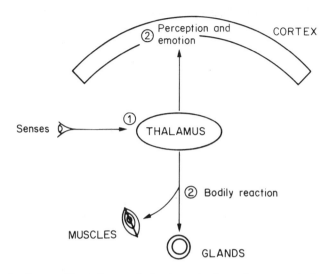

Fig. 3. Cannon-Bard theory: thalamic excitation prior to cortical perception.

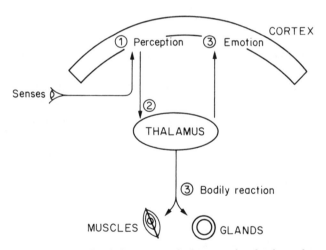

Fig.4. Cannon-Bard theory: cortical perception leads to the
initiation of behaviour via thalamus.

thalamus has been stimulated. Thus, whether the thalamic stimulation takes place before or after perception at the cortex has occurred, emotional feelings are always later than thalamic excitation. Therefore whether the bodily reaction occurs before or after emotional experience depends on the complexity of the bodily changes compared to the perception of emotional feeling.

Note that the two possible pathways are not conflicting theories but reflect Cannon's view that some events immediately trigger thalamic activity — a balloon popping, perhaps — while other events require cognitive activity before their emotional significance is clear — for example, a subtle slur on one's dignity. Indeed, if someone were to pop a balloon the immediate reaction might follow the pathway in Fig. 3 and later realization that it was an affront to your dignity that he should pop a balloon at you might result in a further emotional reaction following the pathway in Fig. 4.

The problem with the Cannon theory seems mainly to be its dependence on the thalamus for producing the different emotions. Strongman (1973) reviews the evidence that well-defined areas of the brain are responsible for different emotional functions and concludes: 'At best we can say that some area of the brain may be a necessary condition for the occurrence of some behaviour; it cannot be a sufficient condition' (p. 37). And further on he writes that all that can be said about subcortical structures and emotion is that such structures seem to be implicated: 'Often it is even impossible to say that they are necessary to emotion, simply that they are implicated' (p. 58).

Both the James and the Cannon theory seem to be rather unsatisfactory, however, as general approaches to emotional experience. No doubt there is interest in the attempt to sketch a causal mechanism in the brain or the peripheral organs of the body, but such mechanisms cannot be more than contributions to the total picture. Moreover, the enterprise is of more physiological than social psychological importance since, just as the view of perception that regarded it as a process of adding meaning to sensation was found unsatisfactory earlier, so the physiological view of emotion as an addition to sensation resulting from brain or body lacks a stance which can cope with the social and cognitive 'accomplishment' of emotional perception.

Recent research, however, has broadened the view of emotional experience and its relation to physiology amongst experimental psychologists such that real social aspects may begin to be investigated. The decisive work was carried out by S. Schachter and colleagues (Schachter and Singer, 1962; Schachter, 1964; Schachter, 1970).

Schachter and his colleagues make the initial assumption, which seems reasonable in the light of the current evidence, that emotional states share a roughly similar pattern of physiological symptoms; that there is little or no differentiation between emotions in terms of bodily state. The experience of physiological arousal, then, merely 'informs' the person that emotion is occurring. The decision as to which emotion the state is to be attributed to must be made on the basis of his current experience — in effect, his definition of the situation.

If the unusual circumstance were to arise in which a person found himself physiologically aroused with no immediate explanation to hand, Schachter would predict that he would search for a label for the emotion in terms of his current situation. Precisely the same physiological pattern could be labelled 'love' or 'anger' depending on the definition of the situation which the person arrived at. (Schachter would hardly suggest this, but it seems to me that James' introspective test of his theory can be adapted successfully in testing Schachter.)

In the normal course of events there is a completely appropriate explanation of the emotional arousal to hand. Here Schachter would expect no need for a search for a label.

A final aspect of Schachter's view of emotional experience is that, while physiological arousal is not a sufficient condition for emotional experience (it must be perceived and labelled), nevertheless it is *necessary* to emotional experience. A person in a given situation will only regard the situation as emotional if he experiences a state of arousal. Although this aspect of the theory reminds one of James' view that visceral changes are prerequisites for the experience of emotion, there is some ambiguity in Schachter's statement of the theory (1964, e.g. p. 53), in that arousal is apparently used interchangeably with experience of arousal, and as we shall see in the work of Valins a person can be deceived as to his state of arousal.

A test of his view of emotional experience required that Schachter should vary the bodily state of individuals independently of both availability of immediate, appropriate labels to explain such states, and environmental circumstances in which explanatory definitions of the situation could be sought.

Schachter and Singer (1962) carried out such experimental tests, in which bodily state was manipulated by either injecting subjects with the hormone adrenaline (= epinephrine) or a placebo, saline solution. By way of explanation, subjects were told that the experiment was to discover the effect of a vitamin compound on vision.

The manipulation of the appropriateness of labels of physiological state was carried out by the experimenter telling those who had had adrenaline administered to them: (i) That the 'vitamin' sometimes had the side effect that 'your hand will start to shake, your heart will start to pound, and your face may get warm and flushed'. These subjects had a quite appropriate explanation of the adrenaline-induced state they would experience. (ii) That 'your feet will feel numb, you will have an itching sensation over parts of your body, and you may get a slight headache'. These subjects had information which would not appropriately explain the state they would be expected to feel, and Schachter would predict that they would require some label — supposedly an emotion label — gleaned from the current situation. (iii) A third group had no instruction about the side effects of the 'vitamin'.

Manipulation of the situation in such a way as to make emotional definitions available to subjects for labelling their physiological state was carried out in this way. Immediately after the administration of the hormone, a subject was left in the room while the vitamin had time to 'get from the injection site into the bloodstream'. The experimental subject was together with a stooge, who the experimenter had introduced as another subject. The emotions of euphoria and anger were investigated. Thus, for one set of subjects, the stooge acted in an extremely elated, euphoric way, whilst in the other condition the stooge began to ask the subject personal and insulting questions, and finally left the room in a rage.

Table 3 indicates the conditions run in the experiment; in all there are seven.

Since the different conditions were intended to have different effects on subjects' experiences, two types of measure of emotional experience were obtained. By observation through a one-way mirror, the behaviour of subjects could be rated in terms of the degree of anger/euphoria exhibited. Also subjects' self-reports of their feelings were elicited.

As far as the euphoria conditions are concerned, on both measures of emotional behaviour and feelings the results were consistent with Schachter's expectation: subjects were more susceptible to the stooge's euphoria when they had no explanation of their own bodily states than when they did. Thus, least euphoria was evidenced by the subjects who had been correctly informed about the physiological symptoms they would experience. They were therefore able to attribute their bodily state to the 'vitamin', and felt no need to search for an explanation by defining the situation as euphoric.

Schachter expected that those subjects who had been administered the placebo saline solution would be comparable in emotional reaction to those given adrenaline injections and correctly informed about the bodily state they would experience. The theory lead to such an expectation because incongruous bodily arousal in the latter group could be adequately explained in terms of the injection, and there should have been no such arousal in the formal group.

The findings, however, did not precisely concord with this expectation. Subjects in the placebo condition were found to be less euphoric than those who had been given adrenaline injections and either misinformed or not informed about the effects (as the theory predicted). But the levels of emotion found in the placebo and adrenaline/informed groups were different: the placebo group being more euphoric.

Schachter accounted for this anomaly in two ways. On the one hand, he found evidence that the subjects injected with adrenaline who had been misinformed or not informed about the effects sometimes correctly attributed their arousal to the injection. When this was taken into account, the difference between the placebo condition and these two conditions was more marked, and therefore, by contrast, the placebo and adrenaline/informed conditions bore a greater similarity to each other. On the other hand, there was also some evidence that the level of euphoria in the placebo group compared to the adrenaline/informed group had been increased because what arousal the placebo group did experience was (correctly, presumably) attributed to the situation, whereas all the arousal experienced by the other group could be attributed to the injection. It seems permissible to suggest that a further explanation is possible to account for the latter effect: that the level of euphoria in the adrenaline/informed condition might be restrained because of the possibility of attributing even that arousal actually due to the situation, to the injection.

In general, the findings in the anger conditions mirrored those for euphoria. Taken together with other supporting studies, Schachter regarded this experiment as providing weighty support for his theory of emotional

Table 3 Experimental conditions in Schachter and Singer (1962)

Emotional situation (i.e. stooge behaviour)	Euphoric		Anger-provoking	
State of physiological arousal	Adrenaline	Saline	Adrenaline	Saline
Adequacy of available account of arousal	Correct Incorrect No account	**	Correct * No account	**

*   In the anger/aroused case, no condition was run where subjects were misinformed as to the physiological side effects of the 'vitamin'.
** In the saline conditions, no unexplained arousal was expected, and therefore no information was given about 'side effects'.

experience. However, there have been some critical reactions to this claim.

Plutchic and Ax (1967) object to the notion that all emotional states are physiologically identical, and differentiation between them is entirely due to the person's cognition of the situation in which the arousal occurs. They prefer to think that there is differentiation in bodily state. But, as Mandler (1975) points out, there is less evidence for this than for Schachter's position. Be this as it may, Plutchic and Ax make several specific criticisms of the experiment of Schachter and Singer (1962). In particular, Schachter did not take into account the well-documented fact that there are wide individual differences in reaction to a given dosage of drugs, such that there is a likelihood that the subjects who participated in the adrenaline conditions were actually at different levels of physiological arousal.

Criticism is also levelled by Plutchic and Ax at the self-report measures used in the experiment, which Zimbardo, Ebbesen and Maslach (1977) also regard as weak. Indeed, the differences between the various conditions in the self-report index are accounted for by a very narrow band of ratings. Clearly the measure lacked sensitivity. Plutchic and Ax mention by way of criticism also the fact acknowledged by Schachter that placebo conditions do not differ significantly from the other three conditions on the behavioural indices of emotion.

Schachter intended that the experience of unexplained arousal would lead subjects to seek to define the situation in such a way as to account for the aroused state. Several objections have been raised to this. There is evidence, in the first place, that unexplained arousal may be in itself anxiety provoking, rather than neutral as Schachter supposed. Again, there is the possibility that the behaviour of the stooge could be viewed in various ways, so that anger or euphoria were not the only emotions available to the subjects.

Mandler (1975) dismisses such objections as these as merely focusing on some aspects of the study which could have been done better, but giving no grounds at all for rejecting Schachter's results or the theory they support.

However two experimental replications of Schachter and Singer (1962) do indicate that the theory requires some adjustment.

Maslach (reported in Zimbardo, Ebbesen and Maslach, 1977) carried out a modified replication in which a new procedure was used in order to avoid the criticisms of Schachter's methodology. Hypnosis was used to induce physiological arousal (thereby circumventing the problem of individual differences in response to hormones). Lack of explanation of arousal was produced by post-hypnotic suggestion of amnesia, whereas 'arousal informed' subjects were not told to forget the instructions given under hypnosis. Various other controls and refinements were introduced, e.g. subjects completed questionnaires which included items about the believability and appropriateness of the stooge's behaviour, and about the precise emotional state he was exhibiting. Thus there was some evidence to support the contention that subjects perceived the experimental situation in' the way the experimenter intended.

The results of Maslach's study indicate that, indeed, unexplained arousal provokes a negative feeling in the subject who experiences it. He also suggests that this might bias the search for an explanatory definition of the situation — one which will not merely account for arousal, but which will account for a negative feeling too. This notion indicates why Maslach's results in the case of anger confirmed those of Schachter, but in the case of euphoria unexplained arousal was not related to the adoption of the elated state of the stooge.

A more exact replication of Schachter and Singer's study was undertaken by Marshall (again reported in Zimbardo, Ebbesen and Maslach, 1977). Adrenaline injections were used, and the general design was the same as Schachter's. Only a euphoric condition was run since it was here that Maslach found results which differed from those of Schachter. Marshall's findings confirmed Maslach's. Negative feelings were provoked by unexplained arousal that appeared in the self-reports of subjects in place of the euphoria expected by Schachter. And there was a difference between the behaviour and feelings of the subjects, for their interaction with the stooge was apparently happy.

The particular revision which these studies force on Schachter's theory seems to me not only to bear on the emotional reaction individuals have to the experience of unexplained physiological arousal, but also to have to do with the ambiguity noted earlier in Schachter's treatment of physiological arousal. For Schachter, arousal is a necessary but not sufficient condition of emotional experience — however, he writes as if arousal and perceived arousal are synonymous. But is it not the *cognition* of arousal which is really involved? It is not that arousal itself is a causal agent in the 'generation' of emotion. Rather, awareness of arousal is part of the normal experience of being in an emotional situation.

If this reconstruction is correct, then awareness of arousal is not surprisingly discomforting if the occasion does not otherwise seem to warrant an emotional reaction. On the other hand, awareness that the situation is worthy of emotional response in patients unable to perceive their bodily state (cf

Hohmann, 1966) should not in itself be discomforting in that their injury gives sufficient explanation of the anomaly.

In sum, the argument is that physiological state is part of the available 'environment' which people draw on in attributing emotion to themselves. It is not that a definition of the situation is a separate phenomenon — rather, cognition or arousal is part of the definition of the situation as emotional. (Note that, although it does seem that the social situation is more informative about the exact nature of the emotion being experienced than physiology — which is hardly surprising since emotions are labelled through the same sort of process of symbolic interaction as other intersubjective meanings — notwithstanding this, our argument would be as relevant were there strong differentiation of emotions at the physiological level.)

If this view is correct, then subjects induced to believe that their bodies are in a state of physiological arousal when this is not true, should act as if it were true. Research by Valins (1966, 1970) bears on this assumption. Here bodily state was perceived falsely by subjects, and this influenced their labelling of emotions.

Valins (1970) deceived his subjects as to their heartrate by making out that heartrate was being recorded by a rather antiquated machine which 'unfortunately' emitted an audible signal at each heartbeat. In fact the signals were prerecorded so as to give the subject a false impression of how his body was reacting. So the information they had was quite incorrect. The study aimed to discover whether emotions would be judged according to this incorrect information or not. In a carefully controlled experimental design the subjects were shown a series of emotion-provoking stimuli, for example a sequence of slides of female nudes were shown to groups of male subjects. The effects of the false heartrate information were assessed by the subjects ratings of the attractiveness of the slides. Valins reports that: 'Nudes to which subjects heard their heart rates change, whether increased or decreased, were liked significantly more than nudes to which they heard no change in heart rates (p. 234).

Valins' results apparently support the view that whether arousal has actually occurred or not, *perceiving* it to have occurred is a factor in a person's attribution of emotionality to himself, and his concomitant definition of the situation as emotional. Other studies have followed Valins' type of methodology, i.e. using a false feedback from 'measuring devices' to indicate to subjects that they are physiologically aroused, with similar results. Wilkins (1971), for instance, used the Valins approach, and showed that subjects who are led to believe that they are physiologically aroused may even misperceive in order to define their situation as emotional. However, Mandler (1975) argues that Valins' method does not demand of subjects that they should regard the false feedback as indicating their bodily state to be aroused. It is open to them to take the feedback rather as giving information about the nature of the situation.

Experimental evidence relating actual arousal, false feedback and reported feelings is provided by Goldstein, Fink and Metee (1972). They showed that the false feedback of increased heartrate was followed by an actual increase in the heartrate of subjects, so there was a flaw in the design of Valins' experiment in that he did not measure actual arousal and merely assumed that the effect of false feedback on emotional experience was a direct one. It might have been mediated by actual arousal. Goldstein and his colleagues replicated Valins' procedure, but included measures of actual bodily arousal, and also ran condition in which male nudes were viewed (which subjects reported as more offensive than the female nudes). The results in the condition in which female nudes were viewed confirmed Valins' findings. But in the offensive male nude condition, changes in false feedback were not related to reported emotional response, whereas actual arousal was.

Goldstein, Fink and Metee conclude that Valins was incorrect to leave out of the account the actual physiological arousal of subjects. In his experiment, false feedback may not have replaced the natural cognition of arousal but rather the false feedback evoked arousal. And in the case of offensive material, false feedback did not evoke arousal itself, and the emotional response related to actual arousal rather than false feedback.

The study of Goldstein, Fink and Metee does not invalidate the main theoretical position of Valins, that perception of arousal is part of the usual experience of emotion rather than there being a direct causal link between physiological arousal and emotion. Neither Valins nor Goldstein prevented subjects becoming aware of their actual state, and so it may well be that in the case of strong emotions, false feedback is not sufficiently convincing in competition with the perception of actual arousal. Indeed it is possible that the measure of heightened emotion used by Valins, which was the choice of one picture as opposed to another, merely indicated a marginal preference and therefore could be taken as showing only slight emotional heightening for which perception of actual bodily state was irrelevant.

Mandler (1975) judges the position of Valins to be as yet unproven. Certainly there is no experimental evidence which unequivocally supports the view that emotional experience depends on perception of arousal rather than being a direct effect of physiological arousal. However, normally perception of arousal is correct perception of actual physiological arousal. Valins' technique fails to vary the two independently. Hohmann's patients, to whom we have already referred provide no evidence since they were not aware of physiological arousal but may indeed have had no such states to experience.

Other research bearing on the viewpoint of Valins includes that of Nowlis (1970), Ewert (1970) and Bloemkolb, Defares and van Gelderen (1971). Generally, the conclusion they point to — but do not establish as categorically correct — is that awareness of arousal is part of the normal experience of emotional state rather than there being a direct causal link between physiology and emotional experience.

In summary, it may be said that the experience of an event as emotional involves the attribution of an emotion by the experiencer to himself, which normally entails the perception of his bodily state as aroused. Definition of the situation may be anomalous in the case of unexplained arousal (Schachter) or apparent arousal (Valins), in which case (i) the very fact of the anomaly is disquieting (Maslach, Marshall), and (ii) the anomaly appears to demand resolution by perception of the situation as emotional.

There is a hint in the work of Laird (1974) that other anomalies in the definition of the situation may also produce a need for resolution. He induced subjects to 'smile' or 'frown' by electrical stimulation of the relevant muscles in such a way that they were not aware of the meaning of the expressions they were displaying. The subjects reported feeling more happy in the 'smile' condition and angrier in the 'frown' condition.

The research reviewed thus far enables a view of emotional experience to be sustained in which the definition of the situation as emotional involves a perception of arousal, a perception of environmental circumstances as being consonant with such arousal, and a self-attribution of some specific emotion in line with this definition.

EMOTION AND SOCIAL INTERACTION

Emotional situations are defined as such by the person in an act of defining the situation (see Chapter 2). Emotion terms are symbols. The theoretical stance of symbolic interactionism is clearly relevant. Before taking this for granted, consideration must be given to an author whose view of emotion is otherwise in many respects sympathetic to the approach adopted in this chapter. As has been argued earlier, the language is a symbol system, and a logical development of the view that emotional situations are defined 'symbolically', i.e. through the use of emotion terms which are then part of the meaning of the situation, is that emotions are experienced by humans through symbolic functioning: language use. In criticism of this approach, G. Mandler (1975) writes: 'Consider the following difficulties if we were to permit the common language to be our guide to the emotional states and terms that a psychological theory of emotion should be able to explain. First, there is little disagreement that such a theory should account for states that are commonly termed anxiety, joy, fear, euphoria, and probably even love and disgust. But is lust an emotion — or is sexual feeling to be handled separately? Are we required to explain feelings of pride? Of accomplishment? Of empathy? Of dislike? Or even worse, are we to construct national theories of emotion so that a German theory may account for *Lust* and *Unlust?*' (pp. 9f).

Mandler writes as if, self evidently, the psychologist will wish to avoid such a messy path! But this is surely precisely the path that a social psychology of emotional experience must take. If a German labels an emotional state using the symbol *Unlust,* defines the situation in such a manner, experiences the emotion as such, and acts in terms of that symbol — then whether or not it is directly translatable into other languages, and whether or not it makes a coherent psychological theory of the emotions more difficult to develop, it would be a falsification of the phenomena with which social psychology concerns itself to avoid this path.

In developing an account of emotion as a social phenomenon after the manner which a symbolic interactionist perspective would require, first some theories of emotional cognition are briefly outlined, then the relationship between culture and emotion is introduced.

Theories of emotional cognition

Lazarus (1966) and his colleagues (Lazarus, Averill and Opton, 1970) have put forward a theory of emotion with a cognitive emphasis, and point out that culture has an impact on emotion through the manner in which emotional events are perceived; the manner of emotional expression; the determination of interaction patterns which perform as stimuli for emotional judgment, and through the establishment of ritualized behaviour of emotional import. He argued therefore that emotions should be studied at the level of individual, culture-influenced cognition. The person is viewed as evaluating events in terms of personal relevance, and an emotional reaction results from a certain kind of appraisal.

Lazarus emphasizes the notion that the world is a dynamic, fluctuating sequence of experiences, and part of the process of coping with such a world is carried out by perceiving emotionally. Emotional responses are part and parcel of the effort of coping, and our own coping activity is itself subject to evaluation.

Kelly (1955) and Bannister and Fransella (1971) also see emotion as part of the process of coping with a dynamic existence in a fluctuating environment. In Bannister and Fransella's interpretation, the first point is that a commonsense distinction often made between rational thought, cognition, and irrational thought, emotion, is an illusion. Rather, the various emotions arise as a result of our awareness of an impending need for change in our constructs. Kelly defines emotions as arising from knowledge, at the back of our minds, that our present perception of the situation is somehow inadequate and change is necessary (although indeed it may not realistically be possible to change the perceptual categories, the constructs). So emotions for Kelly consist in an *awareness that one's construct systems are in a transitional state,* requiring change. Thus, fear is the awareness of an imminent, incidental change in one's core structures — meaning that, when fearful we expect that soon a specific event will alter (i.e. there will be 'incidental change' in) a centrally important category such as the self.

Kelly's definition of fear in terms of perceiving an imminent change in constructs may well appear odd at first sight. After all, the fear relates to the attack rather than to the *idea* of the attack, surely? However, Kelly's stress on the emotion as arising from the *construed* situation is correctly viewed as reiterating the interactionist assertion that man lives in a symbolic environment and does not confront things directly.

Further examples of Kelly's view of emotions are mentioned below. A comparison of his approach and Sartre's is instructive. They are in accord in that both of them are of the opinion that emotions are not meaningless — they reflect a cognitive process, an interpretation of the situation. However, Sartre pointed out something that Kelly sets aside: emotions are not merely *cold appraisals* that one's constructs are in transition. No, they change the state of our awareness — we move from our usual, cool state to an angry, or fearful, or joyful state. Why do we change our state of awareness to an emotional one? It is an attempt, Sartre says, to act magically on the world. We perceive the situation as such-and-such, and without actually changing the situation we alter our state of awareness. Sartre (1962) writes: 'We can now conceive what an emotion is. It is a transformation of the world. When the paths before us become too difficult, or when we cannot see our way, we can no longer put up with such an exacting and difficult world. All ways are barred and nevertheless we must act. So then we try to change the world; that is, to live it as though the relations between things and their potentialities were ... governed ... by magic' (p. 63).

For instance, in the specific case of fear, Sartre argues that the headlong flight from the bear is not rational. It is not calculated behaviour aimed at reaching shelter. No, it is magical behaviour: an attempt to annihilate the relationship between us and the bear. Fear is a state of awareness aimed at negating the thing in the external world by means of magical behaviour.

Perhaps Sartre's language is perplexing (see a later writer of the same philosophical background, Buytendijk, 1962, and for a recent, clear discussion of Sartre's view, Hall and Cobey, 1976). However a solemn experimental psychologist, Pribram (1970), puts forward a view that is not altogether dissimilar, and which helps to underline the similarity between the opinions of Lazarus, Kelly and Sartre. He writes: '... emotions are ... neural programs which are engaged when the organism is disequilibrated' (p. 43). In habitual, uncomplicated behaviour emotions are not aroused, but when hampered in some way the emotional processes emerge.

A couple of caveats must be raised at this point. Firstly, as Leeper (1963) has been at pains to point out, it must not be thought that emotions are disorganized. They are patterned and, in a way, relevant to the situation. It is the habitual pattern of life which is (either pleasantly or unpleasantly) disrupted. Secondly, the cognitive theories reviewed in this section tend to be overindividualistic, at least in the examples they use. It is necessary to emphasize that emotional experiences relate to cognitive appraisal which is *culturally relative*. For example, Lindesmith, Strauss and Denzin (1975) write: 'Even such a strong emotion as fear is not invariably kindled by similar situations. In one society fear may be aroused by the occurrence of a bad omen, such as an eclipse, and in another by anticipation of a collapse of the stock market' (p. 212).

As we have seen, this idea of cultural relativity in emotional experience is opposed by Mandler (1975) — though it is clearly a necessary consideration in the expression and perception of emotions (Chapter 4) as well as in the present context. However Mandler elsewhere provides a useful outline of a model of cognition which has clear parallels with that implied by Mead and which he specifically presents as required for the adequate treatment of emotional experience: 'The minimal requirements of mental structure that we need for later descriptions of the emotional subsystem are: inputs from environmental events; a system of structures that interprets such events and performs the complex transformations on input that is known to be characteristic of human beings; two output systems, one of them an action system and the other a physiological arousal system; and a provision of feedback, in the one case to provide for the perception of arousal, in the other for the monitoring of action' (1975, p. 19).

A 'mechanism' like this would appear to me to work — or to be realized in practice — in a manner which would approximate to the symbolic functioning of the human actor in symbolic interactionism: defining emotional situations.

Human emotions, then, are an aspect of symbolic functioning — and in a specific case need to be understood in terms of the definition of the situation of the actor, which in turn must be viewed relative to his cultural setting.

Culture and emotion

Emotions, then, are culturally relative. However, this general conclusion needs elaboration to cover the phenomena of emotional expression and feeling. The work of Ekman (1970), mentioned in our earlier consideration of the non-verbal expression of emotions, provides a pointer to a more differentiated hypothesis in the case of the non-verbal expression and the perception of emotions — the immediate reaction to a situation may be a universal behaviour pattern, whilst the considered reaction may be culturally relative. If this is so, then the findings of Osgood (1966), Schlosberg (1954) and Frijda (1969, 1970) regarding the classification of expressions of emotions in terms of degrees of similarity and distinctness may be universal for immediate reactions, a supposition supported by research reviewed by Triandis (1964), but more culture-based in the case of considered, later non-verbal reactions to emotional situations.

The perception and expression of non-verbal signals of the emotions may be only to this limited extent culturally relative. However there is no doubt that important cultural differences do exist in the labelling of emotions and the relative emphasis given to such 'cognitively complex' emotions as shame, guilt, embarrassment, and sympathy — and the nature of the situations that give rise to them. By 'cognitively complex' emotions I mean those emotions that arise in the course of perceiving situations which would not provoke an immediate reflex reaction. The startle reaction to a loud bang would be a simple emotional reaction in these terms, and I expect little cultural variation in such a reaction. The later perception of the bang as having been caused by a practical joker taking the mickey — an anger-provoking situation — depends on culturally-dependent labels and therefore would not be expected to be universal. In this case anger is a cognitively complex emotion.

Such a differentiation of emotions is often disregarded. In particular, Davitz (1964, 1969, 1970) has presented an otherwise very useful viewpoint on the emotions which demands, for its further development, some consideration of complexity. He argues that emotions are experienced in terms of labelled states referring to the general situation of the person, and he goes on to analyse the clusters of meanings that emotions are perceived as having, in a manner akin to Osgood and others in their studies of emotional expression. Thus a 'dictionary' of labels for emotions is described. Cultural relativity is not considered, however.

The complex emotions are socialized. This is implicit in saying they are culturally dependent. And a certain group of emotions in each culture appear to have the specific function of aiding the process of social control. This idea rests on the concept of internalization of social control. 'Anxiety becomes associated with punished behaviour and the child comes to avoid behaviour which had previously been punished because, in so doing, he avoids anxiety.' Thus Aronfreed (1968) concludes that the child may become happy or afraid when he thinks of doing something — quite prior to the actual act. This internalization can come about by any means through which an emotional change is attached to a category of behaviour. Aronfreed himself theorizes about this phenomenon using neobehaviourist models but an interactionist view seems more appropriate since, as Strongman (1973) points out, such a process of internalization seems to presuppose an initial attachment to some person, so that the threat of withdrawal of affection is a sanction which can put in train the internalization of social control. We may go further than Strongman and relate internal control of behaviour to the development of the capacity to take the role of the other (Mead, 1934). Possible lines of behaviour are rejected when the child is able to imagine the negative response of the other person (cf Grusec, 1966).

This line of argument provides a context for the empirical finding that cultures differ in the details of the emotional process involved in internalized social control. For instance, Harré and Secord (1972) draw on work carried out by the anthropologist Benedict (1946) in pointing out that, whereas the Westerner tends to regard his behaviour as consistent, the Japanese would not aim at consistency overall, but rather aim to fulfill the obligations placed on them in each of their social roles — which might well produce anomalies when taken together and submitted to the question, Is this person acting consistently? Harré and Secord write, 'In the case of the Japanese, we can hardly begin to understand their social behaviour on any other basis than that of the conscious following of different sets of very well-defined and *independent* sets of rules' (p. 143, my emphasis).

Harré and Secord point out that the emotional equipment of people in a culture based, not on personal consistency but role-playing accuracy might be expected to be quite different. Indeed, the Japanese appear to be much more aware than the Westerner of minor failings in the fulfillment of obligations, and the man felt worthy of respect is the one who shows the most skilful and sensitive performance of roles — involving (as Harré and Secord write) 'the highest degree of conscious self-monitoring and awareness of the social world and its meanings in following the detailed rules of each "circle"' (p. 144f).

What, then, are the differences in the details of the emotional processes involved in internalized social control which we have alleged these facts imply? One indication is that the Japanese feel shame — i.e. the recognition of others' likely antagonism in definite social circumstances — in the face of failure to honour obligations, whereas the Anglo-American culture is commonly regarded as a 'guilt culture' since self-criticism is generally in terms of a failure to match up to a very broad self concept. The emotions of guilt and shame will be further examined later. I suggest that the internalized mechanism of self-regulation of behaviour is a much more generalized one in the Anglo-American case: the self is being viewed from the standpoint of a very abstracted 'generalized other' (cf. Chapter 5). In the Japanese case, the self is regarded from a more role-based standpoint.

Another example of cultural differences in emotion relating to the mode of internalized social control is provided in a paper by Levy (1972) on the Tahitians. After pointing out that contemporary social anthropologists generally argue that refinements are necessary in the typification 'guilt culture vs. shame culture' (a matter dealt with by Piers and Singer, 1953), Levy recounts his field research in which he inquired about the basis of internalized social control by asking whether the informant was aware of impulses which he had but forebore to act on, and if so what the reason was which prevented the action. In general the response was that only the possibility of others coming to know of the action prevented expression of an impulse — the fear of shame and embarrassment. However, another very much less stressed emotional constraint was the feeling of empathy with another who would be wronged by the action, and a sense of pity or compassion arising from such empathy. 'In contrast, the affect of guilt is culturally played down to the point of conceptual invisibility. The Tahitian language has no word which signifies anything like a sense of guilt' (Levy, 1972, p. 294). Respondents reported that, if there were no possibility of detection by others, the likelihood of their carrying out a disapproved impulse would depend only on the strength of the impulse. No notion of guilt in the face of general internalized ethical standards is invoked.

Levy proposes a schema involving the way individuals are integrated in the social structure to account for the difference between Tahitian and Anglo-American internalized control of behaviour. In general the argument is that Tahitians have no awareness of guilt because their culture is in a sufficiently steady state for shame to be a sufficient control. Guilt only appears as an internalized social control mechanism when the culture is in a process of change such that clear criteria of judgment of individual behaviour are not available. And, Levy argues, it is not merely a mechanism of control. He points out that anyone who involves himself in the process of social change is likely thereby to contravene traditional norms and feel guilt. Guilt is here a conservative factor. However, being conscious of guilt enables the person to attempt to separate authentic guilt (where one really contravenes one's ideal self concept) from guilt which can be attributed merely to the outmoded vestiges of an earlier state of society. This schema seems to me compelling, but I cannot hazard a guess as to its general applicability.

Geertz (1959) points out that the vocabulary of emotions, and the social situations regarded by a society as relevant to each emotion, must be determinative in the development of the individuals of that society. He finds, again, in the case of Javanese society, that shame and guilt are undifferentiated, and concludes that this must have 'significant repercussions on the actual personality organization of the Javanese' (p. 262).

The foregoing studies of shame and guilt have been cited merely to indicate that there is some cultural diversity in emotional experience — related no doubt to the historical situation of the specific societies considered. There is also a range of emotional tendencies within our own, pluralistic society. Only some, apparently, are aware of religious emotions. Perhaps more certainly, only some know drug-induced emotional experiences.

This matter of drug-induced emotions is itself very instructive since it relates cultural (or, here, subcultural) influences on emotional experience directly to the type of research Schachter and his colleagues have carried out. Drugs induce bodily changes, but these result in emotional experience *via* a process of labelling, and the labels are provided by the subculture. Becker has written on the social psychology of both marihuana (1953) and LSD (1967).

In his paper on marihuana, Becker argues that no one becomes a marihuana user without going through a process of learning involving three elements. Firstly, he must acquire a technique of smoking that produces bodily effects; secondly, he must label the effects in the correct way (i.e. he must learn to get high); thirdly, he must learn to enjoy the effects — and this involves acquiring the motivation to smoke marihuana. Becker cites interview evidence suggesting that early, naive expectations of the drug are socialized to concord with the perceptions held by the group of smokers. Without the subculture, Becker assumes, a haphazard, idiosyncratic set of beliefs would develop in each smoker.

On LSD, Becker begins by pointing out that evidence as to its danger is not conclusive, and that sociologists are anyway 'unlikely to accept such an asocial and unicausal explanation of any form of complex social behaviour' as is being suggested in the case of an LSD cause of psychosis (Becker, 1967, p. 164). He goes on to argue that several social psychological statements about LSD experiences seem justified on the basis of the available evidence. Firstly, only some effects are perceived as drug-induced, and those that are so perceived may differ from individual to individual. Again, since the drug was taken to obtain unusual effects, it will be unusual effects that are associated with the drug and any more mundane results of taking LSD will tend to go unreported. As in the case of marihuana, the user must go through a process of learning to label as pleasurable certain experiences, and the influence of other users will be of importance to this. Since the use of LSD appeared (at the time Becker wrote) to be increasing, he hazarded the prediction that the incidence of bad experiences would decrease because users would tend more and more to begin taking the drug in the company of more experienced people who could supply labels giving acceptable meanings to initially disliked effects — just as alcohol is fairly well controlled in our culture after very long periods of use and the development of commonly agreed perceptions of its effects. 'The incidence of "psychoses", then, is a function of the stage of development of a drug-using culture' (p. 171).

In these examples of drug-induced emotions it is possible to see the process of labelling of emotional experiences, comparable to the artificial instances of Schachter. We now turn to a consideration of some social psychological aspects of a number of more mundane emotions, in general limited in range of discussion to our culture.

Some specific emotional experiences

Happiness and sadness, pleasure and displeasure, or 'hedonic tone' is, presumably, the most basic emotional continuum. Certainly such authors as Osgood who have sought to discover the most economical model to account for the variety of emotional expressions agree that this is so. Davitz (1970) discovers hedonic tone to be a basic notion in the meaning of emotions as described by non-psychologists, i.e. it is fundamental to the commonsense vocabulary of emotional experience. Studies of emotional development generally support the view that pleasure and displeasure are the first emotions apparent in babies (Singer and Singer, 1969). Such a basic distinction must be universal, though Triandis and Lambert (1958) report that Americans make more distinctions between points on the unpleasant-pleasant continuum than do Greeks.

The greatest amount of social psychological research concerning this emotion has been indirect since it has been in the field of attitudes (Chapter 8). Clearly an area of interest for social psychologists is precisely what objects and events give rise to pleasure or displeasure, and what group and cultural differences exist; these are all questions relevant to attitude research.

Other emotional experiences are, as it were, differentiated variants of happiness or sadness, and are related to certain socially-defined situations, though sometimes bodily arousal and other factors are so clearly implicated that they overshadow the basic hedonic tone aspect.

Guilt and shame have already been discussed at some length in a cross-cultural context which implied that Anglo-American society was uniformly a 'guilt culture'. This might well not be the case. Certainly there are individual differences in the degree to which behaviour is controlled by general considerations of ideal conduct (guilt being the emotional consequence of failure) or by specific group expectations (transgression leading to shame).

The distinction between shame and guilt is admittedly blurred in general conversation. G.A. Kelly (1955) and Bannister and Fransella (1971) define guilt as the awareness of a *dislodgment of the self-concept from one's core role structure.* The idea of core role structure refers to that set of concepts that a person has, which are to do with the important social roles he plays. So guilt arises when he finds himself acting in ways he certainly would not have expected himself to have acted if he really were the kind of person he thought he was. His self concept has slipped, metaphorically speaking, from its place amongst the constructs of social roles — whereas earlier its place was clear.

Certainly Kelly's view is relevant to guilt. But it does not distinguish guilt from shame. Aronfreed (1968) takes pains to do this. For him, 'the distinctive qualitative properties of guilt may be regarded as the experience of anxiety through the filter of the cognition of the harmful consequences of one's actions for others' (p. 247) whereas 'the aversive state that follows a transgression may be described as shame to the extent that its qualitative experience is determined by a cognitive orientation toward the visibility of the transgression. The essence of shame is a cognitive focus on the appearance or display of that which ought not to show. It is this cognitive focus which provides the sense of exposure of vulnerabilty to observation that is so intimately associated with shame' (p. 249).

Aronfreed's treatment of shame seems quite correct, but surely his view of guilt is too narrow. It is not only deeds with consequences harmful to others that can give rise to guilt. In the case of guilt, a view nearer Kelly's would appear more adequate. Aronfreed goes on to review some anthropological studies of shame and guilt paralleling those already treated here. These give him some cause for concern as a behaviourist, the overt signs distinguishing between the two emotions being somewhat too nebulous.

Jenkins' (1950) view of guilt is clearly in line with the generality of opinions reviewed so far: 'The feeling of guilt may be described as a painful emotion ... relating to the realisation of an overwide discrepancy between one's own conduct and the moral or ethical standards one has set for oneself' (p. 353). Margaret Mead (1950) employs this view in her treatment, from the standpoint of psychoanalytic anthropology, of cultural variations in the prevalence of guilt. Apart from discussing the shame/guilt dichotomy, she points out that it is not only Anglo-American society that is guilt-oriented. The Manus people of the Admiralty Islands also are among the guilt cultures, and these people are also puritanical, and fit easily into Western styles of life. Mead argues that a pattern of upbringing 'in which parents differentiate themselves from their children by assuming the moral responsibility of punishing for disapproved acts and rewarding approved acts, in such a way as to encourage the child to take final responsibility for the content of its acts' is one determinant (p. 370). But she also views 'the preoccupation with intake and output of food' as a relevant factor (p. 371). These determinants seem to me less likely to be important than the social structure and language, implicated in the research already cited by Benedict, Levy and Geertz. However, the interrelationship between all these variables must surely be complex. It is not clear how even the most painstaking empirical work could settle this question.

An interesting dimension to shame is treated in a paper by Nuttin (1950). Although writing before the viewpoint was widely accepted, he begins by pointing out that emotions are more than biological: 'the content of emotional experience psychologically originates in a behavioural contact between definite dynamic structures in the subject and the real or imagined situations at hand' (p. 344), that is, the person's perception of the situation is the core determinant of emotion. Nuttin then shows that a sense of shame is only possible because the person construes his conscious experience as 'interior', not immediately accessible to other people. This being so, 'a sphere of privacy is created in human life' (p. 344). Thus, Nuttin argues, if this conscious privacy is absent, as it seems to be in animals, there can be no sense of shame (cf. Riezler, 1943).

However, more is involved in shame than the individual's awareness of privacy in thinking: 'Psychological life is not pure interiority and it cannot be considered as simply impenetrable to others' (p. 345). We express ourselves in words, gestures and actions which others take as indicative of our mental attitude. This fact leads to the possibility that our private sphere of thought and feeling may be violated. Nuttin argues that the two facts of mental privacy and the possibility of unintended exposure constitute the conditions for experiencing shame.

Thus shame, for Nuttin, arises when we betray ourselves: we make available to public view aspects of ourselves which we would rather keep private. This emotion can occur as soon as the person has developed the capacity to view his mental life as private. Although he does not stress this, Nuttin's standpoint implies that shame cannot be felt until the child has acquired the capacity to take the attitude of the other to his behaviour (cf. the discussion of the development of the self-concept in the previous chapter). Guilt, too, depends on viewing our behaviour from an imaginary external standpoint. However, to treat the distinction between shame and guilt in this way requires an elaboration — a considerable elaboration — of Mead's theory concerning the development of self through taking roles. All that need be underlined here is that shame and guilt are intimately linked to these matters.

Empathy and sympathy may profitably be introduced at this point since they relate so clearly to taking the attitude of the other. Empathy, indeed, may be defined so as to be virtually synonymous with taking the attitude of the other — viewing the situation from the standpoint of the other person emotionally (see Stotland, 1969). The relationship between empathy and sympathy has been succinctly expressed by Argyle (1969): 'When a person shares the feelings of another, this is called 'empathy'; when the feelings involved are of distress, it is called 'sympathy'' (p. 192 — cf. Aronfreed, 1968; Lindesmith, Strauss and Denzin, 1975). In my view, empathy is not correctly categorized as an emotion, since the actual content of the empathy may vary depending on the emotion being shared. However sympathy — a feeling of distress due to the perceived situation of another — *is* a distinct emotional entity. Sympathy with a person who is feeling shame does not involve feeling ashamed oneself, but rather distress is experienced.

Scheler (1954) points out that such emotions as sympathy — where the emotion arises in a situation where another is feeling an emotion, and because of the emotional state of the other — such emotions depend on empathy. One could not sympathize, or feel pity or joy because of another's state, unless one first saw the situation from the viewpoint of that other person. He goes on to point out that empathy can indeed carry with it an especial emotional nuance which he terms 'fellow feeling'. All this is true — but empathy itself, I maintain, is better viewed as a skill — an emotional form of taking the attitude of the other — rather than an emotional experience in its own right.

Anxiety and social poise are opposites, in the view of Argyle (1969). He cites research which has uncovered a general tendency to feel anxious in social situations, a tendency which some have to a marked degree — and often betray their anxiety in both nonverbal and verbal behaviour — but which others do not have at all. Argyle describes general lack of social anxiety as 'poise', but of course this lack of an emotional reaction is not to be taken as itself an emotion.

It is important to distinguish anxiety as a general personality characteristic from the emotion of anxiety. The personality characteristic merely reflects a greater proneness to experience the emotion. Kelly's (1955), and Bannister and Fransella's (1971), definition of anxiety seems to me correct and to the point, it is the awareness that the situation with which one is confronted lies mostly outside the range of applicability of one's system of constructs. One is in a situation with undefined, uncategorized, therefore unperceived elements (these often are future implications of the situation). Using such a definition of anxiety, Kelly would explain the experience of anxiety in students approaching a new topic as absolutely necessary and quite non-pathological. If the topic really is new there will be elements which are unperceived though there on the page — we have not the mental equipment to cope with them. Much of the topic lies outside our current system of constructs. We must abandon constructs and develop new ones in order to deal with the topic. It could be said that if you are not anxious in approaching a new topic, then you are not concerned with it sufficiently to be aware of the need to alter constructs in order to learn it. Anxiety is an essential part of the experience of studying. (Fischer, 1970, has developed the notion of the 'emotionally experienced situation' and its place in the flow of life.)

Kelly would deal with Argyle's notion of social anxiety as awareness that one's system of constructs about people and social settings do not entirely apply to this particular social situation. Experience in many situations may be a factor conducive of the development of poise — our earlier anxiety in the company of others gave place to poise as we developed new constructs which applied to more and more social encounters. The same sort of analysis could be made of May's (1950) emphasis on anxiety as arising from any threat to a central value of the person.

Embarrassment is the final emotional experience to be looked at in this chapter — though there is relevant work on other emotions, such as anger and hostility (Stevick, 1971; Bannister and Fransella, 1971) and love (Foote, 1953).

Embarrassment is very strongly related to shame, but is even more dependent than shame on other actual, external people perceiving our actions and appraising us as persons on the basis of these actions. Indeed, Nuttin's (1950) analysis of the preconditions of shame can also be seen as an analysis of the basis of embarrassment, as can be seen when one considers Goffman's (1956) treatment of embarrassment and its social determinants.

Goffman writes: 'Whatever else, embarrassment has to do with the figure the individual cuts ... The crucial concern is the impression one makes on others ... ' (p. 98), and this is certainly also the case with shame. However, embarrassment — whilst a form of shame — is an emotion related to more specific social conditions. By this I do not intend to imply that embarrassment may only be experienced in certain situations; no, as Goffman points out, it is an emotion that can arise in any encounter. Rather its specificity in contrast to shame lies in the actual conditions which cause it.

The theory of Goffman is that embarrassment is experienced when the self-concept one is presenting in an encounter is 'discredited'. 'During interaction the individual is expected to possess certain attributes, capacities and information which, taken together, fit together into a self that is at one coherently unified and appropriate for the occasion' (p. 105). The gardening expert has a self involving special knowledge; the host has a self which is seen as socially skilled and with powers of efficient though discreet organization. At the same time the individual is expected to project his self and perceive correctly the selves projected by others. The interaction proceeds smoothly through such mutual definition of the personnel. But the whole thing can be thrown out of order by a discrediting of the self of a participant. The gardening expert may forget a plant's name or, more difficult to overlook, make an obvious factual error. The host may be rude; let slip a remark; have to confess that his refrigerator has unexpectedly defrosted and spoilt some of the food. The situations differ but the fundamental structure is similar in that the facts that lie open to general observation discredit the self concept that has been claimed.

Given the genesis of embarrassment through such an incident, the person's behaviour becomes flustered and unskilful, and the flow of interaction is flawed. Goffman points out that usually not only the discredited individual is embarrassed but the whole group suffers this emotion. It might be thought that this is to be attributed to empathy on the part of those observing the discrediting, but another source is more usually the cause of the general embarrassment. The discrediting of the self of one participant throws the encounter as a whole out of gear, the mutual definition of personnel itself is disrupted. Therefore there is a general sense of lack of self-definition. No-one is certain how to project himself, so each has a feeling of embarrassment on his own account.

Goffman draws attention to a distinction between 'poise' — which he defines as 'the capacity to maintain one's own composure' (p. 103) even when a potentially embarrassing situation has arisen — and 'tact' or 'graciousness' — which is 'the capacity to avoid causing oneself or others embarrassment' (p. 103) especially by skilfully overlooking a self-discrediting event. In this distinction we see a development of Argyle's concept of social poise, the lack of anxiety in social situations, which underlies both aspects — poise and tact.

Argyle himself (1969) argues that embarrassment is a form of social anxiety, which I dispute since embarrassment occurs when it is only too clear what has happened and that it is a shaming experience whereas social anxiety is surely the awareness that the situation is *likely* to give rise to shame. Anticipated embarrassment may relate to social anxiety, but to draw the parallel further leads to confusion. However, Argyle's other comments are instructive. He wishes to define embarrassment in broader terms than Goffman. Any lack of social skill can give rise to embarrassment, and any failure of 'meshing' in interaction can also be a cause. Lack of a neatly-meshing interaction occurs when there is disagreement over the perception of the situation (one sees it as comic, another as tragic, perhaps) or disagreement over the roles played in the interaction (as when a subordinate acts in a hail-fellow-well-met manner towards a superior). However, these conditions of embarrassment are not mutually exclusive; a child may lack social skill and therefore lack the subtlety to see a situation as requiring tact rather than outspoken honesty, thereby playing an inappropriate role. More importantly, although Argyle's situations may indicate conditions allowing embarrassment, they are not *sufficient* conditions, since we are only embarrassed when we relate the situation to our self concept. Goffman's analysis is more acute in this matter than Argyle's.

Both Argyle and Goffman point out that embarrassment can arise as a sudden event within an otherwise smooth-running encounter, or else can be an emotion felt during the whole encounter. This appears to be especially likely when the self we are called upon to present is so far distant from our real self concept that the role is very hard indeed to sustain. Insights such as this, incidentally, show the truth of Argyle's remark that 'embarrassment is of considerable theoretical interest, since study of it can tell us something about the conditions necessary for interaction to proceed smoothly' (p. 388).

Empirical study of embarrassment has been undertaken by Gross and Stone (1964), who draw for theoretical support on Goffman's analysis, paraphrasing his description thus: 'Embarrassment occurs whenever some *central* assumption in a transaction has been *unexpectedly* and unqualifiedly discredited for at least one participant' (p. 2). Of course, here they can only be referring to embarrassment as a sudden event within a generally well-meshing interaction, otherwise the embarrassing event is not unexpected.

Gross and Stone collected some one-thousand instances of embarrassing events, from students in the main. These were subjected to content analysis, arriving at seventy-four categories (such as 'being caught in a cover story', 'having to make a forced choice between friends', 'misnaming', 'forgetting names', 'body exposure', etc.). These categories were found to be further classifiable, and three general types accounted for most instances: inappropriate identity (i.e. the presentation of a self which did not fit the situation); loss of poise; and disturbance of the assumptions persons make about one another in interaction. Possibly each of these general types of embarrassment can be subsumed under Goffman's typification, though clearly a finer set of distinctions may be drawn. Gross and Stone use their data to examine the conditions of successful interaction.

Other matters of interest about embarrassment may be mentioned in conclusion. It is of course possible to plan to purposely shame and embarrass another by discrediting, perhaps a false front (see Garfinkel, 1956). Further, embarrassment is not necessarily to be thought of at the purely social psychological level. Goffman argues that social structure provides the conditions by which some people are necessarily forced to adopt a false self presentation in certain circumstances which is very much open to discredit. To cite a trite example in the recent experience of the writer, a driving examiner often has to tell a learner driver that he has failed the test, and to do so may well adopt a stereotyped delivery in order to avoid the possibility that his tone of voice be interpreted as sarcastic, apologetic, reproving or whatever. However, the stereotyped speech is itself somewhat odd and could well be remarked on humorously by the disappointed examinee — to the embarrassment of the examiner.

With this brief study of certain emotions this chapter is concluded. The impression which I have intended to convey is that emotional experience is essentially social — just as mind and self, which are required for emotional experience to be possible, are social. Physiology is a substratum of only marginal interest when considering complex emotions such as guilt, shame, sympathy, anxiety or embarrassment.

Mandler (1975) provides in the conclusion to his book on emotion a statement that could not better express the view of emotions adopted in this chapter: 'When all has been said about mental processes, we can return to the importance of the social conditions under which they operate, the realization that life and society determine consciousness, not vice versa' (p. 248).

CHAPTER 7

Being Motivated and Attributing Motives

The study of motivation is concerned with why people act as they do. There are many valid approaches to this broad question, but it is argued that not all are of equal interest to social psychology. Evidence is presented that even 'basic' physiological motives are not precisely causal *motives. Rather, the person acts on the basis of a meaning-ascription which has the physiological event as a focus of perception. Such non-cognitive matters as the physiological state of the person affect experience and action only inasmuch as they are construed as demanding 'motivated' action (Brehm, Zimbardo). Research is then discussed which has a bearing on how we commonsensically account for the behaviour of ourselves and others, and the circumstances under which we view the behaviour as 'intentional' (Heider, Jones and Davis, Kelley) and attribute a conscious motive. The social influences on the categories available for accounting for our behaviour and that of others are discussed (Mills, Scott and Lyman).*

SCIENCE AND SOCIAL MOTIVES

There is no point in hiding the fact that there is a large number of quite dissimilar approaches to the question of why people act as they do — which is the field of motivation. This confusion is, I think, largely because the question is too broadly stated: so many distinct phenomena enter into the arena of motivation, and there is really no reason why the same concept need be stretched to cover them all. So the various theories of motivation centre on one or other of the reasons or causes of human action, and hardly connect with each other at all. They are not different theories about the same thing, but theories about entirely different things. Peters (1958), among others, has shown that the various types of motivation theory focus on different sorts of cause or reason for action.

Consider the various distinct types of motive that can be given to account for the actions of a man who always purchases his goods in bulk where this produces even the minutest saving in the long run. What different views might there be of his reasons for doing this? Firstly he himself really believes he does this in order to save money to bequeath to his nephew. This is, we might say, *his secret reason*. But, when asked by others to account for his behaviour he says 'A penny saved is a penny earned' — *his expressed reason,* the reason he gives to others. The others who know him have their own views as to his motives. 'He's a miser — he's tight,' they say. This is the motive they attribute to him, *the motive attributed by others*. And finally there may be a motive for his actions about which the man and his neighbours are equally unaware. Freud might say his actions are caused by an 'anal retentive' personality due to his personal history. Or a behaviourist might say he is exhibiting conditioned anxiety. A physiological basis for his actions might even be sought. These might be the *underlying causes* of his behaviour.

There is a choice, therefore, as to what phenomena to centre attention on in the attempt to describe the motives for a person's actions. The fact that a person can be wrong in the reasons or causes he gives for his own actions, either because he really does not know why he behaved in that way or because he wishes to present a different — possibly more socially acceptable motive, has led many psychologists to completely eschew the attempt to study the person's own account. Thus motivational theories have often centred on underlying causes.

Before assessing the wisdom of this focus, some clarification of terminology needs to be made. The convention to be adopted for the purpose of this chapter (though the meaning of the words in other contexts may well be different) is as follows:

1. *Motive* is to be an umbrella term covering all inducements to act, whether or not the person is aware of them.
2. *Cause* or causal motive will refer to a motive which induces action without dependence on the conscious awareness of the person. Thus behaviour is to be said to have been caused by something if it is the direct effect of that thing, unmediated by any conscious meaning -attribution.
3. *Reasons* are to be taken as conscious motives for action. Here the behaviour is regarded as intentional.
4. *Accounts* refer to the person's verbal indications of the motives which underlay his actions (he might report a reason for action he accepts as intentional, or a cause which he considers to have produced the behaviour in question).
5. *Attributions* of motive for an action can be made by the actor himself, in which case they are accounts, or by others.

It must be confessed that, while every attempt has been made to adhere to this terminology, the distinctions are often difficult to maintain, especially since 'causal attribution' theory uses 'cause' as the umbrella term rather than 'motive'.

There are many views as to the real causes underlying actions. Thus McDougall in his *Introduction to Social Psychology* (1908) postulated a number of basic instincts, one of the most pervasive of which was 'gregariousness'. He wrote: 'The gregarious instinct is one of the human instincts of greatest social importance, for it has played a great part in moulding societary forms...The instinct is displayed by many species of animals, even by some very low in the scale of mental capacity' (p. 71 — 20th ed., 1926). And he goes on to describe some of the behaviours thought especially due to gregariousness — it is held to be very basic. So this is a hypothesis about a cause of behaviour. However, instinct theories of McDougall's type have lost favour, largely because there seemed to be nothing to prevent the list of hypothesised instincts increasing indefinitely — as Freud foresaw (1949). Further, it seems difficult to test for the reality of an instinct in the form presented by McDougall; if men act socially they are said to have a gregarious instinct, but there is no independent way of investigating the instinct: the social behaviour which the instinct is intended to explain is the only evidence there is of the existence of gregariousness. Other problems with instinct theories are presented by Beach (1955).

A radical behaviourist of Skinner's type goes no further in uncovering the real underlying cause of behaviour than to say that past contingencies of reinforcement are responsible. Other behaviourists attempt to elucidate the basis of reinforcement by arguing that reinforcement of behaviour occurs when a drive such as hunger or thirst is reduced. It might indeed seem intuitively obvious that hunger is the underlying causal motive for behaviour such as searching for and consuming food, so that (whatever the person thinks about the matter) hunger causes eating. Any study of eating should, surely, attempt to discover a physiological mechanism identifiable as the source of the hunger drive.

However there is experimental evidence that it is too simple to regard even so basic a drive as hunger as a purely physiological matter. Some such experiments are reported in a book by Zimbardo entitled *The Cognitive Control of Motivation* (1969), and they are all based on the idea that cognitive factors affect one's experience of physiological drives in a manner akin to their effect on attitudes: situations which are known to bring about attitude change also bring about changes in motive. If this is so, the direct, mechanical view of biological drives as causal motives underlying behaviour needs modification.

Consider this experiment on hunger by J. Brehm (1962), which involved students in the US as subjects (they get a small grade-point reward as a contribution to their course work for taking part in psychological experiments). Brehm invited students to participate, and asked them to refrain from breakfast and lunch before arriving at his laboratory in the afternoon — he told them he was examining the effects of food deprivation on performance on intellectual tasks and tasks involving fine movements. Before carrying out these tasks, the subjects filled in rating scales measuring their degree of hunger. They then spent some time carrying out tasks relevant to the supposed aim of the experiment. At this stage subjects were told that, although they had carried out the task required and would get their grade-point reward, it would be a great help to the experimenters if they would agree to return in the evening for additional testing, not eating at all in the intervening period. In other words they were to undergo further deprivation of food. Moreover, there could be no more grade-point reward for the evening's work, subjects were told. However, subjects were divided into two groups (without knowing that this was the case). One group was left with the situation as stated: they were asked to agree to a further period of hunger without any reward to justify it. The others were told that, although no grade-point reward could be given, five dollars would be paid for further participation in the experiment. So this second group did have some reason for agreeing to further deprivation.

Now the group who were asked to undergo hunger for no reward would, if they agreed, be placing themselves in what, in attitude research, is termed a *dissonant* situation. According to Festinger's (1957) theory of cognitive dissonance, when two 'cognitive elements' are dissonant — as when one holds a certain attitude yet is aware that one is acting contrary to that attitude — then one way of reducing dissonance is to change the attitude (see Chapter 8).

Now, if cognitive dissonance effects were seen in the study of Brehm, hunger would seem to be comparable to attitudes, which would not be expected of a purely physiological, causal motive. Considering hunger as an attitude, then, there should be a difference between the two groups in the amount of dissonance experienced. The group who, although hungry, agree to go without food for a further period without reward are arguably in a 'high dissonance' state: acting contrary to motive. The other group, however, have a reason or justification for carrying on their fast even though they are hungry, since they expect five dollars as payment — their situation is 'low dissonance'.

As soon as Brehm had secured the agreement of both groups of people to further deprivation (though the people were asked individually — not as groups) he immediately asked them to rate again their state of hunger. This was the second measure of hunger. And then they were told that, after all, they did not need to return for later testing and could go and eat their fill.

Now, what can we expect of the two measures Brehm took of rated hunger? If hunger is equivalent to an attitude, and cognitive dissonance phenomena occur, then Brehm would hypothesize that the non-dissonant group of subjects would not feel any pressure to change their view of how hungry they were, but the others *would* feel dissonance (for no incentive they have agreed to stay hungry). This dissonance would be reduced if they de-emphasized their hunger, so that it is no burden to them to stay deprived of food. Well this is exactly the result Brehm obtained. The second ratings of the rewarded group were hungrier than those of the unrewarded group. The unrewarded people had reduced dissonance, it seems, by perceiving their hunger as less strong than they had hitherto.

Well, J. Brehm's experiment indicates that at least *expressed* feelings of hunger (which one would expect to reflect a physiological drive) are susceptible to phenomena which show they have a large cognitive element. A further study by M. Brehm, Back and Bogdonoff (1964) replicated J. Brehm's experiment with a similar result — and, most impressively, also showed that there were differences in the level of free fatty acids in the blood. Normally, hungry people produce more free fatty acids than people who are not hungry. The M. Brehm study indicated that this was inhibited in people who, because of cognitive dissonance, reported themselves as less hungry. In other words, not only did they rate themselves as less hungry than the other group; their bodies actually acted in a less hungry manner.

In the case of hunger, the supposedly basic, causal, physiological motive, which might have been expected to determine action quite independently of conscious awareness, now appears to be less differentiated from 'his reason'. Cognition is taking a central place.

Another experiment by J. Brehm (1962) was on thirst rather than hunger (which overcomes a problem he found in the other study, that too many people positively welcomed a day's dieting, so the proposal that they should deprive themselves of food for a further period of time contained its own hidden justification). The thirst experiment was run on exactly the same lines as the hunger study, with the same result. However, in addition, after the subjects had rated their thirst for the second time (after completing the tasks), they were allowed to drink some water before leaving the laboratory, as they thought to undergo further deprivation. The finding was that group B, who had, as a result of dissonance, rated their thirst as less strong than group A, actually drank less water than that group. So dissonance did not affect merely reported thirst, but also changed actual behaviour: these people actually were less thirsty. Being thirsty is like an attitude.

Other experiments (Zimbardo, 1969; Heckhausen and Weiner, 1972) provide evidence that pain, as a drive leading to the behaviour of avoidance and so on, and many 'social motives' such as the motivation to succeed, are all similarly susceptible to phenomena which show they have a strong cognitive element. The question raised by such findings is: What view of 'causal motives' do they necessitate?

J. Brehm himself writes: 'It is only what the [person] knows about [his] motivational state that affects [behaviour]. Non-cognitive components of motivation, such as the physiological state of the [person], could then affect [behaviour] only to the extent that they affect the cognitive components. That is, a state of deprivation, short of killing the [person], would have to have cognitive representation in order to have any kind of psychological effect at all' (p.75, 1962). This opinion clearly echos the view of Schachter (1964) on emotional experience: motivational factors, like the bodily factors involved in emotion, are perceived 'as categorized' — and it is the perceived drive, not the biological drive directly, which affects behaviour and experience.

At this juncture it is possible to mention other social psychologists who have come to the same conclusion — though without the benefit of the experimental evidence. Presumably they did so because a cognitive approach to motivation seemed intuitively the most promising one from the viewpoint of social psychology. Thus the interactionists Lindesmith, Strauss and Denzin (1975) write: 'A biological condition by itself has little motivational significance except as it is perceived or interpreted by the individual in whom it exists' (p.292).

Another author who has not adopted the common practice of setting aside people's own accounts of their actions, and attempted to get beyond these to 'real, causal motives', but has rather assumed that people act as a result of their construction of the situation is G.A. Kelly (1955; see the exposition of Bannister and Fransella, 1971). Because of this he has been roundly criticized by psychologists such as Foulds (1973) as having no view of motivation and therefore as having nothing to say about the reasons for peoples actions. A specific refutation of Foulds is provided by McCoy (1975), but the general falsity of the criticism is clear. People act according to their definition of the situation, and bodily drives may enter into the perceived situation. If they do, they may influence action.

The authors to be discussed in subsequent sections of this chapter share the view we have suggested. It implies that 'his reason' for acting is, at least usually, the real motive. In their defence of this approach, Harré and Secord (1972) summarize the viewpoint in the following terms:

1. Man is capable of initiating actions which are anticipated in a more or less clear plan. He acts according to his construction of the situation.
2. Most human actions cannot be, and probably need not be traced to ('causal') antecedent events. Indeed it is false to represent an explanation as unscientific because it refers to plans etc., which a person consciously follows, as the basis for his actions.
3. Action cannot be described reductively in terms of pure physiology without losing its essential, 'meaningful' nature.

Before discussing further aspects of accounts of motivation from the social psychological standpoint, consideration needs to be given to the circumstances under which both scientist and commonsense member of society seek to know motives for the action of another person (or, indeed, their own puzzling behaviour).

What behaviour needs explaining?

It will be clear from the line of argument thus far that the discussion that follows will not be concerned with psychologists' theories of real, underlying motives, where such theories are dismissive of actors' reasons for their behaviour. Rather, the commonsense attributions of motive by ordinary participants in social interaction are the focus of interest. (As Mills, 1940, points out in a paper treated below, psychologists and other professional motive-attribution specialists may actually share the general 'rules' with laymen, and merely add a distinct set of motive terms to the commonsense vocabulary).

When is it that we feel we need to look for the motives underlying a person's actions? Now before trying to answer this question we must remind ourselves of the terminological distinctions drawn at the start of the chapter. In asking what motivated another's action we must separate *reasons* for intentional behaviour from *causes* of behaviour, where we do not attribute an intention to the person. The realm of purely causal motivation appears, from the work of Brehm and the others, not to include matters otherwise thought to fall within its boundaries. Nevertheless, the commonsense actor perceives certain actions as caused. For instance, someone treads on your toe — in asking for a motive for the behaviour you ask angrily what he meant by treading on your toe. But this is relevant only if the action is perceived as having a reason. If not, the behaviour might have been merely clumsy or accidental. The motive for the behaviour is outside the sphere of reasons, and we are justified in reintroduce the notion of cause to cover such incidents: occasions where the action had unintended consequences, and where it is hardly relevant to ask for a reason. Thus a condition that has to be met before we commonsensically seek reasons is: the behaviour is not due to some external factor, or chance, but appears to result from an *'internal' and personal* motive—specifically, it is intended.

Sometimes it is inappropriate to worry about people's motives: we know why they acted as they did because we understand (maybe share) their view of the situation. People's motives are not at issue when they take chairs and sit down when they arrive in a room for a scheduled meeting. However there are occasions for motive-seeking. In some situations the reason for an action is hard to interpret. Then we feel the need to attribute a motive to the person who has acted. (And here it is relevant to note that the actor may be oneself, and the puzzlement may arise in later reflection on one's own behaviour.) In sum, then, behaviour needs explaining when *we do not share the actor's perception of the situation.*

Although this may be a start in answering the question of when it is we believe a piece of behaviour needs explaining with an attribution of motive, it has only pushed the question back a step. We now need to ask when it is that behaviour appears to need explaining. And how do we commonsensically decide that it is due to 'internal' motives rather than external causes such as social pressures, chance, the circumstances, etc? Now we will have to sidestep the first question, when it is that behaviour is judged as requiring explanation, because to answer it would require a full description of the culture in which the behaviour takes place and the norms against which it is judged. We will have just to take for granted the fact that we all know unusual behaviour when we see it, and that it is only such abnormal behaviour that is regarded as needing an explanation.

The second question is more easily handled: how do we decide that the behaviour is due to some internal reason — something 'in' the person himself — rather than the result of some external factor (circumstances, chance)? Only if the behaviour has an internal motive may we go on to ask for a reason. Now there is a small-scale theory in social psychology which begins with exactly the question of what basis ordinary people have for judging that an act was the result of the person's own decision or that it was a chance or accidental happening or due to some external factor outside his control. This is attribution theory — so called because it is to do with attributing motive; deciding whether an event is due to the voluntary action of the person.

'CAUSAL ATTRIBUTION'

Clearly the matter of deciding whether an action reflects a deliberate intention of the actor is part of person-perception. So in this section of the chapter we assume that the perception of people as outlined in Chapter 4 is taking place. Within this process, how does the perceiver decide what caused, or was the reason for, the event he has witnessed? (Causal attribution theory unfortunately uses the term 'cause' as we have used 'motive' — to cover both causes and reasons. However the attempt will be made to discuss the theory with the terms already adopted in this chapter.)

F. Heider

The theory of causal attribution (reviewed by Amabile and Hastorf, 1976; Hastorf, Schneider and Polefka, 1970; Heckhausen and Weiner, 1972; Shaver, 1975; and Weiner, 1972, among many authors) is a flourishing area of social psychological research. Its source, and possibly still its best general statement of position, is the work of Fritz Heider (1958).

Heider's concern in this context, then, was to describe the essential characteristics of the search by the commonsense, ordinary individual, for motives of events. Given that a person has been observed to act, and this act has been seen to have certain direct or indirect consequences, what is seen as the cause or reason for the phenomenon? (Implicit in the question — as Heider explicitly stated — is the notion that people are concerned with discovering motives.)

The motive of an event (where 'event' refers to an action plus the consequences of that action) is, first of all, located either in the person who performed the action, or in the environment, or in a combination of the two. This is the most fundamental distinction that the observer must make in attributing causes. Heider writes: 'In common-sense psychology . . . the result of an action is felt to depend on two sets of conditions, namely factors within the person and factors within the environment . . . One may speak of the effective force . . . of the person or of the environment when one means the totality of forces emanating from one or the other source. The action outcome . . . may then be said to be dependent upon a combination of effective personal force and effective environmental force. . .' (p.82).

Internal and external factors, then, are resources for motive attribution. There are distinguishable components of internal forces also pointed out by Heider. Internal motivation can be regarded as a product of ability — the perceived capacity enjoyed by the individual to perform the action and thereby create its consequences — and exertion, which is effort expended in attempting to perform the action.

When intention is also perceived as present in the action (the person wants to perform that action and knowingly aims at the consequences), then we not only regard the action as having a possible internal motive — it is also possible that the motive is 'personal' (i.e. motivated by a reason).

So Heider argues that personal force is composed of ability, effort and intention, but that not all internal motivation is personal, since some behaviour is certainly due to the actor, but is quite unintended — the action was reflex, erroneous, accidental, clumsy; the consequences were not foreseen. This distinction between personal motive and internal motive is most important (see Fig. 5).

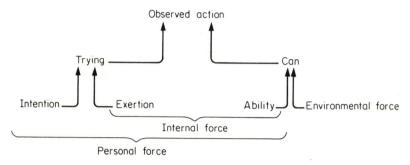

Fig. 5. Heider's view of motivational forces.

Heider points out that, in attributing motives to the person, the perceiver's view that the person was trying is very relevant. Trying is effort expended in an intended direction — so it is an amalgam of percieved exertion and perceived intention. Perception of trying is often obscured because it is not easy, in many cases, to judge intention: many acts may all really have the same intention behind them yet be very different so that the underlying intention in unclear.

Of course internal or personal forces are not the only sources of motivation. The environment may be seen as a source of forces constraining, forcing or negating action. The environment includes, in Heider's analysis: the perceived ease or difficulty of the action and the production of intended consequences; luck; forces which coerce the actor and therefore dictate his actions. Heider treats environmental forces as adding to or substracting from the ability of the actor — so that the two are perceived by an observer in relation to each other. A term was introduced by Heider to cover this synthetic percept: can. (Can is treated as a noun.) The can of an action is the perceived possibility of the behaviour and its consequences, therefore, and is compounded of ability and environmental forces.

The action is perceived as the outcome of trying and can.

So far our outline of Heider has been largely terminological. But the vocabulary has as its basis the attempt to provide a means for analysing the way personal responsibility for events is attributed by observers. The action is perceived in terms of trying and can; responsibility for an action is attributed to the person if his ability is sufficient, the environment does not present insuperable difficulties, and he intended to perform the action, which he expended effort in accomplishing. At least, this is true within limits.

Modifying factors, which indicate that motive-attribution is not a straightforward, logical matter, include the fact that there is a tendency to perceive persons as the instigators of events unless a strong situational force is immediately present. This may be regarded as a systematic bias in the attribution of motives — persons are preferred as the perceived source of events. Again, there is a tendency to lump together persons and events — this is only to be expected in the nature of things, since we form an impression of a person which includes motives and traits of personality — if a 'bad' event is perceived as emanating from an individual, he must be bad. So people tend to be thought of as the source of their behaviour unless some very apparent and forceful external cause is in operation, and even then we may see the person as the source if he is perceived as able and ready to initiate such behaviour; and also perceiving the motive of an action is linked to all the other aspects of forming an impression of the person and cannot be viewed in isolation.

To return to the matter of personal versus internal motivation, it is of course often of practical importance in actual social life that the person is seen, not only as the source of the event (i.e. internal motivation is perceived) but also as the knowing, intending source (so that personal motivation is perceived by observers). In motive attribution, this is a necessary precondition for the search for his reason for acting. Moreover, if he intended the action, then he is praiseworthy or blameworthy — he bears the responsibility for the event.

Shaver (1975) rightly points out that, in all these matters, the judgment by an observer that the actor intended to do it, is crucial. How is intention inferred? Heider discusses three factors that help us to perceive that an intention underlay the action: equifinality, local causality and exertion.

To take exertion first: the fact that the person seemed to expend effort in performing the action strongly suggests intention. If a man aims his boot with force at your shin you are unlikely to believe his protest that the kick was an accident. Equifinality refers to the fact mentioned earlier that many actions with different perceived characteristics may be due to the same intention. As I said, this often hinders the perception of intent. However, if a common thread can be detected, then this is strong evidence for intention. A person who keeps applying for different jobs in Manchester to the exclusion of other towns may well be seen as having a reason. Local causality refers to the fact that intended actions are more likely to be guided throughout by the actor rather than thrown off haphazardly. The man who kicked your shins in the earlier example will be more likely to be seen as intending the action if he aimed carefully than if he merely wafted his feet around.

Heider's reading of the situation, then, is that the more an effect appears to be under the immediate personal control of the actor, the more responsibility will be assigned to him (and therefore the more likely it is that actions whose bases are obscure will lead to concern with his motives).

This position is modified, however, by the fact that Heider detects several 'levels' of perceived responsibility for action. If the event is very serious in that observers strongly seek the why and wherefore (e.g. a fatal accident), then levels of responsibility which would not give rise to blame were the event minor now do take on significance. The 'levels' are as follows (see Sulzer, reported in Shaver, 1975; Shaw and Sulzer, 1964): (1) Association, where the person has no part in the causation of the event — as in 'guilt by association'; (2) Causality, where the person is a cause although the event was quite unintended and unforeseen; (3) Foreseeability, e.g. 'carelessness', though the event was unintended, it is supposed that it could have been foreseen; (4) Intentionality, here the person is fully aware — trying and can are both present — the motivation is personal.

It is, I think, quite clear that these four classes do form a scale of responsibility. Heider adds a fifth level: Justifiability. Here the action is seen as intentional, but environmental circumstances nullify, in the eyes of observers, the personal responsibility borne by the actor, as in a killing undertaken in self-defence. This fifth category seems to me to introduce a consideration which is quite distinct, and a separate matter.

We have now reviewed in some detail Heider's view of the commonsense attribution of motive. Let us take stock. One reaction to his work might be to complain that we knew all this already. Every schoolteacher knows that a judgment of a pupils performance depends on attributions of ability and effort, for instance. A reply to this criticism would not seek to show any surprising information in Heider's analysis — rather the fact is that he was attempting exactly to describe what everyone does commonsensically know about attributing motive. This might seem an odd enterprise — hardly part of science — merely to lay down clearly what everyone knows. But if we are to take seriously the question of how we attribute motive then an essential first step is to clearly describe the basic phenomena (cf. Ashworth, 1976).

This point needs to be firmly grasped. Even some writers on attribution theory (e.g. Shaver, 1975) seem to think that the aim is to lay down scientific guidelines as to how we should go about the task of attributing causes. This is not it at all. The idea is to describe the actual characteristics of attribution rather than any ideal rules.

Another criticism of Heider is more weighty. Hastorf, Schneider and Polefka (1970) point out that his analysis merely indicates some of the relevant factors in attribution. It cannot be regarded as predictive of the way attributions will be made in any specific circumstances. This is true. It in no way casts doubt on the brilliance of Heider's initial contribution. Later writers have been able to elaborate on his basic phenomenology, and these embellishments enable the experimenter to erect testable hypotheses about the process of attribution, which are beginning to indicate general tendencies.

Jones and Davis

The next advance in the description of the attribution of motive was made in a paper of Jones and Davis (1965) *From acts to dispositions: the attribution process in person perception.* They treat as taken-for-granted some of Heider's points. For instance they concur with his view that the perceiver attempts to account for events in terms of either environmental or internal forces. Jones and Davis concern themselves only with the process of attributing motive to the actor — internal motivation. Thus environmental effects — i.e. events outside the perceived range of ability of the actor — are not treated as relevant to their interest by Jones and Davis. A further limitation on the phenomena they deal with is introduced by their concern only with intended actions, or actions perceived as intended. So their focus is not only limited to internal motivation. It is further restricted to *personal motivation:* the search for reasons.

Given internal motivation has been attributed, how is intention inferred so that a personal reason is attributable? If the action and its consequences were observed as associated with the person, the remaining matter is 'to determine which of these effects, if any, were intended by the actor' (Jones and Davis, 1965, p. 220). Unforeseen effects, then, are not a basis for the attribution of intention, even though the motive is internal.

The perceiver, in Jones and Davis' model, is in the situation where he has observed an event which he has taken to emanate from a person rather than the environment. His problem now is to attribute intention: did the person intend to produce that effect? Further, according to Jones and Davis, a motivational basis to the intention may be attributed, answering the question: Why did the actor have that intention? This further stage is the process of attributing personal disposition — clearly it is very relevant to our own concern in this chapter, since it has to do with ascribing motives to account for the behaviour. The model is sketched in Fig. 6.

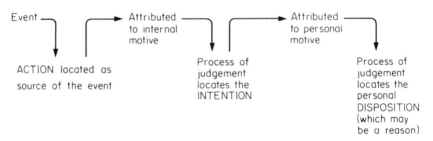

Fig. 6. Jones and Davis' model of act-to-disposition attribution.

How, then, are intentions and personal dispositions perceived on the basis of the observed event? Jones and Davis introduced the term *correspondence* to label the degree of directness and ease with which such attributions may be made. Thus a correspondent inference is one that is made with relative certainty: it is perceived as highly probable that (a) the action reflects a particular intention; (b) the intention is accounted for by a given personal disposition or motive; and therefore (c) that disposition is the basis of the perceived action.

Correspondent inferences are certain, in the mind of the perceiver. They are also extreme (Hastorf, Schneider and Polefka, 1970). Thus one would tend to regard 'He is a very egocentric person' as a more correspondent attribution of disposition than 'He is rather egocentric' because it is more extreme and certain.

Jones and Davis' main contribution was to outline some of the factors which influence this variable of correspondence. Some, it will be noted, are fairly logical in that they seem to be 'objective' features of the situation which necessarily make the task of inference harder or easier. Others are more in the nature of biases. Correspondence is, after all, subjective. It may well be affected by the perceiver's attitudes.

Correspondence is said to vary inversely with social desirability and the number of non-common effects of the action; and directly with hedonic relevance and personalism. This summary statement requires clarification. Consider the factors that weaken correspondence first of all. By *social desirability,* Jones and Davis refer to the perceiver's belief that the actor's behaviour is in keeping with the norms and values of his social group. Thus, for a bus driver to draw up at a bus stop when the bell has been rung is entirely normal and usual. However, were this same bus driver to drive on regardless would be behaviour lacking in social desirability. (Note that desirability is assessed 'taking the attitude of the other': the perceiver attempts to judge the desirability from the perspective of the actor.) Correspondent inferences are more difficult when social desirability is present because, although the behaviour is very likely to be fully intended, it may well be that no strong individual disposition underlies the action. Such behaviour tells the perceiver little about the actor himself. On the other hand, the more the choice of action appears to deviate from the norms to which the actor seems to be subject, the more the action tends to be attributed to a personal disposition (so the motives of the deviant driver may be validly sought). When correspondence is high, this means that it is apparently right to look for motives — though exactly what the motives are is not necessarily easily answered.

A second factor that bears on correspondence is the *number of non-common effects* of the action. Shaver (1975) points out that Jones and Davis implicitly assume actions are always perceived as chosen from a range of possibilities, or at least are chosen as a definite alternative to inaction. This being so, effects which might be produced as a result of several different intentions cannot be used to distinguish the intention and disposition which actually do lie behind the observed effects. For example, an action such as driving a car at high speed might equally be due to an emergency or to 'showing off'. So the action cannot unambiguously be attributed to a disposition: correspondence is low. The more such alternative effects there are of an action — the larger the number of possible intentions and underlying dispositions there may be — the lower correspondence is. The terminology of Jones and Davis is that correspondence varies inversely with the nmber of non-common effects, the notion of 'non-common effects' refers to effects of behaviour that may be attributed to different intentions.

Consider this further example. A man is observed to get his car out of his garage and drive a hundred yards along the road, get out and go into a house. This behaviour could have many desired effects. For instance, were the man disabled, use of a car for such a short journey may be necessary; or he may intend to drive on eventually. More clearly intentional would be such actions as showing the car to the neighbour; testing various components of the car; using the car to transport a very heavy load to the other house, etc. Jones and Davis are not concerned with the earlier examples — which are not attributable to the intention and disposition of the driver. But the intentional effects listed are possible 'non-common effects' — so the fact that there are so many makes the attribution of a specific intention and disposition to the action very difficult. If there were fewer possibilities, correspondence would be greater.

Jones and Davis point out that the same variable affects attribution when more than one piece of behaviour is observed. Say we did later observe the man get back in the car, drive it home and garage it again. This behaviour does not help much, because again the number of non-common effects is large — and taking the two observations together does not eliminate many possible interpretations. If we observed that his house had a badly-maintained appearance and that he had been dressed in a slovenly way, then these observations might well aid the process of attribution because, although the reasons that could be attributed to each individual observation are large in number, taken together there are only a few common effects. We might regard the intention common to each of these effects 'getting the task done with the least trouble' and attribute an underlying disposition or motive of laziness.

A third factor which Jones and Davis regard as influencing correspondence is *hedonic relevance*. (This is something that might well be regarded as a bias in attribution, although the term bias begs some questions since the whole process of attribution is an entirely subjective affair.) They argue that the more relevant to the personal interests of the perceiver a piece of behaviour is, the more ready and willing he is to make a firm attribution. Thus correspondence increases with hedonic relevance. If a brick falls very near you from a building being constructed, the likelihood is that you will be extremely certain and outspoken in attributing intention and disposition. Were the brick merely seen from a distance to fall harmlessly, attribution will be more tentitive, and it may even be that no blame is attached at all.

Finally, Jones and Davis argue that correspondence increases when the perceiver believes that his presence contributed to the action performed. The action is seen as directed particularly at him. The term *personalism* is used to cover this factor. Implications are drawn more strongly when one perceives that the brick was not negligently let fall on *any* passer-by, but was aimed particularly at oneself.

To summarize the contributions of Jones and Davis: correspondence theory argues that the perceiver is more certain about the apparent intention and dispositional cause (or motive) underlying an action when (a) the non-common effects of the behaviour are small in number and (b) they are of low social desirability. But the perceiver can be biased in his attribution by hedonic relevance — especially when he believes that his presence affected the action.

There is experimental evidence in favour of some of these assertions. For instance, Jones and Harris (1967) conducted an experiment that illustrates a point made by Heider — that even if there is a strong external force in evident operation, there are circumstances in which people are still seen as the source of their actions — and also the view of Jones and Davis, that, when actions are of low social desirability, attribution is surer (more correspondent).

Jones and Harris asked subjects to decide whether essays reflected the real views of their authors, who were other students. Some essays were labelled as 'freely written', others as 'assigned'; again, some essays in each category expressed views in favour of the Cuban leader Fidel Castro, others against him. At the time of the experiment the anti-Castro view was far more usual amongst students. Thus the pro-Castro essays were of low social desirability. Not surprisingly subjects tended to view all essays labelled as written freely as expressing the real opinions of the authors, whatever the opinions were. So freely written essays are regarded as attributable to the intended actions of the persons responsible for them. Of those essays labelled as assigned, there was a tendency to regard pro-Castro opinions as more likely to be a true reflection of their authors' attitudes than anti-Castro ones — even though the essays were clearly subject to a strong external force, and subjects might well have guessed that the writers were very likely to share the majority view of Castro. Here the fact that the opinions were of low social desirability led to a bias in attribution which overcame the effect of external constraints.

In another experiment, Jones and de Charms (1957) were concerned with the effect of perceived can and trying on the attribution of blame, and also the influence of hedonic relevance on the process. This is one of the very few studies which has to do with Heider's notions of can and trying — but commonsensically there is a problem in deciding whether a person's success or failure at a task reflects ability or effort.

Two experiments were run. In the first, Jones and de Charms tested the hypothesis that, if another's failure had consequences for the subject — i.e. high hedonic relevance — then that person would be evaluated less positively than otherwise. Clearly the idea is that high hedonic relevance has the effect of increasing the correspondence of attribution of intention and disposition. Several subjects worked on intellectual tasks and one, a stooge of the experimenters, failed. In one condition, only that person failed, so his behaviour was of low hedonic relevance for the subjects when compared to the effect of the stooge's failure in the other experimental condition. Here his failure meant that the whole group failed. The hypothesis that he would be evaluated less positively in the second condition was upheld, but only weakly. Clearly other factors were entering into the situation. It was thought that the fact that the experimenters had emphasized that failure would be due to lack of ability might have been such a factor, since lack of ability is probably not generally viewed as so blameworthy as lack of effort because the intention of the actor is not so clearly implicated. Recent evidence reviewed by Weiner and colleagues (1972) supports this interpretation.

In the second experiment, then, the subjects were given to understand that failure might be due either to lack of ability or lack of effort. Again the results were not strong, but the effect of hedonic relevance was seen. Generally, the influence of hedonic relevance does appear to lead to a difference in the attribution of causes to failure, particularly when trying is seen as the relevant factor rather than can.

Kelley

Let us consider now a second major elaboration of Heider's basic phenomenology of causal attribution. This is the work of H.H. Kelley (1967, 1971, 1972). The concerns of this author are less central to the present chapter than those of Jones and Davis, since they focus on the perception of an event and the search for a cause. Now it may well be that the cause of the event is the action of a person, and from this initial causal attribution the observer may go on to seek a motive (which may itself be a cause or a reason for the action). However the emphasis in Kelley's writing appears to be the attempt to understand an event by deciding on its cause rather than the attempt to understand a person's action by attributing motives.

A brief sketch of Kelley's approach is nevertheless in order for the sake of giving a clearer picture of attribution theory as a whole. Kelley (not, by the way, to be confused with G.A. Kelly who is mentioned elsewhere) takes as his starting point Heider's suggestion that the source of an event will probably be sought in those conditions that vary as the event occur rather than amongst those that remain constant. *Covariation* is thus a key notion for Kelley.

In any attributional situation there will be an *entity* that is the focus of the event being perceived, a *person* who is the possible agent, and an *attributional context,* the time and occasion for the event. Consider the enjoyment of a meal. Is the enjoyment to be attributed to the meal itself (entity), or to the personal characteristics of the eater (person), or to the fact that he has not eaten for a very long time or the circumstance that he is eating in enjoyable company (both of these are aspects of the attributional context)? The perceiver will attribute the enjoyment to one or other factor depending on the pattern of covariation. If it is observed that the person enjoys meals of this sort in many contexts — not only when in company and not only when unusually ready to eat — then the fact that attributional contexts can vary without changing the enjoyment rules this factor out as a source of the enjoyment.

The personal characteristics of the actor may be ruled out as a source of the enjoyment of the meal if it is observed that others will readily agree that the meal is enjoyable. Additional weight would be given to the attribution of cause to the meal if the person was discriminating in his preferences: if he sometimes disliked meals but this one was distinctively enjoyable.

So, consistency over situations rules out the attributional context as a source; consensus with others rules out the person as a source; distinctiveness of reaction to the entity implicates the entity. These ways of locating the source of covariation and attributing cause to this source do not need to be absolutely certain — they merely give a general guide to judgment.

The method of attending to covariation as a means of attribution points to several possible sources of inaccuracy. Kelley cites two. The environmental context of attribution may be only partly known, and there may not be any possibility of comparing the actor's experience or behaviour with others' ('pluralistic ignorance').

Later writing of Kelley (1972) has been concerned with the problem of locating the cause of an event when there are several actually operating. These might be sufficient causes, where each factor on its own would produce the effect, or necessary causes, where every factor must be present in order for the event to occur. Of course the perceiver can be sure that all the necessary causes were in operation if the effect was observed. The case of multiple sufficient causes is more complex. Where many sufficient causes are in action, Kelley postulates a *discounting principle*. This is very similar to Jones and Davis' notion of the relationship between correspondence and noncommon effects, as Shaver (1975) indicates.

With this brief characterization of Kelley's contributions, we complete our account of the central theme of attribution theory. Much empirical work has been carried out in the attempt to test the hypotheses the theory suggests (though the complaint is often raised that work in this area is more concerned with logical, content free structures than with hazarding empirically testable hypotheses). One line of empirical research relating to the theory is concerned with the sources of 'bias' in attribution. However, there is a temptation here which ought to be resisted. This is a tendency to treat attribution as if there were the possibility of a purely rational attribution of motive, which is only flawed by the incursion of biases. It is a misrepresentation, of course. Attribution of motive is part of person perception, only separated for the purposes of exposition. The ambiguity of the overall 'act' of perception, instantaneous yet woolly and revisable, ensures that motive attribution is always less than clearcut.

The self and causal attribution

In reflecting on events in one's life, attribution of responsibility for their occurrence clearly has a bearing on the self concept. Thus there is a link here with the discussion of perception of self in Chapter 5. In deciding that the cause of an event is to be found in one's own action, a search for motive (cause or reason for that action) becomes relevant. And it is obvious that the attribution of motive to oneself will influence the self concept.

It is argued by several authors that, in considering their own actions, people often show a consistent bias towards the view that they are responsible for their behaviour and its outcome, or that they are in the hands of external causes. These constitute two alternative *loci of control.*

Research on locus of control in fact emanates from a theoretical position rather distant from Heider's; the origin is social learning theory (cf. Bandura's work, mentioned in Chapter 2). The basic concern of Rotter (1966, also Rotter, Seeman and Liverant, 1962 and Phares, 1973), in his development of the notion of locus of control as a 'personality factor', was on where the person typically looked for the source of reinforcement. However, it is clear from his characterisation of internal and external control that the viewpoint meshes with the work of Heider, Jones and Davis, and Kelley: 'When a reinforcement is perceived by a subject as following some action of his own but not being entirely contingent upon his action. .it is typically perceived as the result of luck, chance, fate, as under the control of powerful others, or as unpredictable because of the great complexity of the forces surrounding him. When the event is interpreted in this way by an individual we have labelled this a belief in *external control.* If the person perceives that the event is contingent upon his own behaviour or his own relatively permanent characteristics, we have termed this a belief in *internal control'* (p. 1, Rotter, 1966).

Rotter is concerned, then, with a general tendency for a person to expect that his own actions will produce the desired result or that the results will depend on factors outside his control. The focus of interest is on people's attributions of cause for the consequences of their own behaviour or the events of their lives ('cause' is the correct term here, in that the source of an *event* is in question; it may be that a further attribution of motive occurs if the cause of the event is adjudged to be a person's action). General tendencies in attribution of the causes of life events are studied by Rotter by means of his *I-E scale* — a questionnaire assessing 'internal-external' attributive tendency. Research using the I-E scale does indicate widespread individual differences in this tendency (see Phares's, 1973, review).

Phares, Wilson and Kylver (1971) used Rotter's I-E scale in an experiment which showed that people who tend to attribute causality to external factors are less likely to blame themselves for failure in an intellectual task. Failure is seen as blameworthy when one is the cause of the failure.

Other studies (Streufert and Streufert, 1969; Johnson, Feigenbaum and Weibey, 1964) have shown that, quite apart from any general I-E bias, people tend to attribute success at a task to internal motives and failure to external causes. This holds true when it is *their* success or failure that is in question — the attribution of the success or failure of others may be different. This seems to indicate a defensive bias which accepts praiseworthy behaviour as one's own intended action, but rejects events to which blame might be attached (see also studies by Polefka and by Gross, reported in Hastorf, Schneider and Polefka, 1970).

A further aspect of the attribution of failure is shown in work by Fitch (1970). He looked at the relationship between self esteem and attribution when subjects had been given to understand that they had failed on a task. He asked them to estimate the number of dots in a rapidly-presented display. When told they had failed, they were invited to explain why they thought they had been mistaken. Some attributed the cause to internal, others to external factors. This was related to a questionnaire measure of self esteem — i.e. the degree of value the person puts on himself. It was found, not surprisingly, that people who placed a low value on themselves were more ready to blame themselves for failure.

One interpretation of some of these results that internal attribution for failure is anxiety provoking, so the tendency is to externally attribute causes of failure (though the complex relationship with self esteem requires a further explanation). With this in mind, Watson's (1967) finding that general anxiety is related to the overall tendency to attribute cause externally (as assessed using Rotter's I-E scale) is intriguing. The problem is that it is unclear whether the belief that the causes of events are external gives rise to anxiety ('things are outside my control'), or whether general anxiety leads to a sense of impending failure which tends to give rise to external attribution. Obviously this tightly-interconnected area requires empirical and rational clarification.

Jones and Nisbett (1971) have presented evidence that the attribution of causality concerning one's own behaviour and its consequences is systematically biased towards external sources, whilst others are perceived as the cause of events associated with them: '...there is a pervasive tendency for actors to attribute their actions to situational requirements, whereas observers tend to attribute the same actions to stable personal dispositions' (p. 2). Jones and Nisbett suggest several reasons for this, amongst which is the defensive tendency to deny the possible attribution of blame.

Obviously the work of Schachter and Valins reviewed in our previous chapter is relevant to the study of the way people attribute causes to their own actions (in these authors' work, their own 'emotional' bodily states). Nisbett and Valins (1971) also cite the writings of D. Bem (1972, for instance) on one's perception of one's own attitudes. This is relevant to the next chapter. But to end the consideration of work on attribution of causality for events involving the self, the study of Storms and Nisbett (1970) on insomnia is instructive.

This experiment provides some support for the view that many attribution phenomena can be accounted for by the belief that attributing events to external causes means we are not responsible and therefore need not be anxious. Storms and Nisbett gave a placebo pill to two groups of insomniacs. One group was told the pill would be arousing, making them less able to sleep. The other group was told that it would calm them and help them sleep. It turned out that the first group — who thought the pill would arouse them — fell asleep quicker than the group who had been told the pill would calm them. Storms and Nisbett argued that the reason for this result was that those who thought the pill would arouse them were able to attribute their sleeplessness to this external cause, and this allayed their anxiety about not sleeping, so soon they fell asleep. The other group found that, even though they had taken a pill they had been told was calming, they remained awake. This increased their anxiety. (See also Totman, 1976, for an experiment manipulating cognitive dissonance, in the manner of J. Brehm, to combat insomnia. Note that Kellogg and Baron, 1975, were unable to replicate the Storms and Nisbett phenomenon.)

Storms and Nisbett may only be giving one aspect of the relation between external cause and anxiety, as we have already seen in the work of Watson.

A final note on causal attribution

Our study of the literature on how people commonsensically attribute causes of events was necessitated by the earlier conclusion that motives are only sought when a person's behaviour is not understood because we cannot see what perception of the situation led him to act in that way, and the event is seen as due to his intentional action. Thus to seek a motive implies that the source of the event is personal.

Given that an attribution of cause to personal sources has been made, and given that the behaviour is not directly explicable, then a motive is sought. Two very important points need to be made about this. Firstly, note that this view of motive-seeking implies that people need to be able to account for others' actions to some extent. (To recall a theme in the last chapter, people are anxious when they see that they lack a perceptual category necessary for coping with a situation.) When social interaction appears to be undermined by an inability to understand the actions of another person, then it is necessary to fill in the lack. So motive-attribution serves the purpose of 'plastering over a crack' in one's understanding of the other's perception of the situation — enabling one to take the role of the other. This view of motives is central to an important paper by Blum and McHugh (1971). They state that the aim of their paper, entitled 'The social ascription of motives' is not to talk about 'causal motives' in a scientific way — postulating a number of causes that lie behind people's actions — but rather to 'describe how ordinary actors employ motive (statements) as a practical method for organising their everyday environments' (p.98). So motives are attributed to people in order to make their actions understandable, to enable one to interact with them, since interaction demands that one is able to take the attitude of the other. (The rest of Blum and McHugh's paper has to do with the taken-for-granted assumptions made when we attribute motives — many of which attribution theorists have also treated — e.g. we assume intention on the part of the actor; we attribute a personal disposition.)

The second point is somewhat less important. It is that much of the work of attribution theorists, and others concerned with the description of commonsense ascription of motives, is not really about a psychological process that has to be undergone in order to decide: (a) whether the source of an event was an action, (b) if so, whether the behaviour demands a search for motive; and (c) whether such a motive ought to be considered to be found in a cause of the behaviour or in an intention, a reason. Although it is sometimes the case that such a sequential, conscious process is experienced particularly in those problematic instances where the reason for a person's action does have to be sought (cf. Fig. 6), in most instances of attribution, there is a self-evident motive which is 'given' in the instant of person perception. Here the clarification provided by attribution theory is of the 'logical' structure of attribution. In these cases, Heider and his followers are effectively pointing out that an ascription of motive has a number of implications (e.g. that the environmental force is adjudged to be weaker, in some sense, than the personal force). Thus in unproblematic instances, no one goes through a process by which the environmental and personal forces are weighed — rather, the source of the act as, say, intentional is immediately given in the perception of the act itself. There is no need for a search for motive: you and the actor share the definition of the situation.

COMMONSENSE VOCABULARIES OF MOTIVE

Attribution theory goes no further than indicating the circumstances under which a reason or cause of a person's actions might be sought if the definition of the situation does not of itself supply a motive. Because of this limitation on its scope, it gives the appearance — irritating to some readers — of being a content-free, *a priori* structure. However, elsewhere in the social psychological literature is a body of research on the actual motives people attribute to each other in order to 'patch up' the knowledge they have of others' actions. This work was initiated by C. Wright Mills (1940), and has been carried on, spasmodically, by a quite different group of writers to the attribution theorists. It is part of the scandal of the division of social psychology into sociologically and psychologically oriented people with few links between them. The literature on causal attribution and on vocabularies of motive contains few if any cross-references.

Mills' paper had as its theme the idea that a group of people shares a repertoire of possible reasons for behaviour than can be drawn on in order to account for problematic actions: a vocabulary of motives.

Mills takes as his starting point the fact that motives are stated or called for when there is some question arising from unexpected actions, or when people make a choice about programmes of action. We have noticed before that people are only questioned about their motives when the perception of the situation that led to an action is not clear — but Mills alerts us to the fact that this may be apparent either because the person has done something odd (i.e. the question arises from unexpected actions) or because he has chosen to do one thing when there are other, perhaps equally likely programmes of action open to him (a point that resembles in some respects Jones and Davis' view that causality is less correspondent when there is a number of noncommon effects).

Mills then goes on to ask what counts as an appropriate thing to reply when a person is asked his reasons for acting, after all (as he says): 'Men discern situations with particular vocabularies, and it is in terms of some delimited vocabulary that they anticipate consequences of conduct' (p. 906); since the reasons people give are about their perception of the situation (and often this involves the anticipated consequences of action in that situation) there must be a limited set of appropriate reasons for actions. So Mills wants to inquire about the nature of the vocabulary of motives.

One characteristic of this vocabulary is that it is acquired in the process of primary socialization, and perhaps extended or modified in later adult socialization situations. Mills writes: 'The mother controls the child, 'Don't do that, it is greedy.' Not only does the child learn what to do, what not to do, but he is given standardized motives which promote prescribed actions and dissuade those proscribed. Along with rules and norms of action for various situations, we learn vocabularies of motive appropriate to them. These are the motives we shall use, since they are a part of our language and components of our behaviour' (p. 909).

In this part of his paper Mills is asserting that we are provided socially with a vocabulary of motives — a repertoire of accounts that we may draw on when our motives are unclear to either ourselves and others. He also seems to be suggesting that these motives actually guide behaviour. Thus Mills is another of the authors, some of whom were listed at the end of our consideration of 'science and social motives' who regard people as acting in accord with their perception of the situation. However he goes further than this in arguing that a culture provides members with a set of motives against which to consider possible ways of acting. For instance, often our action is guided by remembering the various ways in which we could subsequently justify it to others. The action is chosen which meets the situation and which we could later link to an acceptable motive. In a way, the 'motive' has been causal — although the causal link is not of the sort that those interested in uncovering the 'real causal motives' would respect.

Wright Mills goes on in specifying the nature of the vocabulary of motives by saying that accounts are only possible within the framework of the motives usually stated by people in specific situations. And this is important, because it means that we reject accounts of actions when these do not fit the vocabulary of motives we use in that situation. Mills' example is of a mediaeval monk who states that he gave food to a poor but pretty woman 'for the glory of God and the eternal salvation of his soul'. Mills thinks that most contemporary westerners would not accept that account as the real reason but will impute sexual reasons as more correct as an account. Mills is quite ready to think that the monk's religious motive was the actual motive, and regards our modern questioning of the monk's reason as due to the fact that religious motives are not part of the average man's vocabulary of motives applicable to such a situation.

Wright Mills also claims that motivational systems like psychoanalysis are merely the vocabulary of motives of an 'upper bourgeois patriarchal group with strong sexual and individualistic orientation'. He does not grant such systems any special status: they are on a par with commonsense vocabularies of motive. This argument appears to me to be of special interest in that it implies that the 'real causal motives' for behaviour which social psychologists have listed — such as dependency, aggression, achievement (see for instance, Secord and Backman, 1974) — are of concern to us, not as an approach towards a universal explanation of human behaviour in terms of motivating drives, but rather as an indication of the sort of motives that are within the vocabulary of a given segment of humanity (possibly Western man, maybe only a number of social scientists). This appealing suggestion is, of course, far in advance of the evidence.

Finally Mills states a programme for future research, with the aim of relating the vocabularies of motive used to the social situations in which they are used, and to the nature of the groups using them and the historical setting of the groups. It must be said that hardly a start has been made on this programme. The sort of research to be done would be like this. Consider social work. Have people given different reasons in the past for entering this occupation to the reasons given now? If so, why is this? Does it mean that the place of social work in society has changed? Or have the members of the occupation changed? And consider other aspects of the social work vocabulary of motives besides those used to explain why people become social workers — those motives used to explain why social workers do certain things that seem to the populace at large problematic. What reasons are given for the actions that make newspaper headlines? Are these reasons 'honoured' — by which is meant, Do they find acceptance as genuine, relevant motives that satisfactorily explain the behaviour? And so on. This research, as I say, is barely begun (but see L. Taylor, 1972; B. Taylor, 1976).

A second major theoretical contribution to the study of vocabularies of motive was made in a paper entitled simply *Accounts* by Scott and Lyman (1968). They are again concerned with the reasons people give for their actions or the problematic actions of others. By an account, then, Scott and Lyman mean exactly what we have termed a motive. 'He did that strange thing because...' and then we attribute a motive, give an account. Scott and Lyman write: 'By an account...we mean a statement made by a social actor to explain unanticipated or untoward behaviour — whether that behaviour is his own or that of others' (p. 46, 1968). And they go on to agree with Mills that the nature of acceptable accounts depends on the situation, the group and the culture.

The central observation of their paper is that there are in general two kinds of accounts: *excuses* and *justifications*. When making a justification of some behaviour, one accepts responsibility for the action (it was intended and the consequences realized) but one denies the pejorative implication. Thus a person questioned about speeding in his car by a policeman might accept that he was intentionally going faster than the speed limit, but point out the very ill person lying in the back of the car whom he is taking to hospital.

Excuses, on the other hand, involve admitting the act in question is inappropriate, but denying full responsibility for it: the speedometer must have been wrong.

Scott and Lyman betray no acquaintance with the attribution theorists — but it cannot be denied that there is a strong relationship between the distinction between excuses and justifications, and that between internal and personal motivation. The difference between an excuse and a justification is a denial of responsibility because of a lack of intention in the former: the behaviour and its consequences were unintended and so should be excused. Again, the difference between attribution to internal factors and to personal factors is that the former case does not imply intention. If the behaviour is intentional it is personally attributed. So, in general we may say that excuses deny the attribution of responsibility since the event was unintentional; justifications accept the attribution of to the person.

After distinguishing excuses and justifications, Scott and Lyman give a long description of examples of such excuses and justifications — together with some of the social implications — but this (though of interest) I leave out of our present consideration. Of more central importance is the discussion of the circumstances under which accounts are (as they say) *honoured* or not honoured. An honoured account brings equilibrium back to the relationship, and they give as an example of situations in which almost any account will do the case of a slip or social gaffe in an interaction that causes embarrassment. Any account enables equilibrium to be restored — so it is very likely to be honoured. So one variable governing the honouring of an account is the ease with which such honouring will heal undesired disruption of interaction.

Another important factor (and this clearly connects Scott and Lyman to Mills' favourite theme) is the character of the social circle in which the account is offered. A drug addict may be able to justify his conduct as related to his state to his bohemian circle, but not to a court.

An important aspect of honouring accounts relates to the fact that people will tend to give reasons for their actions that will be likely to be honoured by those being told the reason. And this often leads to the situation where a person gives one reason for his action to one group of people and a quite different reason to another group. Hartung (1965), for example, suggests that delinquents may use accounts relating to 'middle class' ideologies of deviance such as cultural deprivation when taking to such agents of social control as social worker. Accounts that they probably would not honour themselves.

Wootton (1975) makes a case for the view that such possibilities pose problems for social scientists since the account a person gives may not be the one he believes. Wootton cites Taylor's (1972) use of magistrates to distinguish between 'valid' and 'invalid' accounts of their behaviour by sex offenders as further evidence of the difficulty of deciding what status an account has. It appears to me that this is only a problem if the wrong questions are being posed of accounts. It must be borne clearly in mind that accounts are always erected in the service of explaining untoward behaviour. (A fact Wootton, incidentally, denies on the grounds that the same sentence may be construed as having other meanings than accounting for behaviour. Of course it is true that an account is only such if the interacting parties define it as such, but this merely reminds us of the importance of the study of definitions of situations. The attempt to undermine the idea of motive-ascription in this way is unavailing.)

In an experimental study, Blumstein and several of his students (1974) investigated some of the factors involved in the honouring of accounts. Subjects imagined themselves as bystander observers, and in that role read short descriptions of an interaction containing an offence committed by one person against another, the wronged person's reaction which called for an account, and an account by the offender of his action. The context, offence, nature of the account, and the relationship between the offender's status and that of the wronged person were all systematically varied. Subjects judged the validity of the account by the offender — i.e. they decided whether or not it should be honoured.

Honouring was dependent on the moral worth of the offender, his penitence, his superior status compared to the wronged person, and the degree of offensiveness of the action. In fact the findings of Blumstein are quite in accord with the results of attribution theorists — although we might argue that the decision about honouring accounts is a stage removed from attribution of causality: having attributed cause and responsibility, the observer waits to hear the actor's account which may lead to reattribution.

To return to Scott and Lyman's paper, they also consider the various strategies people use for *avoiding* the necessity of giving accounts of their actions. For instance, there are conventional institutional rules preventing the questioning of the actions of some members of an organization by other specified members. Men must not question officers' actions in military organizations. But there are strategies more intricate than mere refusal to give account. One is called *mystification* by Scott and Lyman: 'There are good reasons for my action, but the facts are complex or secret', or simply 'Its a long story'. Another is *identity-switching*. A boy playing with his father criticizes the way he flies the kite, and the man, hurt, remarks, 'Don't speak like that to your father'. He is no longer a playmate — from whom an account for behaviour may be asked — but a stern father above giving excuses or justifications.

The example of identity-switching reminds us that accounts related to the presentation of self, or image, or self-concept, of the individual — a point also made explicitly by Blum and McHugh, and by such attribution theorists as Jones and Davis. It is for this reason that it is possible to avoid giving accounts, by emphasizing suddenly your identity as a well-intentioned person with good motives. Another example would be to say, 'Surely you know me better than that' or, if you are a manager whose decision has been called into question, 'I assure you all this was thoroughly discussed at the planning stage'. Both these examples involve suddenly drawing attention to one's identity and therefore avoid giving accounts. But of course the line between this ploy and mystification is hard to draw.

Scott and Lyman's list of ways of avoiding giving account of your actions may readily be supplemented. For instance J. Fukuda (reported in Hastorf, Schneider and Polefka, 1970) supplies the information that Japanese contains a grammatical form (the 'passive causative') which enables one to communicate the idea that his behaviour was caused, ordered, coerced by somebody else. Clearly this is a form of excuse that refers the questioner to another person for an account. It is not an excuse in the sense of Scott and Lyman since there is an intention involved.

Hewitt and Stokes (1975) have extended the argument of Scott and Lyman by the introduction of the notion of the *disclaimer*. Whereas accounts are given after the event, disclaimers are issued at the time of an offensive utterance — or any piece of behaviour that might appear to disrupt interaction — in order to reduce its importance, in observers' eyes, as a cue. Hewitt and Stokes treat disclaimers in a way that makes comparison with Goffman's view of embarrassment easy. Embarrassment arises when a person's image has been discredited in interaction (see the previous chapter). A person who sees that a projected action could lead to embarrassment might issue a disclaimer: 'I'm not an economist and am perhaps mistaken, but what I think is...'; 'I know you might think this odd, but...'; 'Strictly speaking I'm out of order in saying this, but...'. Hewitt and Stokes present many types of disclaimer.

A disclaimer can be seen as not only loosening the link between the presented self and the action, but it can also be viewed as an attempt to reduce the likelihood of being called to account. The level of intention is lowered, by implication. 'I have no strong motive for the following statement. Take it or leave it.'

As Hewitt and Stokes point out, disclaimers, like accounts, are devices which enable interaction to proceed relatively normally even when shared definitions are either lacking or are about to be disrupted.

RETROSPECT

The points raised in this chapter possibly require brief summary. Initially, the question of motivation was raised, and it was concluded that generally people act according to their perception of the situation. However, in everyday life, occasions arise when one's actions or those of others are problematic. The events seem to be the result of intentional behaviour, but the perceptions that led to the behaviour cannot be readily inferred. In these circumstances, motives are sought. Attribution theory supplies a model of how events are perceived as resulting from actors' intentional behaviour. The work of Mills and of Scott and Lyman indicates the factors involved in ascribing some *particular* motive to the actor. The importance of motive-attribution lies in the fact that the lack of an understanding of the perception of the situation that lay behind an action makes taking the role of the other, and therefore interaction, difficult. The ascription of a motive to account for the problematic behaviour enables interaction to continue relatively undisrupted.

CHAPTER 8

Holding Attitudes

Some debates in the realm of attitude theory which have attracted recent research efforts are outlined, and a few of the conceptual connections with interactionism are suggested in this chapter.

'Attitude' compares with the notion of 'symbol'. But also, attitude is found to be a conceptual synthesis. The nature of this synthesis is discussed. It is noted that use of the term 'attitude' often carries the implication that man is a meaning-ascribing being.

Discussion of the relationship between attitudes and behaviour leads to a re-emphasis of the importance of 'definition of the situation' and of motivation analysed in terms of reasons rather than causes.

The view that attitudes are not isolated but structured suggests a search for the principle of structuring. This is found in the idea of 'subjective consistency with values'. But such consistency is provisional. Festinger's theory of cognitive dissonance has generated much research which, by indicating limitations on the dissonance effect, can be taken as providing evidence that attitudinal consistency involves conscious self-monitoring. This reflection is taken up in the Conclusion of the book.

THE CONCEPT OF ATTITUDE

The study of attitudes has been a dominant area of research in social psychology throughout almost the whole of the history of the discipline (McGuire, 1969). Indeed, Allport (1954b) points out that social psychology has been defined by several writers as the study of attitudes. The reason for this is largely due to the interface position of social psychology stressed in the Introduction: social psychology links individual psychology and sociology. This being so, the notion of attitude is rightly given great importance, since it points to individual mental phenomena which, supposedly, directly reflect societal facts. As Thomas and Znaniecki (1918) argue, social psychology is the science concerned with the subjective side of culture and therefore it must have as its central concept one which directs attention to data which link individual and society. They, like the majority of subsequent authors, select the concept of attitude.

157

In our earlier chapters, particularly where interactionist ideas were being introduced, the notion of symbol was very much to the fore, since the whole theoretical standpoint of that school of social psychology rests on the symbol and its source in interaction. Analysis shows that symbol and attitude are used analogously, even if they are not entirely synonymous. Romanyshyn's (1971) work on the phenomenology of attitudes certainly suggests such a relationship, and careful consideration of Rose's (1962a) treatment of symbols in his summary of interactionist theory shows that this is very much in line with the way attitudes are assumed to behave by social psychologists who write about them.

It is relevant to review some of the points Rose makes about symbols as a prelude to a discussion of attitudes. He writes: 'Through communication of symbols, man can learn huge numbers of meanings and values — and hence ways of acting — from other men' (Rose, 1962a, p. 9). Again: 'Through the learning of a culture. . . men are able to predict each others' behaviour most of the time and gauge their own behaviour to the predicted behaviour of others' (pp. 9f) — and the learning of culture is the acquisition of symbols, in large measure. Rose also writes: 'The symbols — and the meanings and values to which they refer — do not occur only in isolated bits, but often in clusters, sometimes large and complex' (p. 10). We will see in this chapter that all these attributes apply to attitudes. Thus, the study of attitudes is only artificially separated from the study of language and other systems of symbols.

Definitions of attitude

Several authors have reviewed the available definitions of attitude. As early as 1935, Allport was able to cite over a hundred, yet he concluded that there was a common core to all the definitions, since they all seemed to identify 'the essential feature of attitude as a preparation of readiness for response'. On this basis, Allport constructed the following, very influential definition: 'An attitude is a mental and neural state of readiness, organised through experience, exerting a directive or dynamic influence upon the individual's response to all objects and situations with which it is related' (Allport, 1935, p. 810).

Even if that were acceptable in 1935 as a synthesis of the contending approaches to attitude, it is unlikely that any single definition could be agreed today. The divisions have perhaps sharpened. McGuire (1969) has examined a wide range of approaches to the study of attitudes, and firmly rejects the idea of an agreed definition. Indeed, he attempts to differentiate the field into five quite distinct treatments, whose underlying conceptions of attitudes are irreconcilable. Among these approaches, two broad categories are worth consideration. These are, on the one hand, firmly behaviourist notions of attitude, which regard the concept as labelling a *probability* of a certain response to a certain stimulus, and, on the other hand, the more cognitive view of attitude as referring to a mental state, a 'latent process', a *disposition* which one hypothesises as accounting for the observed behaviour.

A definition of the behaviourist sort is exemplified by De Fleur and Westie's (1963) view: 'The attitude — is an inferred property of the responses, namely their consistency. Stated in another way, attitude is equated with the probability of recurrence of behaviour forms of a given type or direction' (p. 21).

Apart from Allport, many authors have suggested dispositional or cognitive definitions of attitude. Some, such as Campbell (1950), have attempted to frame a probability definition yet have made dispositional assumptions too: 'A social attitude is (or is evidenced by) consistency in response to social objects' (Campbell, 1950, p. 31). This is a probability definition if the emphasis is placed on the idea of attitude as consistency, but a dispositional definition if the view of consistency as providing evidence of attitude is emphasized.

A more thoroughgoingly dispositional viewpoint is given by Newcomb, Turner and Converse (1966), who argue that attitudes may be viewed as both cognitive and motivational entities: 'From a cognitive point of view...an attitude represents an organization of valenced cognitions.' ('Valenced' means that emotional associations accompany the cognitions.) 'From a motivational point of view, an attitude represents a state of readiness for motive arousal. An individual's attitude toward something is his predisposition to be motivated in relation to it' (p. 40). Clearly, Newcomb, Turner and Converse would view behaviour as indicating an underlying attitude rather than viewing attitude as a term which merely draws attention to behavioural regularities. Attitude is a mental disposition: the holder of an attitude is ready to display certain tendencies of thought and feeling as well as action.

It will be obvious that the question of defining attitude, central as it has been in the history of social psychology, enables clear theoretical tendencies to emerge. Recalling the final section of Chapter 2, concerning the claim that Mead may be described as a 'social behaviourist', we see in the contending definitions of attitude a specific example of the distinction drawn there between positivist behaviourism and cognitive models.

The probabilistic treatment of attitude is in line with the positivist standpoint, which generally regards science as demarcated from other forms of knowledge by its focus on *observable* events and the relationships amongst such observables. The unobservability of Allport's 'mental and neural state of readiness' would lead the positivist to reject his definition. De Fleur and Westie believe that no mental process need be invoked. Attitude for them is merely a term which registers the observer's acknowledgement that there are certain regularities in the response to particular stimuli.

The probabilistic account accords the concept of attitude the status of 'intervening variable', a link between stimulus and response which allows formal acknowledgement to be made of their relationship but which is not to be taken as referring to any 'hidden' process, such as the participation of conscious awareness.

Brannon (1976) points out that most social psychologists have been unwilling to accept definitions of this sort. They regard attitudes as mental phenomena which involve more than can be drawn from the perusal of behavioural regularities. For example, the clustering of attitudes so as to form political ideologies seems to require a view of the attitude-holder as actively organizing his attitudes. As Eysenck (1954) says in this context, 'There can be no doubt whatever that attitudes do not occur in splendid isolation but are closely linked with other attitudes in some kind of pattern or structure. Indeed, the very existence of parties and political labels implies as much; to say that a person is a Socialist or a Conservative immediately suggests that he holds not just one particular opinion on one particular issue, but rather that his views and opinions on a large number of different issues will form a definite pattern' (p. 107). As we shall see, a cognitive or dispositional account of attitudes seems more capable of dealing with attitude structuring.

Dispositional accounts treat attitudes as 'hypothetical constructs' (see Chapter 2): they do not merely connect stimulus and response, but involve the participation of influences (here 'dispositions') not observable in the manner of stimuli and responses. Without question, an interactionist view of attitudes must be dispositional, rather than probabilistic, since attitudes, like symbols, entail a meaning construction of events. Indeed, even the cognitive approach to attitudes as hypothetical constructs might be regarded as too near to the positivist view, in that an attitude could be treated as a 'variable' which influences the translation of stimulus into response — and the social psychologist be expected to look for the causes which determine that variable's activity.

Therefore, although the approach of symbolic interactionism to attitudes may be characterized as dispositional and cognitive, it is only so characterized with the proviso that such cognitions and dispositions are not seen as links in a causal chain from stimulus to response, but rather as an aspect of the perception of the 'stimulus' by the individual. Thus 'attitude' is the social psychologist's term, allowing him to abstract for special consideration some characteristics of the perception of, and behaviour towards particular objects. The earlier discussion of perception as of meanings, and of definition of the situation is therefore of direct relevance to the study of attitude theory, in that our view of attitudes is intended to carry the implication that man is a meaning-ascribing being.

Most authors in this area, then, adopt dispositional definitions of attitude. Typical is that of Secord and Backman (1964): 'The term attitude refers to certain regularities of an individual's feelings, thoughts and predispositions to act towards some aspect of his environment' (p. 97). There are attractions in this as a definition, but it also raises an issue about the nature and interrelationships of the 'components' of attitude which they have specified.

Components of attitudes

Secord and Backman (1964) follow their definition with this sentence which introduces a conventional terminology: 'Feelings are often referred to as the *affective* component (of attitudes), thoughts as the *cognitive* component, and predispositions to act as the *behavioural* component' (p. 27). This alerts us to an important fact to be faced in dealing with attitudes as mental dispositions: the term attitude does not refer to one mental phenomenon, but an amalgam.

The cognitive component acknowledges that the individual knows or believes something, which is the object of his attitude. A person who is not conversant with Christianity at all cannot know what 'the Church' refers to and so one supposes that he cannot have an attitude about it. Even within a culture affected by Christianity, everyone may recognize the term 'the Church' — but in fact will doubtless have a range of beliefs as to what it means. So if we are to study attitudes towards 'the Church' we must not neglect consideration of the question of what people mean by the term: the cognitive component of that attitude.

The emotional, or affective, component of an attitude is probably the usual meaning of 'attitude' when the term is used in everyday conversation. It focuses on the feelings of like or dislike which the holder of an attitude entertains towards the attitude object.

The behavioural component ought to be distinguished from actual action related to the object of the attitude — it rather refers to an intention to act or a tendency to act. The reference of Secord and Backman to 'predispositions to act' denotes the behavioural component of an attitude. In discussion Fishbein's approach to the relationship between attitudes and behaviour in this chapter, problems associated with an emphasis on the behavioural component of attitude are raised.

The three components of attitude can be described as if they were distinct, as we have seen. However, this separateness is ambiguous. Feeling, thought, and intention to act can be distinguished conceptually, but in any particular instance of an attitude these three components will be present as an inextricable system of interrelationships. In general it could be said that any strong emotional reaction to an object implies a certain belief or knowledge, and a marked tendency to act. In empirical study, the three components would be expected to intercorrelate. Audi (1972) summarizes the situation by writing that relationships between measures of at least the first two components are high, but the components are not identical. (See also McGuire, 1969.)

Audi (1972) concurs with the view that social psychologists' conclusions about attitude tend to resolve the concept into three components, but he goes on to discuss the relationship between this scientific analysis and the assumptions about attitude made by ordinary people in their everyday commonsense use of attitude-related terms. To assess everyday usage, he assembled 'a list of more than fifty terms which, quite apart from any psychological or technical philosphical notions of an attitude, seemed to denote clear cases of attitudes' (Audi, 1972, p. 184). Examples are 'prejudice', 'approval' 'condescension', 'self-esteem' and 'nationalism'.

The next stage was to analyse the commonsense assumptions about attitudes that 'would "account for" all these attitude-denoting terms, in the sense that it provided necessary and sufficient conditions for our application of them in everyday situations' (p. 184). The analysis specified these conditions. Firstly, there is always an *object* of the attitude. Secondly, that an attitude is a personal disposition with the following components (and here we have a focus of interest in Audi's article, since such components of commonsense attitude-attribution may be compared and contrasted with the components of attitude specified by social psychologists): (a) a belief or some beliefs involving evaluations of the attitude object; (b) a want or some wants, by which Audie means roughly *desires* concerning the object.

Now the analysis thus far seems comparable in some respects to social psychologists' components of attitude as a scientific concept. The cognitive component of scientific theory allows for the commonsense assumption that each attitude has an object. The affective component is directly translatable as an evaluative belief aspect. However, it is very important that Audi does not directly reproduce the behavioural component but replaces it with a desire aspect.

Audi elaborates by saying that, where the attitude object is positively evaluated, the desire is that it 'should be maintained in an already favourable' state, or that 'it should prosper ...advance ...increase, etc.'. Where it is negatively evaluated, the desire may be that it 'should be modified in what the person considers to be a desirable direction, or ...be maintained in an already unfavourable' state, or that 'it should be destroyed ...hindered, etc.' In the possible situation of neutral evaluation, the concomittant desire is that the attitude object 'should be neither favoured nor disfavoured, or that it should be given further study, or that it should be left to follow its own course, etc.' (p. 185).

Audi is not able to specify the desires related to each evaluative situation in a neat formula, but merely lists the sort of possible desires each situation brings. The reason for this lack of neatness is, I suppose, that the relevant desires depend not only on the evaluation made of the object but also on the nature of the object itself: one's desires for a favourite pet dog are different in detail from one's desires concerning a favourite musical composer.

Audi's suggestion that desires be regarded as more relevant to the description of attitudes than behavioural intentions is a valuable contribution in that it enables the introduction of a concept to the analysis of attitudes which demands that the user should adopt a cognitive, dispositional approach to attitudes which entails an awareness of the meaning-attributing nature of the attitude holder.

The notion of attitude, then, is a conceptual sythesis, since it is a general conclusion that a description of attitudes which is at all true to their nature as dispositions must have reference to the various components we have discussed.

It may be that some of the problems of attitude measurement are due to the ambiguities of this synthesis, rather than to problems of attitudes as phenomena — but this possibility cannot be investigated further here.

Audi's conclusion that desires are more central components of attitudes than behavioural tendencies importantly affects both our view of the personal functions attitudes subserve for the individual who holds them and our view of the relation between attitude and behaviour. The attitude/behaviour relationship is the topic of the section *Attitudes and behaviour* in this chapter. We turn now to the personal functions of attitudes.

Personal functions of attitudes

Audi argues that attitudes (not only in everyday usage, but also in science) have as an essential component one or more wants concerning the attitude object. His analysis will be adopted here. Newcomb, Turner and Converse, in their treatment of attitudes as 'a state of readiness for motive arousal', are perhaps the authors nearest to Audi.

The work of D. Katz (1960) indicates the way the personal needs or desires of the individual may affect his attitude (especially his evaluation) of an object. Katz, then, is concerned with the personal functions that an attitude may subserve. He argues that knowledge of attitudes is incomplete unless we are aware of the reasons why an individual holds the attitudes he does. Certainly it is a temptation in attitude research to consider attitudes in the abstract, apart from the person who holds them. For instance, after conducting a survey of political attitudes we might classify a number of people as right-wing. But there is a danger here. Although all those people might hold the same views — and they might even share the same attitudes in great detail, believing the same things, feeling the same about them, and acting the same way as well — nevertheless the reasons why they hold the attitudes might be quite different.

Katz has discussed four such reasons; these are desires that people have (in Audi's terms) which lead them to evaluate attitude objects in particular ways. The attitudes subserve these four functions for the individual: (1) *Instrumental function,* where the holding of a certain attitude has a 'pay-off' of some sort; (2) *Ego-defensive function,* which is due to the fact that attitudes reflect on the attitude holder, thus the holding of a certain attitude may serve the function of setting him off in a good light, beguiling both himself and others; (3) *Value-expressive function,* which is subserved when the individual expresses an attitude because it is appropriate to his values. Values here are taken as superordinate attitudes, very general. Thus someone who has a general value which elevates economic concerns to a high position, this will dictate his attitude towards many things which he might not have given individual attention to at all. He will experience desires concerning certain objects and antipathy towards others. These will influence his attitudes (cf. Allport, Lindzey and Vernon, 1951); (4) *Knowledge function,* which is seen in the desire to give structure to the experiences with which he is confronted. Attitudes certainly have the general function of ordering experience (cf. symbols), so this function refers to the desire to structure giving rise to attitudes.

As an example of the effect on one of these functions, Katz, McClintock and Sarnoff (1957) carried out an experiment in which the susceptibility to attitude change was related to questionnaire measures of ego-defence. The subjects were initially given a number of personality tests designed to measure defensiveness. They were also asked to fill in a stereotype checklist devised as an indicator of anti-Negro feeling. In a second session, a fortnight later, they read a booklet about 'mechanisms' by which antagonistic attitudes are projected onto others. This constituted an attempt to influence their attitudes. In this session they were again given the stereotype checklist. In a third session, five weeks later, they were again assessed on anti-Negro feeling, but this time the relevant questions were interspersed among many other questions irrelevant to the study.

The idea was that, since ego-defence is hypothesized to be a major source of prejudice (i.e. the desire is to bolster up one's self image and this is carried out by adopting an unfavourable attitude to some group of people), the susceptibility to change one's view of Negroes will depend on ego-defensiveness. Moreover an attempt to influence attitudes by an attack on the desire rather than directly on the attitude was involved.

It was found that the medium ego-defenders were influenced more than either the high ego-defenders (for whom the prejudice could not easily be abandoned presumably because its function was too important) or the low ego-defenders (since for them the prejudice did not have its basis in ego-defence at all, but in some other desire). Thus the hypothesis of Katz, McClintock and Sarnoff was upheld, and some evidence for the ego-defensive function is provided. Further evidence on the various functions subserved by attitudes is reviewed by McGuire (1969).

ATTITUDES AND BEHAVIOUR

It will be recalled that Allport's influential early definition of attitude treated it as a dispositional concept which involved a readiness to respond in a certain manner to the object of the attitude. This implies that attitudes will reveal themselves in behaviour. Campbell's (1950) view that consistency in response to social objects is to be taken as evidence of an underlying attitude similarly requires that behaviour and attitudes be related. Quite apart from the definitions of social psychologists, the idea that behaviour is guided by attitudes is in agreement with common sense.

This being so, it is very embarrassing that research aimed at disclosing a link between attitudes and behaviour often arrives at the conclusion that the relationship is, at best, weak. (Reviews of such studies are numerous: Brannon, 1976; Calder and Ross, 1973; Thomas, 1971; Wicker, 1969.) The bold assertion of Krech, Crutchfield and Ballachey (1962) that 'The actions of the individual are to a large extent governed by his attitudes' (p. 146) seems, in face of the evidence, incorrect.

Of course, there is no problem of a relation between behaviour and attitudes-as-dispositions for those authors who adopt a probabilistic definition of attitude. If attitude is no more than concept labelling behavioural regularities, then without a behavioural consistency there is nothing to label as an attitude. This holds true even when one behaviour is expressing an opinion and the other is acting in a situation relevant to that opinion: if the behaviours are inconsistent, then no attitude is present. Thus for authors such as De Fleur and Westie (1963) the problem of attitude-behaviour inconsistency does not arise.

However, Weissberg (1964; see also Alexander, 1966) argues that the abandonment of dispositional views of attitude for a probabilistic one would reduce research on attitudes to a very barren state: the theoretical term would be virtually devoid of meaning. The problem of the attitude-behaviour relationship disappears only because the idea of attitude is sacrificed.

The most widely cited evidence for an inconsistency between attitudes and behaviour is the early study by La Piere (1934). He travelled extensively with a Chinese couple, staying at 66 hotels, motels etc. and visiting 184 restaurants and cafes throughout the USA. Often La Piere attempted to keep himself out of the picture so that the behaviour of the hotel and restaurant personnel could be shown as directed purely towards the Chinese couple. They were refused service only once out of so many visits. Six months later La Piere sent postal questionnaires to the places visited which asked, 'Will you accept members of the Chinese race as guests in your establishment?' Replies were obtained from 47 of the hotels etc., and 81 of the restaurants and cafes: 91 percent of the former and 92 percent of the latter replied 'No'. The remainder gave equivocal replies, 'Uncertain, depends on circumstances', except for one 'auto camp' proprietor who gave the only 'Yes' reply.

Although there are obvious flaws in the experimental control La Piere exercised in his study (noted for instance by Kiesler, Collins and Miller, 1969), it is clear evidence that a problem of the relationship between attitude and behaviour exists: the establishments actually served Chinese yet denied that they would do so.

In a more recent study, De Fleur and Westie (1958) assessed verbal attitudes towards Blacks. In the process of assessment the subjects viewed a number of colour slides showing interracial pairings of males and females posing in a setting arranged as a lounge: a relaxed friendly situation. Later the subjects were asked whether they would pose for such pictures, since more were needed for various purposes. They were asked to sign their assent, against as many uses as they would agree to, the list ranging from private laboratory experiments to a nationwide publicity campaign urging racial integration. Here the comparison was between expressed racial attitude and the intention to behave in various ways which were supposed to reflect a scale of increasingly liberal views. In this study attitude and behaviour related well, although, as Kiesler, Collins and Miller (1969) point out, even so a third of the subjects behaved in a way inconsistent with their expressed attitudes.

De Fleur and Westie's study was more formal and controlled than that of La Piere. An even more tightly controlled study was reported by Tittle and Hill (1967) who adopted a 'testing approach' (Calder and Ross, 1973) in which attitudes were assessed using carefully designed multi-item questionnaires to give attitude scores (which compares favourably with La Piere's single question), and behaviour was also assessed by recording a number of instances (rather than one) and deriving an index for behaviour. The two types of score — attitude and behaviour — could then be correlated to produce a gauge of consistency.

The attitude scales of Tittle and Hill were aimed at assessing views concerning personal participation in student political activity and four behaviour indices: actual voting as recorded in returns from an election held one week prior to the attitude assessment; the respondent's report of his voting behaviour for the previous four elections; and two indices based on responses to questions about various forms of student political activity.

The relationships among the attitude scales themselves varied from a correlation of 0.796 to one of 0.337. Different ways of measuring the same attitude may produce markedly different results. In comparing attitudes and behaviour indices, Tittle and Hill report only a moderate degree of correspondence. However, they were able to argue that the relationship was improved when the behavioural measure incorporates several activities relevant to the attitude rather than just one.

The studies considered so far suppose a consistent attitude underlying behaviour. Calder and Ross (1973) point out the relevance of studies in which attitude *change* has been produced: do changes in attitude give rise to changes in behaviour?

Very few studies have been carried out on this question. Festinger (1964) was only able to review three studies which incorporated measures of both attitude and behaviour, and in none of these did a behaviour change accompany a change in attitude. More recent work reviewed by Calder and Ross gives no conclusive evidence for behaviour change.

Given the generally equivocal relationship between attitudes and behaviour shown in these studies, and the many other studies which he reviewed, Wicker (1969) argued that researchers in the social sciences should not claim that a piece of attitude research has any serious implications for actual behaviour. Brannon (1976) observed that: 'By the late 1960s the old commonsense assumption that attitudes influence actions was rapidly disappearing from the technical and professional literature' (p. 147).

However, this situation is an uncomfortable one: it has been an underlying assumption of earlier chapters that mental processes and actions are of a piece. Other authors, including Wicker and Brannon, have also been dissatisfied merely to leave attitudes and behaviour as distinct domains. They have speculated, and sometimes experimented, on the reasons for the lack of an attitude-behaviour relationship. The general viewpoint guiding such speculations and research is that this *is* an impact on behaviour from the individual's attitudes, but the conceptualization and measurement of attitudes and behaviour is inadequate to reveal this; and that often a potential attitude-behaviour correspondence is lacking because other factors apart from the relevant attitude affect observed behaviour. The rest of this section will be largely devoted to reviewing the reasons why a given attitude may not be predictive of an actual action.

Attitudes and behaviour: conceptual problems

It is often argued that a clearer conceptualization of 'attitude' would assist researchers in their attempts to demonstrate a relationship between attitudes and behaviour. The three components of attitude, for instance, may relate differently to behaviour.

Along these lines, Insko and Schopler (1967) has argued that though the three components of attitude may relate differently to behaviour, but that there will be a general tendency for the person to attempt to keep the components consistent. As Calder and Ross (1975) point out, this would lead one to expect a convergence between attitudes and behaviour. However, Insko and Schopler maintain that such a convergence depends on the monitoring of his attitudes by the individual. It is not automatic. They also argue that 'other variables' (which we shall review shortly) affect the relationship between attitudes and behaviour.

Other authors have stressed the possibility of an inconsistency between the components of attitude — at least, as they actually appear in measurements — and behaviour. For example, Kothandapani (1971) showed that assessments of the action-tendency or behavioural component (using Secord and Backman's version of the three component model) are more clearly related to actual behaviour. His study was concerned with the use of contraceptives. Note that this does not really imply an inconsistency between the three components. Rather, as Brannon (1976) has suggested, asking people about their intended actions, instead of about their beliefs and feelings, allows them to reply in a way much more relevant to actual behaviour.

Again, Fishbein (1967,1973) argues that behavioural intentions are virtually the only way specific behaviours can be predicted with any success. Moreover the assessment of this component must be aimed precisely at the particular behaviour being predicted. In effect the subject is apparently being asked to predict the likelihood that he will do that thing. Brannon considers that this makes people consider other variables that might influence their behaviour. So the very pointed assessment of behavioural intentions seems to be moving away from attitude research into the realm of predicting one's own behaviour. If this means that attitudes are not centrally involved in such prediction — or that they are only one factor — at least this tells us a certain amount about attitudes. And it leads us to a position in which the lack of an attitude-behaviour relationship matters less.

Empirical studies which have tried to relate very specific behavioural intentions to actual behaviour, however, have still produced only very small correlations (Wicker and Pomazal, 1971) or none at all (Linn, 1965).

The version of the three-component model presented by Audi (1972), in which 'desire regarding the attitude object' replaced the behavioural component of attitude, was specifically intended to assist conceptualization of the attitude-behaviour relation. Audi writes, 'The commonsense psychological generalization ...which seems to guide at least the most thoughtful of our everyday inferences from people's attitudes and wants to their behaviour seems to be approximately this:

'If a person wants something (G), has no equally strong or stronger incompatible want(s), believes that his doing A is necessary to (or will enable him to, or may well enable him to) realise G, has the ability to do A, and does not believe there is some other action which will be at least as good a way to realise G, then he will very likely do A' (Audi, 1972, p. 193).

This view seems to me to be very important indeed. It is clear that the replacement of action tendency with 'the wants and desires linked to the beliefs and evaluations of the attitude object' enables a much more acceptable statement of the attitude-behaviour relation to be made. Moreover, the three components seem to cohere logically. Action-tendency is not in the same category as belief and feeling — desire is.

Another model of attitude in relation to action which, in this case, has received empirical attention is the expectancy/value view of M. Fishbein (1967). Fishbein builds on the view that behavioural intentions are the closest quasi-attitudinal approximation to behaviour. He goes on to argue that behavioural intentions are a composite of the person's attitude towards the proposed action and the person's beliefs about the social norms surrounding that action, so that the intention to perform an action will only be expressed if the positive aspects of his attitudes to the action and the norms about it outweigh the negative aspects.

Fishbein details the model further. The person's attitude towards the action is made up of the sum of all his attitudes towards all its aspects — and *these* attitudes in turn are the product of the strength of belief in that attitude-aspect, and the degree of positive or negative feeling about that belief. Thus my attitude to writing a particular letter is composed of a number of mini-attitudes, all of which must be summed to give an overall attitude. Each mini-attitude (such as the attitude concerning the effectiveness of the letter in conveying my thoughts) is made up of a belief (yes, it can convey my thoughts well) and an evaluation of that belief (good).

On the matter of social norms, Fishbein argues again that the person's overall belief about others' expectations may be broken down into a number of beliefs about particular norms. These in turn are modified by the person's motivation to comply.

Expressed algebraically, the relationship between attitude and behaviour is given by:

$$B \approx BI = \left\{ \sum_{i=1}^{n} B_i\, a_i \right\} w_0 + \left\{ \sum_{j=1}^{m} (NB_j)\,(Mc_j) \right\} w_1$$

where:

B   is actual behaviour
BI   is behavioural intention
n is the number of beliefs concerning proposed behaviour
B_i is the strength of such a belief
a_i is its evaluative component
m is the number of normative beliefs concerning proposed behaviour
NB_j is the strength of such a norm
Mc_j is the motivation to comply

and, w_0 and w_1 are weightings which are associated with a person's tendency to act in accordance with norms or his own attitudes (Fishbein, 1967).

Ajzen and Fishbein (1970) review studies based on the model. They all report a high degree of conformity of actual attitude-behaviour relationships with the model. Even if a careful conceptual model of the attitude-behaviour relationship, such as those of Audi and Fishbein, is constructed, the problem of *operationalization* remains. Technical considerations of questionnaire design are outside our scope here (see Oppenheim, 1966), but suffice it to say it is undeniable that an attitude-as-assessed is only an approximation to the actual attitude.

Tittle and Hill (1967) found that different measures produced rather different views of what attitude an individual held. Triandis (1964a) showed that even the behavioural component of attitudes is a complex entity, not unidimensional. The attempts of Cook and Selltiz (1964), and Sherif and Sherif (1967) to develop methods of assessment which more validly reflected the respondents' views have met with no outstanding success (Audi, 1972). As Roiser (1974) points out the attitude questionnaire often appears to the aware respondent to be 'asking silly questions', frustratingly caricaturing the opinions which he would like to be asked to express. In view of these problems of assessing attitudes, it would be perhaps surprising if the attitude-behaviour relationship were very strong.

Kiesler, Collins and Miller (1969) and Brannon (1976) point out that answering an attitude questionnaire is itself a form of behaviour. Thus the real question in attitude-behaviour studies is the extent to which both forms of behaviour relate to the hypothetical attitude governing each. Brannon writes: 'In practice...attitude-behaviour studies are empirical comparisons between measures of two different forms of behaviour. This ... should not be confused with a true causal relationship. We don't normally believe that Jones discriminates against Blacks because he checked "yes" on a questionnaire, but rather that he has racist attitudes which influenced both forms of behaviour' (p. 171).

Apart from the problem of conceptualizing attitude and operationalizing this conception, Brannon (1976) suggests that behaviour raises problems of conceptualization and measurement. Certainly Tittle and Hill (1967) showed that the attitude-behaviour correlation could be increased by careful selection of cases of attitude-relevant behaviour and combining these to give an index of behaviour. But Brannon also suggests that the relevance of attitudes to the guidance of behaviour in a given situation is subject, not to objective, logical decisionmaking, but to the 'apparent fit' or 'congruence' of attitude and behaviour. He writes, 'the degree of normally-perceived fit between an attitude and a behaviour under standard conditions, the relation which knowledgeable members of the culture would expect without knowing any of the special circumstances of the case' (p. 173) is congruence.

Thus, whether an attitude should guide such-and-such a piece of behaviour depends on certain social norms about congruence. Doubtless there are also individual factors: one man will perceive more situations as relevant to attitude than others do. Definition of the situation, therefore, involves definition of the situation as calling forth an attitude. Kiesler, Nisbett and Zanna (1969) suggested that the cue of another person stating an attitude can make one's own attitudes salient. A stooge was heard by subjects to agree to go out to persuade people in the street on an opinion topic, and say 'Okay, I wouldn't mind convincing people about something I really *believe in*. I guess that's the important thing'. A control group heard the stooge say, 'Okay, it would be good to be in a study that really *shows something*. I guess that's the important thing'. (The experimental group, therefore, heard an attitude-relevant statement, the control group an attitude-irrelevant one.) The experimental group later showed a strong correlation between attitude and the effort they planned to expend in carrying out the persuasion task whereas the control group did not display such a correlation.

On this same matter, Brannon argues that the same act may be seen as relevant to attitude in one context but not in another, for instance whether the politician knows the baby he is kissing.

Attitudes, 'other variables' and behaviour

We have seen that the detailed definition of attitude and of behaviour, and the way these definitions are operationalized can affect the expected and observed relationship between attitudes and behaviour. The more successful of the redefinitions of attitude and behaviour also allowed the possibility of other factors besides attitude affecting behaviour. Thus Audi presents a number of variables which might lead a person to think that the desire involved in his attitude would or would not be furthered by acting in an attitude-related way in a given setting. Fishbein points out that group norms and the motivation to obey them may affect behaviour; Kiesler, Nisbett and Zanna point to the individual definition of the situation as affecting the perceived relevance of attitudes, a factor very much related to Brannon's notion of congruence.

Other authors have suggested a host of 'other variables' that might — and in some cases have been shown experimentally actually to — affect behaviour, and therefore the attitude-behaviour relation.

Wicker (1971) showed that the behaviour of attending church was predicted more accurately when such measures as self-ratings of 'the likelihood that the person would attend church if he had non-churchgoing weekend guests' were added to religious attitude. This is an instance where attitude is translated into action in the absence of other factors. Brannon argues that the greater relationship between a measure of behavioural intention and action is due to the fact that a person may take other variables beside attitude into acount in expressing his intention to act.

Festinger (1964) suggests that a reason for the lack of attitude change being seen in changed behaviour may be that attitude change is unstable and environmental support (Fishbein's group norms perhaps) is required in order to sustain such change and allow behaviour to flow from it. Along the same lines, Calder and Ross (1973) argues that the lack of stability in attitude-change may be a consequence of commitment to the earlier attitude so that habits of thought and behaviour tend to encourage the person to revert to his former opinion.

Not unconnected with these observations is the viewpoint of Brannon (1976), who argues that attitude and action have different consequences for the individual. In general action is more costly than attitude, but this is not an iron rule. Thus it may be that the attitude has to be very strong to cause a behavioural expression in certain contexts. Calder and Ross (1973) make a similar point in connection with attitude change, saying that the graph of attitude versus behaviour may be a very steep curve such that a large attitude change prompts only a small behaviour change. Yet they go on to say that the curve may have a different slope at the upper and lower ends. This idea is useful heuristically, though a graph of this sort would only express an empirical relationship and would, in itself, give no hint of the reason for the relationship between attitude and behaviour.

The same can be said of Campbell's (1963) notion of 'behavioural threshold'. He argues that findings such as La Piere's can be explained by assuming that, rather than holding attitudes inconsistent with their actual behaviour, the hoteliers and restauranteurs found it easier to express the attitude in questionnaire response than in face-to-face interaction: the behavioural thresholds of the actions were different. Although this is appealing as an explanation, looked at critically it is no explanation at all but a restatement of the phenomenon of attitude-behaviour inconsistency. The real question is why there is the observed difference in behavioural threshold (Calder and Ross, 1973).

The conceptualization of the attitude-behaviour relation by Audi (1972) is one of the most helpful aids to an understanding of the situation. If behaviour is not perceived as furthering the attitude-associated desires of the person, then it will not necessarily be in keeping with the attitude. I suppose this is one aspect of the notion of the 'personal functions of attitudes' (Katz, 1960) discussed earlier: the functions that attitudes subserve are not necessarily enhanced by actual behaviour. The functions of attitudes and behaviour may be quite different for a given person in a certain context. If this is so, then no relationship need be expected. As Davey (1976) points out, attitudes are not to be expected to be causally related to behaviour, but an individual may choose to express his attitude through behaviour. Such choice depends on the sort of considerations of relevance, payoff, satisfaction of desires and wants, etc., outlined above.

Given the indirectness of the link between attitudes and behaviour, when the relationship is considered as a causal one, it is not surprising that the attempt to change people's behaviour through changing their attitudes — by education or by group training techniques — is so often ill-fated (cf. Chinoy, 1975). And the larger premise, that changing people's attitudes can change society ought to be regarded with similar caution. Attitude change can relate to behaviour change but only under conditions which are very favourable, such that personal desires and environmental circumstances are in tune with the change.

As has been often demonstrated, behaviour change is more likely to give rise to attitude change than attitude change is to behaviour change (Insko and Schopler, 1967; Kiesler, Collins and Miller, 1969). Some of the characteristics of this reversed relationship will be discussed in the context of research on cognitive dissonance (Cohen, 1960; Greenwald, 1970).

Attitudes and behaviour: an interactionist perspective

The foregoing discussion has allowed some approach to be made towards an understanding of why it is that there is an equivocal relationship between measured attitude and observed behaviour. It can be seen that attempts to explain the relationship have often been rooted in different ways of handling the conceptual synthesis 'attitude'. Thus authors such as Insko and Schopler have suggested that the components may vary in the directness of their behavioural implications, and that if there is a relationship between attitude (taken as a coherent structure) and behaviour, this is due to the conscious monitoring of his attitudes by the individual. Authors who discuss circumstances under which the situation may or may not be defined as relevant to an attitude also show an awareness of the possibility that attitudes and behaviour relate in an equivocal way because the maintenance of the required attitude structure demands a level of awareness which may not always exist.

Other authors deal with the problem that attitude is a synthetic notion by focussing on just one, 'pure' component. This is done by Fishbein, of course. His concern is with *prediction,* and for his purposes the idea of attitude seems less important than the collection of a number of cognitive variables that can be relied on to correlate well with behaviour.

This distinction between the treatment of attitudes as aspects of conscious awareness and the use of them as variables for predicting behaviour is akin to that drawn earlier between probabilistic and dispositional views. For Fishbein, and for those who use mechanistic descriptive terms like 'behavioural threshold', it is apparent that attitude functions as an intervening variable rather than as a hypothetical construct. Their notion of cognition hardly involves conscious self monitoring; rather, the cognitive 'arena' is a 'locus' for the interaction of a number of variables which are held to have a causal influence on behaviour — an influence which may be upset by the effect of 'other variables'.

We must be aware, then, that there is a certain ambiguity in the formulation which was used to introduce this section: the expectation that attitudes should 'reveal themselves in behaviour' may, on the one hand, be read as suggesting a direct *causal* relationship, or, on the other hand, be taken as indicating that an attitude will often be a *reason* for the choice of a line of behaviour (Davey's view is obviously relevant here).

These reflections enable some statement to be made of an interactionist view of the attitude-behaviour relationship. It must take the concept of attitude to be dispositional rather than probabilistic, and understand behaviour to be motivated by reasons (in general) rather than causes (see Chapter 7). The idea of 'defining the situation', treated in Chapter 2, forms our starting point.

'If men define situations as real, they are real in their consequences' directs attention to the meaning of the situation for the person. His perceptual activity is the focus of interest for the interactionist study of behaviour, since behaviour is the person's response to his definition of the situation. The reason for his action is to be sought by inquiring as to his perception of the situation.

Within this context, then, 'attitude' is a term which refers to *perceptual* regularities. Holding a certain attitude, the person's perceptual activity will focus on certain elements of a situation which may well differ from those to which another person attends. The situation calls forth particular beliefs, feelings and desires — indeed, it is already perceived as 'embodying' a reference to such components of attitude, insofar as the perceptual activity of defining the situation is, like all perception, a perception of meanings (see Chapter 4).

Attitude, as was noted at the beginning of the chapter, is comparable to symbol as a theoretical concept. Thus the earlier argument in this book concerning the major symbol system, language, and its relationship to perception, may be recalled. And it can be extended. Like symbols in general, attitudes 'motivate' and 'suggest the meaningful content' of perception. They motivate it in the sense of giving the perceiver reasons for attending to certain facts. They 'suggest the meaningful content', in that perception, being of meanings, already meshes with various attitudes, so that the person not only holds a given attitude prior to an act of situational definition, but perceives immediately that the meaning of the situation 'contains' the attitude. (Concrete examples of the phenomenon are gives in the section of .Chapter 4 concerned with implicit personality theories and stereotypes.)

Thus definition of the situation implicates attitudes. And the definition of the situation provides the person with a *scene* within which to act. The choice of behaviour is made with that scene in front of one, or rather, one makes the choice while immersed in that situation. One acts relevantly given the definition of the situation, but it would be odd to suggest that definition of the situation *determines* behaviour. Rather, it give the person reasons for his choice of a line of action.

This sketch of an interactionist understanding of the relationship between attitudes and behaviour is obviously of-a-piece with the treatment in earlier chapters of such matters as motivation, perception, and symbolic functioning.

Two very recent reviews, one entirely concerned with the attitude-behaviour relationship (Schuman and Johnson, 1976) and the other having this as one of its main themes (Eagly and Himmelfarb, 1978), provide invaluable bibliographies on this matter. Both are able to adopt a rather more sanguine view of the empirical relationship between measured attitude and behaviour, since they stress studies carred out in the last five or six years which take account of the viewpoint of Fishbein concerning the need to measure specific behavioural intentions rather than very general attitudes, and which also attempt to take account of 'other variables'. There is no doubt that predictions based on the improved causal model pay off. Therefore we must emphasize here that it is *not* dubiousness concerning the predictive capability of the model, which links attitudes and behaviour by a causal chain, that leads us to suggest that social psychology might investigate the possibility of a different conceptualization of the relationship. Rather, it is that, when attitudes and behaviour are both situated in a more encompassing view of social action, it seems proper to argue that a less mechanistic, less causal model would better illuminate the facts. Hence, the cognitive/perceptual (or, as we shall argue later, phenomenological) stand which has been outlined above. In other words, insofar as symbolic interactionism is able to give a coherent account of social interaction and its relationship to conscious awareness in general, then in applying the theory to the attitude-behaviour relationship it is found more congenial to the overall standpoint to suggest a conceptualization which plays down the notion of a causal chain.

THE NOTION OF ATTITUDE STRUCTURING

Cognitive theorists in general have taken the view that attitudes are not haphazard, but that they have a certain structure, predictability or consistency. Such consistency is an assumption that lies behind scientific concern with the relationship between attitudes and behaviour. We have seen that there are good reasons why an expectation of consistency here is only sometimes fulfilled.

Again, the notion of structure and consistency leads authors to assume that the three components of attitudes do not contradict each other: we do not feel strongly unless we believe something, for example. Insko and Schopler (1967) have put forward arguments in favour of 'triadic consistency'. But the assumption is not uncontroversial. For instance, Brannon (1976) argues that the triadic view of attitudes is not supported by evidence. The model has rarely been empirically tested, but when it has 'the data have seldom even vaguely supported the model' (p. 155). It may be that Brannon is missing the point here. Generally, authors have not treated the three component view of attitudes as an empirical matter, but as the conclusion from a rational consideration of the very idea of holding an attitude. It appeared from such consideration that, for a mental stance towards an object to count as an instance of an attitude, then a belief, a feeling and an action-tendency or desire must be present — as it were, by definition. This in itself does not preclude the possibility that each of the components might often stand alone.

It is certainly possible to view triadic consistency as part of the definition of attitude; if it is not observed empirically in a given case, then what is being observed is not an attitude. However, if we are to adopt that view, it must be conceded that 'attitude' is no longer to be regarded as *synonymous* with 'symbol'. Perhaps this is correct: not all symbols are attitudes; however, attitudes are symbols with the structure implied by triadic consistency.

A further aspect of the general assumption that attitudes have structure rather than being haphazard is that within the whole system of an individual's attitudes there is rational structure, and that this allows some consistency and order to be seen by the person when perceiving his world (Kiesler, Collins and Miller, 1969; Kelvin, 1970). It is this aspect of the idea of attitude structure that requires elaboration.

The most straightforward principle governing attitude structuring in individuals would be found if attitude systems conformed to the laws of *logic*. This would mean that each attitude held by a person was related to each other attitude entirely consistently. Such logically-interrelated attitudes would be demonstrated if inferences from any one attitude found no contradiction in any other attitude. The structure of attitudes would in such a case be in conformity with logic. Certainly Zajonc (1960) has argued that people do attempt to think and act rationally. To what extent do such attempts meet with success?

Experimental study of the logicality of human thought processes has largely been concerned with the syllogism — such deductive arguments as 'All swans are white, this object is not white, therefore this object is not a swan'. Clearly, any evidence that human thinking is not logical puts in doubt the idea that attitudes are structured according to logical principles. Woodworth and Sells (1935) showed that people do indeed make errors of logic when dealing with syllogisms. Chapman and Chapman (1959) reject Woodworth and Sells' explanation of this finding, but certainly do not dispute the quite general view that people are rather bad logicians (but see Henle, 1962). Thus, McGuire

(1969) lists prominently amongst a number of reasons for individual inconsistency in attitudes, that people make logical errors so that they fail to see that one attitude leads to conclusions that conflict with another attitude.

However, if it is wrong to view a person's attitudes as likely to be logically structured, it is also a mistake to abandon all search for a principle of structuring. Certainly, attitudes, like symbols in general, 'do not occur only in isolated bits, but often in clusters, sometimes large and complex' (Rose, 1962, p. 10).

Abelson and Rosenberg (1958) try to cope with this problem by suggesting rules of 'psycho-logic' which are formal principles of structure in attitude systems but which are rather different from the laws of logic. Similarly, G. Kelly (1955) argues that, although 'personal constructs' (his term replacing symbols or attitudes) are sufficiently well structured to allow a person to make some sense of the events of his world, nevertheless, one cannot assume that the system is all-of-a-piece. One construction of the world may be 'inferentially incompatible' with another. The attitude system is somewhat fragmented. Logical rules apply in only limited areas. Presumably the individual is often unaware of his illogicality because the attitude areas do not come into contact. The contradictory attitudes never confront one another. In severe instances of this phenomenon, the person's illogicality becomes apparent to everyone but himself.

If logic is not the principle of attitude structuring, and yet we are forced to view attitudes as nevertheless consistent to some degree, then we must search for an alternative structuring principle or system of principles. Several authors have suggested that *values* serve this function of providing a basic system giving order to attitudes (Kelvin, 1970; Rokeach, 1972, 1973). In effect, attitudes are seen by Kelvin as giving order to a person's perception of the world, and values structure the attitudes.

Kelvin's (1970) *The Bases of Social Behaviour* has the subtitle 'an approach in terms of order and value'. It is a main argument of the book that, if a human being is to be able to act in the world, or just think about the people, objects and events in the world, he must perceive order. So people have to construe some sort of order in their environment. Kelvin writes: 'man can only cope with his environment if that environment is relatively orderly and predictable...' (p. 1). Now, if this is taken as true, how does the person impose order on his social environment? How can other people's actions be construed as orderly and therefore predictable? Kelvin suggests that we impose order by perceiving the social environment in terms of our values — hence the subtitle of his book.

For Kelvin, attitudes are viewed as fairly specific perceptual categories which relate to particular objects. These attitudes are structured by a far more general system of values. Thus, in the examination of individual behaviour, 'the first task is to consider the psychological processes whereby values come to affect the person's perception of the world, and his response to it. The fundamental psychological processes here are attitudes' (Kelvin, p. 39).

So Kelvin is arguing that, because the individual needs to be able to construe the environment as ordered and predictable, he imposes order on it in the form of value-judgements. Thus attitudes to particular objects are manifestations of the person's values. Further, although Kelvin does not stress this implication, we may add that the individual's system of attitudes is structured inasmuch as the individual attitudes reflect consistently particular values. (Other views paralleling Kelvin on this matter include those of Katz and Stotland, 1959, and Reich and Adcock, 1976).

As concrete example of Kelvins view consider this: One common value that people hold which gives order to part of the social world is 'justice' — so in order to think about, and maybe to act towards some things in our social environment we evaluate them as 'just' or 'unjust'. And our attitudes towards these things will reflect these values. Logical inconsistency between attitudes is not ruled out: it is quite likely that the total set of attitudes serving a given value will contain items which are logical contradictions, unless conscious monitoring of attitudes (presumably carried out under the auspices of a value favouring logical consistency) is actively maintained. As Zajonc (1960) points out the situation is anomalous: 'While the concept of consistency acknowledges man's rationality, observation of the means of its achievement simultaneously unveils his irrationality' (p. 281).

There are strong similarities between Kelvin's view and that of Katz (1960). His insistence that one cannot fully understand the attitudes held by a person unless one has some idea about the functions they serve for him, led to a detailing of four specific functions: instrumental, ego-defensive, value-expressive and knowledge. Clearly there is much in Kelvin that immediately reflects Katz's views. Kelvin says that values, like knowledge have the function of making the world orderly and predictable. And is not ego-defence a process that reflects the value we place on our selves? So Kelvin would argue that values and ego-defence and the knowledge function of attitudes are all part of the same thing. Kelvin does not really deal with the instrumental function of attitudes. If we express an attitude, not because we actually hold that attitude, but rather because the act of expressing the attitude itself has a useful result, then the attitude expressed does not reflect a value. So Kelvin's view that attitudes reflect values is not always true. In the case of attitudes with an instrumental function, it is the act of expressing the attitude that reflects the value, not the attitude itself.

The instrumental function of attitudes points to a fact which is often implicitly ignored in research on attitudes. Attitudes are *contextualized*. The meaning of an attitude is not clear unless the situation to which it relates is included in the analysis. Notions of attitude structure tend to assume that situation may be ignored, or that the fact that attitude structures include particular attitudes concerning situations means that such structures may be considered as self-contained. Thus, structures of attitudes are pictured by psychologists as if they were as structurally coherent as, say, a chemist's molecular model: separate attitudes being 'bonded' to others.

Such a picture is not helpful. If some degree of consistency is attained by an individual, this subjective consistency with his values must be provisional only. That is, insofar as he is living in a world, and is open to experience. New situations will initially be defined in old ways, using the conceptual apparatus available, but the disjunction will throw that apparatus — that substructure of the symbol system — into disarray, calling for reconstruction.

This was part of what the idea of 'negotiation' of situational definitions implied (Chapter 2), and was what lay behind some aspects of embarrassment (Chapter 6), and so on. Just as language is intimately related to the context of speech, so attitudes are dialectically related to the lived world of their 'owners'. So that attitudes will, as has been argued, 'motivate' a certain definition of the situation, and 'suggest a content', yet the situation defined through the influence of attitudes may, on occasion, appear unsatisfactory to the perceiver. There is an undefined element on the 'horizon' of awareness which demands attention. The 'real situation' (so to speak) is refractory in the face of his attempt at definition. The attitude structures which were implicated in that attempt are sent into disorder.

It is likely that reconstruction of attitudes which have become 'discredited' in such a way will be piecemeal. Consistency with other attitudes will not be a central concern immediately. Later reflection may enable an approach to consistency to be regained, but consistency requires conscious monitoring of attitudes.

At this stage we need to consider a theory of attitude structure which attempts to treat attitudes as open to events.

COGNITIVE DISSONANCE THEORY

Festinger's *Theory of Cognitive Dissonance* (1957) is an account of attitude structure and change. It assumes that some principle of consistency governs attitude structuring, and that the perception that attitudes are inconsistent with each other or with some other 'cognitive element' (which might, for example, be the understanding that interpersonal negotiation of situational definitions has broken down) is 'dissonant', and demands the recovery of consistency. Thus cognitive structures are liable to cycles of partial breakdown and repair, in response to external circumstances especially.

In this section of the chapter, a fairly thorough review of the debates surrounding dissonance theory is attempted. The original theory and the types of experimental evidence thought to support it are described first. This is followed by a consideration of the main lines of criticism and elaboration of the original theory — though the various alternative models which radically depart from the dissonance theory are merely mentioned. Finally, an interactionist comment on the field is given.

Since dissonance theory attracted such a wealth of empirical and conceptual treatment throughout the 1960s, it presents a case study, so to speak, of the approach to a cognitive process which orthodox, cognitive social psychology takes. The detailed treatment which is accorded this case study is intended to indicate the seriousness with which we view the approach. However, the final subsection is designed to show that the elaborations and revisions of dissonance theory actually move it closer to the understanding of human social consciousness seen in symbolic interactionism, and that the insights developed in this book can accommodate even this field of work — which has been laboured at by social scientists who are, I suspect, far from sympathetic to the interactionist approach.

The original theory and paradigms for experimental confirmation

Festinger (1957) presented a definition of dissonance; a view of the effects it produced; a way of predicting the magnitude of dissonance to be expected in a given situation, and a statement of the various modes by which dissonance might be resolved. (See also Aronson, 1969;. Brown, 1965; Kiesler, Collins and Miller, 1969; Leventhal, 1974; and Zajonc, 1960.) In the wake of his theoretical statement, several situations have come to be regarded as especially appropriate for the experimental testing of the theory (Brehm and Cohen, 1962; Totman, 1973). We will here first expound the main tenets of the original theory and then describe experimental evidence which illustrates their practical operation.

The theory is one of the family of consistency theories: there is assumed to be a tendency towards consistency between the various attitudes held by a person at a given time. The focus is on the circumstances giving rise to inconsistency and the ways inconsistency may be resolved. Festinger argues that, taking just two attitudes a person holds (or, as he says, taking two *cognitive elements)* three relations may obtain between them: there may be no relationship, the one element being quite irrelevant to the other; they may be consistent with each other, or they may be inconsistent (dissonant). In defining dissonance, Festinger writes: 'Let us consider two elements which exist in a person's cognition and which are relevant to one another. The definition of dissonance will disregard the existence of all other cognitive elements that are relevant to either or both of the two under consideration and simply deals with these two alone. *These two elements are in a dissonant relation if, considering these two alone, the obverse of one element would follow from the other.* To state it a bit more formally, x and y are dissonant if not-x follows from y' (1957, p. 13, italics in original). Kiesler, Collins and Miller (1969) point out that 'obverse' is misused by Festinger — but his meaning is conveyed by the replacement of 'obverse' by 'negation' or 'opposite'.

A cognitive element is 'any knowledge, opinion, or belief about the environment, about oneself, or about one's behaviour' (Festinger, 1957, p. 3). 'Knowledge of one's feelings, behaviour and opinions as well as knowledge about location of good objects, how to get them, what other people believe, and so forth, are examples of cognitive elements' (Brehm and Cohen, 1962, p. 3).

Cognitive dissonance occurs when an element implies the negation of another element. It can result from logical contradiction, but more often the contradiction is psychological: the one attitude may psychologically contradict cultural mores as embodied in another attitude: one specific opinion may be out of keeping with the wider general opinion a person holds (I approve of a certain Conservative politician yet I am a Socialist); again, a new experience which contradicts past experience may give rise to dissonance.

What is the effect of dissonance? It is 'psychologically uncomfortable', i.e. it is experienced as a sort of 'stress' (Tannenbaum, 1968) or 'tension'. This aversive state can be lessened and perhaps removed only by achieving greater consonance between the two dissonant elements. The psychological contradiction must be overcome somehow. The urgency of the tension, as it were, depends directly on the magnitude of dissonance. Dissonance is supposed to be related to the proportion of dissonant elements compared to the total number of cognitive elements, all relationships being weighted by importance.

Total dissonance, D, is given by

$$D = \sum_{i=1}^{n} (a_i P_i) / \sum_{j=1}^{z} (b_j P_j)$$

where

a_i is the ith dissonant element and P_i is its importance.
b_j is the jth element in the total structure and P_j is its importance.
n is the number of dissonant elements.
z is the total number of elements in the structure.

From this we learn that Festinger does not wish to restrict his theory to the assumption that only the relationships between the two elements being considered affect magnitude of dissonance. There is an incoherence in the theory here, which will be discussed later.

Dissonance may be resolved in many ways. The cognitive elements may be changed. Other elements could be added so as to remove the dissonance or reduce it. Festinger predicts that the mode of resolution will be chosen which subjects those elements to change which are least resistant. In particular, cognitive elements which can be easily tested by reference to reality will be resistant to change if they are in concord with the person's perception of reality — otherwise they will be relatively easy to change. Relationships of consonance with other elements also lead to resistance to change.

The above account gives the main strands of the original theory. Two situations in particular have come to be regarded as especially appropriate for the experimental test of cognitive dissonance theory: those in accordance with the 'forced compliance' paradigm, and those assessing 'post-decision dissonance'. The only reason why these two types of experiment are to the fore is that a tradition of research has centred around them. As Totman (1973) and

Brown (1965) point out, very many situations can be seen as likely to arouse dissonance. However, often these other situations can be studied using theoretical frameworks far less elaborate than Festinger's. Forced compliance and post-decision dissonance on the other hand sometimes give rise to situations where cognitive dissonance theory makes surprising predictions, and therefore the theory can be rather more rigorously tested here.

The forced compliance paradigm has as its classical example a study by Festinger and Carlsmith (1959). Actually the term forced compliance is rather strong. What actually happens in these studies is that a person is asked to make a statement of some sort advocating a point of view contrary to the one he himself holds. This is supposed to be dissonant, because cognitive element 'I believe X' and cognitive element 'I expressed the viewpoint not-X' are inconsistent. So the studies would test the prediction of cognitive dissonance theory that the person will act or change his attitudes in a way that reduces the inconsistency.

Festinger and Carlsmith invited students to participate in an experiment as a normal part of their class activities. The experiment involved the very tedious work of turning pegs a quarter of a turn, and putting spools on and taking them off a rack, for a total of an hour. Subjects took part individually, and at the end of the hour each was told (falsely) that he had been a member of a control group in an experiment concerning the effect of prior expectations on manual tasks. They had been given no prior expectations — others would be. At this stage one-third of the subjects were asked to go to another building to fill in a questionnaire. (The impression purposely conveyed was that the questionnaire was quite unconnected with the tedious experiment.) The questionnaire included an item about the 'last thing the student had done before coming in to fill in the questionnaire' — was it dull or fun? In this way a rating of the task was obtained.

For the other two-thirds of the students, the rating was not obtained immediately the task was over, but instead the experiment continued in the following manner. As if as an afterthought, the experimenter told the student that the person who usually performed the role of giving prior expectations to experimental subjects was ill — would they do this job just the once? There was a subject in the waiting room. Would they tell the subject that the task was fun? One-third of the students were told that they would earn twenty dollars if they agreed to act the role of 'expectation-inducer'. The remaining third were told that they would be paid one dollar.

Having agreed, the job of persuading the person that the task would be fun was carried out, payment collected — and the student was sent to fill in the questionnaire.

Festinger and Carlsmith argued that the forced compliance situation induced dissonance in the two-thirds of students who agreed to tell another person that the task was fun, since 'The task is dull' and 'I said it was fun' are incompatible. They had evidence from the control group's ratings that the task was perceived as very dull indeed. However they predicted the magnitude of dissonance in the two experimental groups would differ: the twenty-dollar group would be able to regard this very large payment as an element which justified the falsehood. Thus for them there was an element of consonance between 'The task is dull' and 'I said it was fun' — since 'I said it was fun for twenty dollars'. The one-dollar group could not draw on a justification like this: their reason for lying was small.

Thus the prediction was that the one-dollar group would feel dissonance which could not be reduced by denying that they had said the task was fun so easily as it could be reduced by changing their view of the task. If the task actually had been fun, then there was no dissonance induced by the fact that they had said so. Festinger and Carlsmith therefore argued that, whereas the twenty-dollar and control groups would rate the task as very tedious, the one-dollar group would give a more favourable rating, thus lessening their own cognitive dissonance. This is in fact what they found by inspection of the ratings of the three groups.

In response to the possible criticism that the effect might have been due to the one-dollar group for some reason expending more effort in trying to persuade the waiting 'subject' that the task was fun, and thereby persuading *themselves* (something that King and Janis, 1956, had shown), Festinger and Carlsmith produced the evidence that judges who rated tape-recordings of the persuasive efforts of all experimental subjects without knowing which group they belonged to, found the twenty-dollar subjects slightly more 'hardworking' than the one-dollar group. Thus this alternative explanation of the results can be discounted.

Post-decision dissonance is a second paradigmatic situation used to study the viability of cognitive dissonance theory. The argument is that dissonance is very likely to arise whenever a free choice is made between alternatives. In deciding to buy product x in preference to y and z, for instance, it is probable that there will be a certain amount of regret that one had to reject y and z, which had some positive aspects, and buy product x, which was not totally good. Prior to the decision, the experience may be one of conflict, but only after commitment does dissonance occur. The magnitude of this post-decision dissonance is supposed to depend on such factors as the recency and importance of the decision; how wide the range of alternatives was (the greater the number, the greater the dissonance since the likelihood of error is magnified); how similar in attractiveness the objects were, and how different in kind they were (very different objects give rise to less dissonance since they are less comparable).

Post-decision dissonance may be resolved, it is hypothesized, by emphasizing in one's own mind the positive aspects of the chosen object and the negative aspects of those objects rejected, and also by depreciating the positive aspects of rejected objects while ignoring the negative aspects of the object that has been chosen.

An example of an experiment concerned with post-decision dissonance is Cohen's on the effect of becoming engaged to be married on the man's attitude to his fiancée (Cohen, reported in Brehm and Cohen, 1962). The attitudes towards their prospective fiancées and towards engagement were assessed in thirty Yale students who were considering becoming engaged during the Christmas vacation. The attitudes were measured just before the end of term.

Cohen argued that those with a more negative attitude towards engagement could be expected to experience greater dissonance when they actually got engaged. This dissonance might be resolved by an increase in positive attitude towards their fiancées. On return from the vacation, the twenty students who had actually become engaged were divided into two groups on the basis of their earlier high or low estimate of engagement. There was the predicted effect, in that the two groups differed in the change of attitude expressed concerning their fiancées, the greater positive change being expressed by the 'low estimate of engagement' group.

A further experiment using a 'post-decision dissonance' situation was reported by Knox and Inkster (1968). This was carried out in the natural setting of a racecourse — far removed from the laboratory. Sixty-nine people were interviewed immediately prior to placing two-dollar bets to win. They rated the chances of the horse they were backing on a seven point rating scale, the average rating being 'fair chance of winning'. Seventy-two other people were interviewed immediately after placing their bets, and their average rating was significantly higher: 'good chance of winning'. A second study successfully replicated this one. Both sets of data supported the prediction of dissonance theory that post-decision dissonance may be reduced by mental emphasis of the positive aspects of the choice that has been made.

Criticisms and elaborations

A major source of articles discussing various features of dissonance theory in the context of cognitive consistency theories in general is the book edited by Abelson and colleagues (1968). One of Abelson's own contributions (1968a) is a summary of various views of cognitive structure, and indeed the main criticisms of Festinger's theory stem from the fact that his view of cognitive structure is not clear. The production of dissonance when certain conditions of 'psychological implication' between elements are fulfilled is only predictable if a clear model of cognitive structure is given. Other problems with the theory have a similar basis. They are outlined below.

The question of psychological implication

The question of psychological implication between elements is not treated fully by Festinger. He argues that dissonance arises when one element implies the negation or opposite of another element, but the conditions under which this situation obtains are left unclear.

Aronson (1969) suggests that the problem of the nature of psychological implication between elements may be tackled in a particular situation by actually empirically testing whether people expect two cognitions to be related in a certain way; if they do, then dissonance will be aroused when the cognitions do not relate in that way. For example, the likelihood of cognitive dissonance in the Festinger and Carlsmith study would be shown by asking people, 'Students who did the experiment found it boring. What do you think they told other people?'

Aronson's solution is unsatisfactory and *ad hoc*. Kiesler, Collins and Miller (1969) point out that it seems inevitable that, except in the case of logical contradiction, some knowledge of the beliefs, cultural background or personal experience of the particular individual is required before the prediction that two cognitive elements will produce dissonance can be made. A plain description of the two elements is not usually sufficient.

On this matter, Brown (1965) points out that, in everyday language, the use of contrastive conjunctions (but, however, nevertheless, although, even so, yet...) often signal dissonance. Thus another empirical approach to discovering a psychological implication which produces dissonance is to ask what conjunction they would use in the sentence, 'Students who did the experiment found it boring...they said it was fun'.

The fact that other parts of the individual's cognitive structure as well as the two elements under scrutiny affect the dissonance felt between the two elements is obvious. The meaning of the elements, and therefore the implications each has for the other, is partly derived from related conitions. Festinger is naive to suggest that the two can be considered alone — and naive also to suggest that one can draw any conclusions, from just considering two elements, about their implications each for the other.

Further to this, Truzzi (1973) points out that the limitation Festinger places on elements that may be considered — that they must be relevant to each other — demands that we know intuitively which elements fulfill this specification. But this depends on all sorts of factors which have to do with the larger cognitive structure in which the elements are 'embedded'. Festinger gives us no guidance as to our approach to this structure.

Suppressed premises and the value basis of cognition

The fact that, as we have said, a plain description of the two elements is not sufficient in itself to enable a prediction of dissonance to be made indicates 'suppressed premises'. Brown (1965) points out that 'I found the experiment dull' is dissonant with 'I said it was fun' only because 'I tell the truth' or 'I try to be consistent' or whatever. In other words, whatever it is that makes the elements dissonant is not an integral characteristic of the elements but is an extra cognition. Aronson (1969) agrees, and goes on to suggest that two elements that might seem to an observer likely to give rise to dissonance may not do so if the person has some other cognition that makes them seem to him consonant.

These arguments lead to a consideration of what we earlier termed the underlying 'principle of structuring' of dissonance theory. In discussing what principle underlay consistency in attitude structures, we concluded that psychological concordance with *values* must be the answer. Brown and Aronson indicate that it is lack of such concordance with respect to values that produces dissonance. As might be expected, Katz (1968) argued that dissonance theory ignored 'the motivational level' — by which he referred to the attitude functions mentioned earlier in this chapter. The situation could be remedied if it were recognized that dissonance occurred because the functions performed by the cognitions were at risk when they were dissonant. Most of these functions (the possible exception is the instrumental function) reflect the value basis of cognitive structure.

A specific example of the value basis of dissonance is emphasized by Aronson (1969) who argues that many studies implicitly assume that people place a high value on the self concept. Indeed, he cites experiments that have indicated that people with *low* self esteem feel dissonance when they are led to believe they have acted *well*. Presumably the Festinger and Carlsmith experiment would not have shown a dissonance effect if lying were consistent with the self concept of subjects.

Aronson goes so far as to say that dissonance occurs only if the individual's behaviour is inconsistent with his self concept. This is in line with the view of Bramel (1968) who, after stating that dissonance arises 'if and only if an organism attends to some information which is contrary to what it expected' (p. 355) — a radical reformulation of the concept — goes on to point out that there are often a number of sources of dissonance. When a person feels reponsible for a bad decision he has made, two sources of dissonance: encountering an event which is contrary to expectation and the discovery that one has chosen incompetently.

Bramel decides that dissonance should be reserved for 'anxiety associated with social rejection. The feeling of unworthiness, incompetence, unlovableness is probably aroused both by the failure to predict accurately and the failure to behave competently or ethically. The consequences of anxiety about one's worth are likely to be such things as self-justification and the search for information that will reflect favourably upon the self. These responses seem much less probable following the arousal of other kinds of anxiety...' (p. 365).

An experimental test of Aronson and Bramel's view that the crucial determinant of dissonance is whether the disparity between cognitive elements threatens the self concept was carried out by Nel, Helmreich and Aronson (1969). The attitude change results upheld the hypothesis, indicating that cognitive dissonance is a function of the value one places on oneself.

Aronson argues, then, that the value of self esteem supplies the missing principle of structuring for cognitive dissonance theory. However there seems *a priori* no reason why other values might not also serve this function. It may be that Aronson's theory allows other values to slip into the picture surreptitiously, since the threatening of a value is often also a threat to self esteem.

Kelman and Baron (1974) argue that the effect of incentive in reducing dissonance postulated by Festinger and Carlsmith depends on the nature of the dissonance. When dissonance is due to acting in a way that has very low payoff (e.g. engaging in a boring task), the 'hedonic dissonance' is reduced by payment; when one experiences 'moral dissonance' on the other hand, high payment increases dissonance — one has acted contrary to values for a high payment. Their argument seems open to debate, and it is by no means clear that the distinction is sharp or the different effects of payment certain. However, they do alert us to the possibility that different values and different personal functions of attitudes (Katz) may require quite distinct modes of dissonance resolution.

'Magnitude of dissonance' and associated problems

It will be recalled that dissonance is supposed to be proportional to the ratio of the number of dissonant elements to the total number of elements, each element being weighted by its importance. This formula raises problems for several reasons. One is that it is incompatible with the general definition of dissonance, where two elements are considered alone. Festinger is tacitly admitting that the dissonance is not due merely to the implicative relationships between the two elements.

Another problem, pointed out by Kiesler, Collins and Miller (1969), is that the magnitude of dissonance is a function of the importance of relevant elements, which in itself is very difficult to measure. Indeed it may be that the subjective importance of an element is high simply because it *is* in a dissonant relationship with another element. If this is the case, the formula is very difficult to apply. Kiesler, Collins and Miller argue that the quantification of the magnitude of dissonance is so problematic that Festingers' thoughts on the subject merely indicate the difficulties that would be faced were we to attempt measurement.

The situation is further complicated by the problem of predicting how dissonance is to be resolved (Abelson, 1968b). It is suggested that the cognitive element least resistant to change will be the direction resolution takes. This again might be expected to relate to the importance of elements. So it seems that independent measures cannot be made of the importance of elements, the resistance to change of elements, and the magnitude of dissonance — and thus prediction cannot be certain.

Brehm and Cohen (1962) argue that dissonance theory should be limited to instances where the person has a feeling of voluntary commitment to the action. Commitment may be assumed if he 'has decided to do or not do a certain thing, when he has chosen one (or more) alternatives; when he actively engages in a given behaviour or has engaged in a given behaviour' (p. 7). Such a restriction, they argue, means that 'the specification of dissonance and the manner in which it is likely to be reduced are relatively unequivocal' (p. 10).

Certainly, if commitment can be manipulated experimentally, and therefore the strength of resistance to change of one element ascertained, the number of alternatives amongst the various modes of resolution of dissonance is reduced. Thus predictability is enhanced. However, as Kiesler, Collins and Miller point out, this says very little about real life situations and their typical forms of dissonance and dissonance reduction — all that has happened is that experimental control in the laboratory has been intensified.

Other necessary conditions for cognitive dissonance

Brehm and Cohen (1962) suggest restricting dissonance theory to situations where voluntary *commitment* can be secured. Other authors have provided experimental evidence that unless voluntary commitment *is* present, cognitive dissonance does not occur (e.g. Helmreich and Collins, 1968; Collins and Hoyt, 1972).

Cooper and Worchel (1970) showed that the *seriousness* of the counter-attitudinal behaviour must reach a certain subjective level before the cognitive dissonance effect occurs. They conducted an experiment replicating Festinger and Carlsmith (1959) but in which half the subjects were told that their attempt to convince the 'waiting subjects' were successful, the other that they were unsuccessful: their listeners still believed the task would be dull. The dissonance effect was only found in subjects who were 'successful' in convincing those waiting.

The importance of *freedom of choice* in agreeing to act contrary to attitude in the forced compliance situation, which was emphasized by Brehm and Cohen (1962), has been shown experimentally by Linder, Cooper and Jones (1967). It seems that a low inducement arouses dissonance and leads to greater attitude change only when subjects remain free to decide against compliance after they have been fully informed about the reward. Otherwise, the incentive effect (more attitude change for greater reward) rather than the dissonance effect (more attitude change the less the reward) is found. All these experiments help to clarify the situations which give rise to cognitive dissonance. Psychologically, the experience of dissonance seems to be one of personal regret for behaviour which seems to reflect on one in that it runs counter to one's values.

Stress and the motivating nature of dissonance

Apparently, Festinger himself regrets the emphasis given in the original theory to dissonance as a stress, an aversive discomfort (Tannenbaum, 1968). Brehm and Cohen (1962) give less emphasis to this aspect of the theory. In a summary of views about inconsistency as a 'motivational' construct, Tannenbaum claimed that there was agreement on a 'unanimous rejection of a unitary, drive-reduction nature of inconsistency — essentially, that inconsistency is an aversive state, and generates activity for its own resolution' (p. 343). However, there is some agreement as to a basic need for consistency. There is no reason why we should not regard this merely as an aspect of man's nature, as a being that tries to make sense of his world; ambiguity is a problem to be solved in order to act. The notion of a 'causal motive' underlying this behaviour clouds the actual situation.

In this subsection the main criticisms and elaborations of the original theory have been briefly surveyed. Within the present context, treatment of the various models which have been put forward to account for (especially) forced compliance effects without using any concept of dissonance can only be mentioned. The most prominent examples are: Rosenberg's (1965) 'evaluation apprehension' model; the 'incentive/biased scanning' model of Elms, Janis and Gilmore (Elms and Janis, 1965; Janis and Gilmore, 1965; Elms, 1968); Bem's (1965; 1967; 1972) 'self perception' theory; Tedeschi, Schlenker and Bonoma's (1971) 'impression management' formulation and Nuttin's (1975) 'response contagion' theory.

Dissonance theory and an interactionist view of attitudes

Bannister and Fransella (1971) argue that dissonance 'theory' is merely a sketchy idea, lacking the precision and clarity required of a properly developed theory. Certainly there was vagueness and ambiguity in Festinger's original proposal, and, although later writers have done much to make it more specific and definite, there is still a general unsatisfactoriness about the idea.

Considered as a causal model of attitude change, the theory does not specify sufficiently clearly the conditions which are necessary and sufficient for dissonance to occur. Because of this, dissonance studies have proved hard to replicate (Kiesler, Collins and Miller, 1969; Collins, Ashmore, Hornbeck and Witney, 1970; Nuttin, 1975).

Brown (1965), in a similar vein, argues that 'The outcome of almost any dissonance experiment can be explained without recourse to the principle of dissonance. And usually there are several ways of doing it' (p. 603). This is a weak criticism since absolutely any empirical observation may be explained in several ways. If this is an objection to dissonance theory, then all other theories in every science fall foul of it. The correct line of defence is that of Brehm and Cohen (1962), who reason that dissonance theory prevails over other views because of the number of apparently distinct examples of attitude change which it can economically explain. However, Brown counters this with the observation that it can only perform such apparent feats of explanation because it is so ill defined — the theory can be adjusted to suit the circumstances. Thus, the argument returns to the complaint of Bannister and Fransella.

On another tack, Chapanis and Chapanis (1964) protest that 'To condense most social situations into two, and only two, simple dissonant statements represents so great a level of abstraction that the model no longer bears any reasonable resemblance to reality' (p. 21). In reply, Kiesler, Collins and Miller make the point that science is concerned with erecting models that account for events, not with picturing the subtleties of the events themselves. This parallels the fact that H_2O does not have to refer, in itself as a formula, to the wetness of water. Surely it is true that scientific symbol systems do not directly evoke the phenomena to which they eventually refer. But on the other hand an explanatory model should not *distort* understanding of these phenomena. The molecular theory in chemistry does not distort understanding, but is true to the phenomena it is intended to explain. Dissonance theory may well distort attitude change by oversimplification. The elaborations to which dissonance theory has been subjected since its original statement indicate that it was at the start too simple an account of attitude change processes — for instance, there were suppressed premises. And even in the original statement, the formula for magnitude of dissonance tacitly acknowledged that more than two cognitive elements were involved in cognitive dissonance events.

These various complaints against Festinger's theory might lead the reader to wonder whether too much space has not been devoted to it. Certainly the theory is not sufficiently clear to enable immediate use to be made of it, either in embellishing an interactionist account of attitudes or in indicating limitations to such an account. Yet the history of the theory is instructive, and gives an opportunity to show further features of attitudes from an interactionist standpoint. Surely the amount of concerted research effort which has been devoted to dissonance theory means that it ought to be accorded serious attention?

Let us consider first the consistency assumption which underlies this theory — as it does a whole family of related approaches to the study of attitudes (Zajonc, 1960). As the previous section of this chapter showed, symbolic interactionism does not dissent from the notion that attitudes are structured in terms of consistency, and it has been suggested that Kelvin's principle of subjective consistency with values has much to recommend it.

Kelvin, it will be recalled, suggested a motive for consistency, which was the need to perceive the social world as predictable if one is to act in it. Thus a consistent ordering of attitudes enables the holder to impose a degree of orderliness on his environment. Now, lying beneath this view is the idea which has been stressed in this book that perception is inevitably in terms of meanings. Thus the 'need for consistency' is not to be thought of as a causal motive to which human beings are prey, and which willy-nilly orders their attitude structures and systems of symbols. Rather, the nature of the 'need for consistency' is best viewed as part of the activity of perceiving: where an event is a focus of inconsistent attitudes, the meaning of that event is necessarily unclear, and a sort of 'functional blindness' must surely come over the perceptual field. But this description is a conjecture, because ambiguity over meaning is largely prevented by the attempt to maintain consistency in the attitude system.

Attitude structuring, then, avoids ambiguity in the meaning-laden perception of situations. In this connection it may be suggested that the special emphasis placed on the importance of maintaining a consistent attitude structure with respect to the value of *self* (e.g. in the work of Aronson and of Bramel) can be justified because of the centrality of the self concept. As Chapter 5 might suggest, ambiguity in self-perception would have very general consequences — depending on the degree to which the social circumstances of the individual require a coherent self concept.

The proviso just entered concerning the generality of the effect of attitudinal inconsistency with respect to a certain value reminds us of the situated nature of attitude structures. The end of the previous section of this chapter was concerned with this matter. There it was argued that attitude structures are only 'provisionally' consistent. In particular, repair of consistency when an attitude has been 'discredited' is likely to be piecemeal. This can be taken further. It may well be that such discrediting of an attitude when it has been responsible for the construction of a certain definition of the situation will be limited to that situation, so that the same attitude will be maintained in other contexts. There is no empirical evidence which bears directly on this point, largely, it must be confessed, because attitude theory has been notoriously bad *social* psychology, in general. The task of mapping relationships between attitudes in a variety of social settings has not been of interest to workers in this field. Yet it may be hazarded as a reasonable guess that, just as the self may not be too consistent across situations, so attitudes structured in terms of other values may vary.

This brings us to the dissonance postulate of Festinger. Two inferentially inconsistent cognitive elements will give rise to dissonance (assuming they are relevant to each other). Objections to this have already been mentioned. In this part of the theory and also in the treatment of magnitude of dissonance — and in the idea that dissonance is a sort of stress which acts as a causal motive in re-establishing consistency — a major problem is the pretence of building a tight, predictive model, which purports to explain in causal terms how certain attitude changes occur.

This is a matter of central importance, because it appears to be a general flaw in the whole enterprise represented by dissonance theory. Discussion of it will indicate that those more recent authors who have attempted to elaborate the theory in terms of other factors relevant to dissonance (voluntary commitment, seriousness of effect, freedom of choice of action) are moving the theory towards a symbolic interactionist position.

It appears to the present writer, then, that there is a systematic ambivalence running through dissonance theory, and which later elaborations have still not entirely eliminated. On the one hand, the model is couched in terms which suggest an almost mechanical predictability of attitude change in certain circumstances. Yet, on the other hand, the application of the model in any concrete instance requires an interpretative understanding of the point of view of the subject. In stating the circumstance which will cause dissonance, for instance, Festinger presents a picture of automatic discomfort arising from a clash of cognitions. But in order to know that dissonance is likely in an actual individual case, the psychologist has to be aware of quite a number of facts to do with the lived world, the perceived situation, of that person. Often, in reports of dissonance experiments, the degree to which such information has been necessary is not made explicit simply because the experimental subjects, the experimenters, and the readers of the report all share (for all practical purposes) the same perception of the subjects' situation. But the information which they have is nevertheless an unexplicated part of the prediction of dissonance. (The *ad hoc* empirical tests of dissonance suggested by Aronson and by Brown acknowledge this.)

The formula for magnitude of dissonance also appears on the face of it a tight predictive model. But the notion of importance, by which elements are weighted, indicates again that reference to the person's viewpoint.

The ambivalence which these examples indicate is lessened to some extent by the efforts of the later authors in their elaborations of dissonance theory. But even here a similar tendency may be seen, insofar as these authors present their work as providing a set of further *variables* to be taken into account in the prediction of dissonance. Rather, such considerations as whether or not the subjects in a dissonance study saw their choice of behaviour as free ought to be regarded as part of the subjects' definition of the situation. It is not, surely, that perceived freedom of action is a causal factor in the lawful determination of a necessary response to a clash of cognitions. Rather, whether or not a person saw his behaviour as due to his own internal and personal motivation (see previous chapter) is used by him in monitoring his own attitudes. If he was not free to act otherwise, then the fact that he acted in a way inconsistent with his attitudes needs no excuse or justification.

Festinger's theory brings out clearly a distinction that has been hinted at elsewhere in this book (especially at the end of Chapter 2). This contrasts the view of consciousness as merely the field in which a number of variables interact, with the view that consciousness is awareness of situation, and involves the capacity to plan actions and monitor one's own behaviour. Both are cognitive approaches. Both appear to regard cognitive processes as having the status of hypothetical constructs, or at least as more than intervening variables. But some distinction must be drawn. It is in line with a widespread usage to label the second viewpoint *phenomenological*.

Throughout this book, even in its particular interpretation of Mead's thought, phenomenological understandings have been preferred to other, merely cognitive, ones. The person has been seen as immersed in a social context. His point of view has been regarded as primary — his definition of the situation, his self concept, his meaning-laden perception of emotions and motives. The same preference is appropriate in making sense of the welter of research on attitudes.

Conclusion

In every event of symbolic interaction, the conscious awareness of participants, by which they monitor, interpret, respond to each other's actions may be viewed as consisting in a number of components. Chapters 3 to 8 of this book take, in turn, certain components, certain aspects of this stream of conscious participation, as topics for detailed consideration. But of course the division into such 'topics' is somewhat arbitrary. The event of interaction/conscious awareness is, in itself, a unity, and each of the aspects gives a partial account — insufficient even to deal with the focal concerns to which it is addressed (hence, motivation is not adequately treated by motivational concepts, for instance: perception, thought, attitudes are implicated).

Can an organizing concept be found to give a degree of unity to the separate accounts of the 'topics'? There is a case for the view that the central topic is perceiving. Attributing motives and emotions to oneself and to others in the course of interaction are, in a sense, merely special instances of perceiving. But a theme which has recurred throughout the book is the pervading influence of symbols, especially language, on thought and on meaning-laden perception. There is a dialectical relationship between symbol and experience. Thus an organizing notion which contends for primacy is symbolic functioning — and the very term 'symbolic interactionism' would seem to demand such a solution. (Also the treatment of attitudes as perceptual categories links this aspect centrally to the idea of symbolic functioning.) Again, should not a work concerned with social interaction and consciousness be more specific in the type of perceptual-symbolic behaviour with which it deals and treat 'defining the situation' as the very basic notion?

Such a quest for a primary organizing concept is unnecessary. As a careful reading of this book should reveal, each concept implies the others, since each is merely a means of abstracting or isolating a particular, relatively coherent but certainly not independent aspect of the stream of social interaction/consciousness for consideration. Insofar as interaction-and-awareness can be viewed as a continuous, flowing process, so the concepts which organize the chapters of this book are interlinked parts of a whole.

However, this perspective implies that a full understanding of the social interaction/consciousness nexus requires a 're-contextualization' of the conceptual 'packages' which have been isolated for examination. It is a heuristically advantageous policy to perform such an abstraction, but the reader must reintegrate the matters discussed and relate them to the concrete instances of interaction observed in daily life if the abstract considerations are to inform his comprehension.

Romanyshyn (1971) has indicated the direction which such a re-contextualization of the concept of attitude must take initially. He reminds us that an attitude is an abstraction by an observer of a certain *meaning* of a segment of experience for the subject. If research and reflection on attitudes in general provides some fruitful insights, to benefit from an awareness of such insights in considering a particular attitude which someone actually holds it is necesary to re-contextualize the concept by recalling that an attitude is an 'intentional [i.e. conscious, and therefore having cognitive content] and situational [i.e. connected to social interaction] phenomenon which relate an individual to some aspects of his own history, to other people and to a project unfolding in time'.

The further study of a particular attitude, then, requires an interpretative approach to the person's definition of the situation, his self and other perceptions, his attributions of motive, and so on. The emphasis being on the meaning of the attitude to him in his social situation.

In a final perspective on the material treated in this book, then, two matters require consideration. Firstly, the suggestion of the preceding paragraphs is that the justification for our study of the social interaction/consciousness nexus is only to be found by showing that the enterprise of abstracting and analysing components of that unity actually increases understanding of interaction and awareness when the aspects are re-contextualized. The judge of success in this direction is the reader. But a summary of some of the basic conclusions of the book may assist him to reach a favourable verdict.

Secondly, the insistence of Romanyshyn that the study of a certain attitude of a particular person may only be undertaken by an *interpretative understanding* of its place in the total context of his lived world, is not only true of attitudes, but of each of the abstracted components of social interaction and awareness with which this book deals. Once the 'topics' are re-contextualized, conceptual familiarity with them becomes part of a background structure of the social psychologist's understanding, but in the foreground is the subject's lived world. The centrality of meaning in symbolic interactionism demands that social psychological understanding be in terms of the meanings by which the subject perceives and thinks his world. Now this leads to a certain way of viewing the relationships between social psychology and the disciplines at whose interface it lies — psychology and sociology. And it also allows a connection to be seen between interactionist social psychology and some recent versions of psychoanalysis. These ideas relate to the orientation sketched out in the Introduction to this book, yet they go beyond what might be expected of a Conclusion in that they point to areas of research in the human sciences which certainly lie outside the book's own scope. Nevertheless it seems right to indicate these natural connections: no body of knowledge is self-contained, and least of all that of an interface discipline.

To pursue the first of these objectives, in the service of providing a final perspective on this book, let us draw out some of the more central assertions of the eight chapters. Chapters 1 and 2 sketched out the general stance of symbolic interactionism, and discussed recent work of both conceptual and empirical sorts which allowed some judgement to be made on the ambiguities and flaws in Mead's theory. The primacy of the interactive experience in the development of mind and full symbolic interaction is the main impact of Mead. The concomitant emphasis on symbolic functioning suggests that language as a symbol system is of fundamental importance (which was borne out in Chapter 3). It also leads to an awareness of the overarching influence of society, in that society is the context of that initial interaction from which mind proceeds, and it provides the major symbol system which structures both thought and interaction.

Notions such as 'defining the situation', 'self-monitoring' and 'taking the attitude of the other' are among the conceptual tools which interactionism provides. These enable the insight that conscious awareness and interaction are an indissoluable whole to be carried through. Behind each of them stands the presupposition that meanings (made concrete in language and other symbol systems) 'motivate' action, and that perception of self, other and situation is immediately meaning-laden (Chapter 4).

Chapter 5 on perception of self, Chapter 6 on emotion and Chapter 7 on motivation all continue into different aspects of consciousness/interaction the basic understanding developed in earlier chapters of perception as meaning-laden, of language as the socially-constituted carrier of meaning, and of behaviour as situated in a social context.

It was Chapter 8 in which some of the more detailed arguments concerning the nature of personal symbol systems emerged. Attitudes, though perhaps best viewed as special sorts of symbols, in that various distinguishable components are seen (belief, feeling and desire), show certain characteristics which must typify symbols in general. They connect in a fairly structured way with other attitudes — a similar consistency must underlie symbol systems, since perception would be put at risk if there were regular ambiguity in the meaning of events because of inconsistency in symbol use.

Yet attitude systems are only 'provisionally' structured. They are situated, in that they refer to external matters, and are not to be considered as self-contained. Part of what this means was discussed in connection with the vexed attitude-behaviour relationship. Rather than picture that relationship as akin to a causal connection, the idea was put forward that attitudes 'motivate' and 'suggest a content' for situational definitions. Within the definition thus perceived a person may choose various lines of action. And interpersonal negotiation of situations, and other processes of drift or invalidation of situational definitions may feed back to attitudinal structures.

Such a sketchy review of the content of this book perhaps does no more than underline the claim that, in invoking interactionism as a theoretical framework, we are able to see a degree of coherence in an otherwise fragmented discipline.

The second line of consideration, in suggesting a final perspective within which to view this book, has to do with the idea (which surely may be deduced from symbolic interactionism) that, since *meanings* are central in human action, investigation of human action should proceed through the interpretative understanding of such meanings.

Mead's own work is somewhat ambivalent on this point. The possibility of characterizing his approach as 'social behaviourism' (though rejected, after some consideration, in Chapter 2) does at least indicate a tendency towards a deterministic view of human action. A causal, deterministic view would treat definitions of situation and other such 'meaning attributions' as variables in a field of causes and effects — cognitive variables, no doubt, but variables none the less.

Such a standpoint does not take conscious awareness seriously. Consciousness is treated as a 'field' for the interaction of variables. Yet symbol-use, thinking, meaning-laden perception, definition of situations, and so on, all refer to consciousness as 'constitutive'. Symbolic interactionism is not merely a cognitive theory, it is a phenomenological one. Cognitive processes are certainly more than intervering variables, but they also transcend the status of hypothetical constructs. They are 'owned'. Consciousness involves *someone's* awareness of a lived world.

Thus the re-contextualization of social psychological concepts puts them into service as background structures which assist the interpretative understanding of a person's lived world — his meaningful experience.

Recalling the Introduction, it may be asked how this theoretical stance relates to the relationship between social psychology and the 'parent' disciplines of sociology and psychology. Symbolic interactionism — as will have been seen in this book — enables the development of a true 'Janus faced' social psychology; one which is continually aware of the social nature of the individual and the human nature of society. Surely the evolution of social psychology itself, in the solution of its own particular problems may be permitted to suggest a considered point of view which the neighbouring disciplines ought to heed? If so, sympathetic stances are readily available. In the case of psychology, the ethological approach is one which locates the individual in a lived world (Thinès, 1977), and phenomenological psychology generally has a venerable history (Giorgi, 1970, 1975). In sociology, several contending approaches can be viewed as compatible with interactionist social psychology, perhaps the most viable being that based on the work of Merleau-Ponty (see Spurling, 1977). These opinions can only be mentioned in the present context. To demonstrate their accuracy is not relevant to a study of interactionist social psychology, yet mention of them does appear relevant in that an interface discipline cannot pretend to command a body of knowledge which is entirely distinct from that of its neighbours.

It has been stressed that the concrete social event, the interaction/

consciousness flow, requires investigation by means of the interpretative understanding of the individual points of view involved. One advantage of seeing the material in this book as contributing a conceptual framework, as the background to such attempts at interpretative understanding, is that it allows a connection to be made with some recent developments in psychoanalysis. If the movement towards re-contextualization takes us to the individual's meaning-laden perception of the situation, then we will find that all is not clear in his account of his perception. The unravelling of the meaning of his situation is akin to psychoanalysis (cf van den Berg, 1972).

The constructs, symbols, linguistic elements, attitudes which a person employs to organize his perception of events and his interaction with others are, as we have seen, part of structures — systems of implication and connotation. These may be largely undisclosed to their 'owner'. The explication of his perceptual tendencies, then requires a 'hermeneutic' approach.

Several influential recent contributions to psychoanalytic theory (e.g. Lacan, 1953; Rycroft, 1968; Ricoeur, 1970, 1971) have argued forcefully that psychoanalysis is to be regarded as a linguistically-based procedure aimed at the interpretation of the patient's communicative behaviour (verbal or non-verbal), akin to the historian's or theologian's attempt to interpret the meaning of an ancient text. Hermeneutics is the art of interpretation of texts (see Harney, 1978).

As Steiner (1976) points out, Freud's own unrealized hope that his scheme for interpreting 'symptoms' would be found to have some sort of physiological basis can be seen as a 'desire to escape from the hermeneutical circle of language seeking to deal systematically with language' (p. 253). Within the perspective of symbolic interactionism it is not surprising that there is no such escape, for if social interaction generally is mediated by symbols, then the scientific attempt to understand interaction is no less a symbolic enterprise. Thus, as Steiner writes, commenting on Lacan: *'La parole du patient* is the sole medium of psychoanalytic action' (p. 255).

These final paragraphs have attempted to set the material of the book in a wider context than the limited sphere of interactionist social psychology. It is not possible to pursue these matters further here. However, social psychology does not stand alone, and it is with these approaches within neighbouring human sciences that a symbolic interactionist social psychology has the greatest affinity.

Bibliography

Abelson, R.P. (1968a). 'Discussion: minimalist versus maximalist positions on cognitive structure', in Abelson and colleagues (1968).

Abelson, R.P. (1968b). 'A summary of hypotheses on modes of resolution', in Abelson and colleagues (1968).

Abelson, R.P., Aronson, E., McGuire, W., Newcomb, T., Rosenberg, M. and Tannenbaum, P. (1968). *Theories of Cognitive Consistency,* Chicago, Rand McNally.

Abelson, R.P. and Rosenberg, M.J. (1958). 'Symbolic psychologic: a model of attitudinal cognition', *Behavioural Science,* **3,** 1-13.

Ajzen, I. and Fishbein, M. (1970). 'The prediction of behaviour from attitudinal and normative variables', *Journal of Experimental Social Psychology,* **6,** 466-487.

Alexander, C.N. (1966). 'Attitude as a scientific concept', *Social Forces,* **45,** 278-281.

Allport, G.W. (1935). 'Attitudes', in C. Murchison (ed.) *Handbook of Social Psychology,* Worcester, Mass., Clark University Press.

Allport, G.W. (1943). 'The ego in contemporary psychology', *Psychological Review,* **50,** 451-478.

Allport, G.W. (1954a). *The Nature of Prejudice,* New York, Doubleday.

Allport, G.W. (1954b). 'Attitudes in the history of social psychology', in N. Warren and M. Jahoda (1973), *Attitudes* (2nd ed.), Harmondsworth, Penguin.

Allport, G.W. (1968). 'The historical background of modern social psychology', in G. Lindzey and E. Aronson (eds., 1968), *The Handbook of Social Psychology,* (2nd ed., vol. 1). Reading, Mass, Addison-Wesley.

Allport, G.W., Lindzey, G. and Vernon, P.E. (1951). *A Study of Values,* Boston, Houghton.

Allport, G.W. and Odbert, H.S. (1936). 'Trait names: a psycholexical study', *Psychological Monographs,* **41,** 1-211.

Amabile, T. and Hastorf, A. (1976). 'Person perception', in B. Seidenberg and A. Snadowsky (eds)., *Social Psychology,* New York, Free Press.

Anderson, N.H. and Lopes, L.L. (1974). 'Some psycholinguistic aspects of person perception', *Memory and Cognition,* **2,** 67-74.

Argyle, M. (1969). *Social Interaction,* London, Methuen.

Argyle, M. (1975). *Bodily Communication,* London, Methuen.

Arnold, M.B. (1968). *The Nature of Emotion,* Harmondsworth, Penguin.

Arnold, M.B. (1970). *Feelings and Emotions,* London, Academic Press.

Aronson, E. (1969). 'The theory of cognitive dissonance', *Advances in Experimental Social Psychology,* **4,** 1-34.

Aronson, E. and Rosenbloom, S. (1971). 'Space perception in early infancy: perception within a common auditory-visual space', *Science,* **172,** 1161-1163.

Aronfreed, J. (1968). *Conduct and Conscience: the socialisation of internalised control of behaviour,* New York, Academic Press.

Asch, S.E. (1946). 'Forming impressions of personality', *Journal of Abnormal and Social Psychology,* **41,** 258-290.

Ashworth, P.D. (1976). 'Some notes on phenomenological approaches in psychology', *Bulletin of the British Psychological Society,* **29,** 363-368.

Ashworth, P.D. (1977). 'Alfred Schutz, the assumptions of everyday experience, and the human sciences', *Bulletin of the British Psychological Society*, **30**, 147-148.

Audi, R. (1972). 'On the conception and measurement of attitudes in contemporary Anglo-American psychology', *Journal for the Theory of Social Behaviour*, **2**, 179-203.

Ball, D.W. (1972). '"The definition of the situation": some theoretical and methodological consequences of taking W.I. Thomas seriously', *Journal for the Theory of Social Behaviour*, **2**, 61-82.

Bandura, A. (1967). 'Behavioural Psycotherapy', *Scientific American*, **216** (3), 78-86.

Bandura, A. (1969). 'Social learning theory of identificatory processes', in D. Goslin (ed), *Handbook of Socialisation Theory and Research*, Chicago, Rand McNally.

Bandura, A. (1971). *Social Learning Theory*, New Jersey, General Learning Press.

Bandura, A. and Walters, R. (1963). *Social Learning and Personality Development*, New York, Holt, Rinehart and Winson.

Bannister, D. and Fransella, F. (1971). *Inquiring Man: the theory of personal constructs*, Harmondsworth, Penguin.

Bateson, M.C. (1975). 'Mother-infant exchanges: the epigenesis of conversational interaction', *Annals of N.Y. Academy of Sciences*, **263**, 101-113.

Beach, F.A. (1955). 'The descent of instinct', *Psychological Review*, **62**, 401-410.

Beach, L. and Wertheimer, H. (1961). 'A free response approach to the study of person cognition', *Journal of Abnormal and Social Psychology*, **62**, 367-374.

Beattie, G.W. (1978). 'Floor apportionment and gaze in conversational dyads', *British Journal of Social and Clinical Psychology*, **17**, 7-15.

Becker, H.S. (1951). 'The professional dance musician and his audience', *American Journal of Sociology*, **57**, 136-144.

Becker, H.S. (1953). 'Becoming a marijhuana user', *American Journal of Sociology*, **59**, 235-242.

Becker, H.S. (1963). *Outsiders*, New York, Free Press.

Becker, H.S. (1967). 'History, culture and subjective experience: an exploration of the social bases of drug-induced experiences', *Journal of Health and Social Behaviour*, **8**, 163-176.

Becker, H.S., Geer, B., Hughes, E.C. and Strauss, A. (1961). *Boys in White: a study of student culture in medical school*, Chicago, Chicago University Press.

Becker, H.S. and Strauss, A.L. (1956). 'Careers, personalities and adult socialisation', *American Journal of Sociology*, **62**, 253-263.

Beloff, J. (1973). *Psychological Sciences*, London, Crosby, Lockwood, Staples.

Bem, D.J. (1965). 'An experimental analysis of self persuasion', *Journal of Experimental Social Psychology*, **1**, 199-218.

Bem, D.J. (1967). 'Self-perception: an alternative interpretation of cognitive dissonance phenomena', *Psychological Review*, **74**, 188-200.

Bem, D.J. (1972). 'Self perception theory', *Advances in Experimental Social Psychology*, **6**, 1-62.

Benedict, R. (1946). *The Chrysanthemum and the Sword*, London, Routledge and Kegan Paul.

Bennett, S. (1971). 'Infant-caretaker interactions', *Journal of the American Academy of Child Psychiatry*, **10**, 321-335.

van den Berg, J. (1972). *A Different Existence*, Pittsburgh, Duquesne University Press.

Berger, P. and Luckmann, T. (1967). *The Social Construction of Reality*, Harmondsworth, Penguin.

Bernstein, B. (1970). 'Social class, language and socialisation', in P.P. Giglioli (1972), *Language and Social Context*, Harmondsworth, Penguin.

Berry, J.W. (1971). 'Ecological and cultural factors in spatial development', in Berry and Dasen (1974).

Berry, J.W. and Dasen, P.R. (1974). *Culture and Cognition*, London, Methuen.

Bertocci, P.A. (1945). 'The psychological self, the ego, and personality', *Psychological Review*, **52**, 91-99.

Bindra, D. (1970). 'Emotion and behaviour theory', in Black (1970).

Birdwhistell, R. (1968). 'Kinesics', *International Encyclopedia of the Social Sciences*, **8**, 379-385.

Bjerg, K. (1968). 'Interplay-analysis. A preliminary report on an approach to the problems of interpersonal understanding', *Acta Psychologica*, **28**, 201-245.

Black, P. (1970). *Physiological Correlates of Emotion*, New York, Academic Press.

Blanshard, B. and Skinner, B.F. (1967). 'The problem of consciousness — a debate', *Philosophy and Phenomenological Research*, **27**, 317-337.

Bloemkolb, D., Defares, P. and van Gelderen, G. (1971). 'Cognitive processing of information on varied physiological arousal', *European Journal of Social Psychology*, **1**, 31-46.

Bloom, S.W. (1965). 'The sociology of medical education: some comments on the state of a field', *Milbank Memorial Fund Quarterly*, **43**, 143-184.

Blum, A. and McHugh, P. (1971). 'The social ascription of motives', *American Sociological Review*, **36**, 98-109.

Blumer, H. (1962). 'Society as symbolic interaction', in Rose (1962).

Blumer, H. (1966). 'Sociological implications of the thought of George Herbert Mead', *American Journal of Sociology*, **71**, 535-544.

Blumstein, P.W. (1974). 'The honouring of accounts', *American Sociological Review*, **39**, 551-566.

Blumstein, P.W. (1975). 'Identity bargaining and self-conception', *Social Forces*, **53**, 476-485.

Bramel, D. (1968). 'Dissonance, expectation and the self', in Abelson and colleagues (1968).

Brannon, R. (1976). 'Attitudes and the prediction of behaviour', in B. Seidenberg and A. Snadowsky (1976), *Social Psychology*, London, Collier-Macmillan.

Brehm, J.W. (1962). 'Motivational effects of cognitive dissonance', in M.R. Jones (ed), *Nebraska Symposium on Motivation* (1962), Lincoln, Neb., University of Nebraska Press.

Brehm, J.W. and Cohen, A. (1962). *Explorations in Cognitive Dissonance*, New York, Wiley.

Brehm, M.L., Back, D. and Bogdonoff, M. (1964). 'A physiological effect of cognitive dissonance under stress and deprivation', *Journal of Abnormal and Social Psychology*, **69**, 303-310.

Bromley, D.B. (1977). *Personality Description in Ordinary Language*, London, Wiley.

Bronowski, J.S. and Bellugi, U. (1970). 'Language, name and concept', *Science*, **168**, 699.

Brown, L.B. (1973). *Ideology*, Harmondsworth, Penguin.

Brown, R. (1956). Appendix to J.S. Bruner, J.J. Goodnow, and G.A. Austin (1956), *A Study of Thinking*, New York, Wiley.

Brown, R. (1965). *Social Psychology*, London, Collier-Macmillan.

Brown, R. (1976). *A First Language*, Harmondsworth, Penguin.

Brown, R. and Herrnstein, R.J. (1975). *Psychology*, London, Methuen.

Bruner, J.S. (1957). 'On perceptual readiness', *Psychological Review*, **64**, 123-152.

Bruner, J.S. (1977a). 'The ontogenesis of speech acts', in P. Collett (ed.), *Social Rules and Social Behaviour*, Oxford, Blackwell.

Bruner, J.S. (1977b). 'Early social interaction and language acquisition', in Schaffer (1977a).

Bruner, J.S. and Sherwood, V. (1976). 'Early rule structure: the case of "peekaboo"', in R. Harré (ed), *Life Sentences*, London, Wiley.

Buytendijk, F.J.J. (1962). 'The phenomenological approach to the problem of feelings and emotions', in H. Ruitenbeek (ed), *Psychoanalysis and Existential Philosophy,* New York, Dutton.

Calder, B.J. and Ross, M. (1973). *Attitudes and Behaviour,* New Jersey, General Learning Press.

Campbell, D.T. (1950). 'The indirect assessment of social attitudes', *Psychological Bulletin,* **47,** 15-30.

Campbell, D.T. (1963). 'Social attitudes and other acquired dispositions', in S. Koch (ed), *Psychology: a study of a science,* (Vol. 6), New York, McGraw-Hill.

Cannon, W.B. (1927). 'The James-Lange theory of emotion: a critical examination and an alternative theory', *American Journal of Psychology,* **39,** 106-124.

Chaikin, A. and Derlega, V. (1974). *Self Disclosure,* New Jersey, General Learning Press.

Chapanis, N. and Chapanis, A. (1964). 'Cognitive disonance: five years later', *Psychological Bulletin,* **61,** 1-22.

Chapman, L.J. and Chapman, J.P. (1959). 'Atmosphere effect reexamined', *Journal of Experimental Psychology,* **58,** 220-226.

Cherns, A. (1975). 'What is left of social psychology?' British Psychological Society Conference, *Social Psychology in Context,* Loughborough University (8 March 1975).

Chinoy, M. (1975). 'How not to resolve a conflict', *New Society* (4 Sept. 1975), 513-516.

Chomsky, N. (1959). 'Review of Skinner's *Verbal Behaviour',* *Language,* **35,** 26-58.

Cohen, A.R. (1960). 'Attitudinal consequences of induced discrepancies between cognitions and behaviour', *Public Opinion Quarterly,* **24,** 297-318.

Collins, B., Ashmore, R., Hornbeck, F. and Whitney, R. (1970). 'Studies in forced compliance XIII and XV. In search of a dissonance-producing forced compliance paradigm', *Reports of Research in Social Psychology,* **1,** 11-23.

Collins, B. and Hoyt, M.G. (1972). 'Personal responsibilty for decision. An integration and extension of the "forced compliance" literature', *Journal of Experimental Social Psychology,* **8,** 558-593.

Collis, G.M. (1977). 'Visual co-orientation and maternal speech', in Schaffer (1977a).

Collis, G.M. and Schaffer, H.R. (1975). 'Synchronisation of visual attention in mother-infant pairs', *Journal of Child Psychology and Psychiatry,* **16,** 315-320.

Condon, W.S. and Sander, L.W. (1974). 'Neonate movement is synchronised with adult speech', *Science,* **183,** 99-101.

Conklin, H.C. (1955). 'Hanunóo colour categories', *South Western Journal of Anthropology,* **II,** 339-344.

Cook, M. (1971). *Interpersonal Perception,* Harmondsworth, Penguin.

Cook, S. and Selltiz, C. (1964). 'A multiple-indicator approach to attitude measurement', *Psychological Bulletin,* **62,** 36-55.

Cooley, C.H. (1902). *Human Nature and the Social Order,* New York, Charles Scribner's Sons.

Cooper, J. and Worchel, A. (1970). 'Role of undesired consequences in arousing cognitive dissonance', *Journal of Personality and Social Psychology,* **16,** 199-206.

Cromer, R.F. (1974). 'The development of language and cognition: the cognition hypothesis', in B. Foss (ed), *New Perspectives in Child Development,* Harmondsworth, Penguin.

Darwin, C. (1872). *The Expression of the Emotions in Man and Animals,* London, Murray.

Davey, A.G. (1976). 'Attitudes and the prediction of social conduct', *British Journal of Social and Clinical Psychology,* **15,** 11-22.

Davitz, J. (1964). *The Communication of Emotional Meaning.* New York: McGraw-Hill.

Davitz, J. (1969). *The Language of Emotion,* New York, Academic Press.

Davitz, J. (1970). 'A dictionary and grammar of emotion', in Arnold (1970).

De Fleur, M. and Westie, F. (1958). 'Verbal attitudes and overt acts', *American Sociological Review,* **23,** 667-673.

De Fleur, M. and Westie, F. (1963). 'Attitude as a scientific concept', *Social Forces,* **42,** 17-31.

Deutsch, J.A. and Deutsch, D. (1973). *Physiological Psychology* (Rev. ed.), Homewood, Ill, Dorsey.

Doob, L.W. (1964). 'Eidetic images among the Ibo', in Berry and Dasen (1974).

Dornbusch, S., Hastorf, A., Richardson, S., Muzzy, R. and Vreeland, R. (1965). 'The perceiver and the perceived: their relative influence on categories of interpersonal perception', *Journal of Personality and Social Psychology,* **1,** 434-440.

Durkheim, E. (1964). *'The Rules of Sociological Method',* New York, Free Press.

Duval, S. and Wicklund, R.A. (1972). *A Theory of Objective Self Awareness,* New York, Academic Press.

Eagly, A.H. and Himmelfarb, S. (1978). 'Attitudes and opinions', *Annual Review of Psychology,* **29,** 517-554.

Ekman, P. (1970). 'Universal facial expressions of emotion', in R.A. Levine (ed. 1974), *Culture and Personality,* Chicago, Aldine.

Ekman, P. (1971). 'Universals and cultural differences in facial expressions of emotion', in J.K. Cole (ed) *Nebraska Symposium on Motivation, 1971.* Lincoln, Neb, University of Nebraska Press.

Ekman, P. and Friesen, W. (1969). 'Nonverbal leakage and clues to deception', *Psychiatry,* **32,** 88-106.

Ekman, P. and Friesen, W. (1971). 'Constants across cultures in the face of emotion', *Journal of Personality and Social Psychology,* **17,** 124-129.

Elms, A. (1968). 'Role-playing, incentive and dissonance', *Psychological Bulletin,* **68,** 132-148.

Elms, A. and Janis, I. (1965). 'Counter-norm attitudes induced by consonant versus dissonant conditions of role-playing', *Journal of Experimental Research in Personality,* **1,** 50-60.

Ewert, O. (1970). 'The attitudinal character of emotion', in Arnold (1970).

Exline, R.V. (1972). 'Visual interaction: the glances of power and preference', in J.K. Cole (ed) *Nebraska Symposium on Motivation* (1971), Lincoln, University of Nebraska Press.

Eysenck, H.J. (1954). *The Psychology of Politics,* London, Routledge and Kegan Paul.

Fantz, R. (1961). 'The origin of form perception', *Scientific American,* **204,** 66-72.

Fantz, R. and Nevis, S. (1967). 'Pattern preferences and perceptual-cognitive development in early infancy', *Merrill-Palmer Quarterly,* **13,** 77-108.

Feffer, M. (1970). 'Developmental analysis of interpersonal behaviour', *Psychological Review,* **77,** 197-214.

Fehr, F.S. and Stern, J.A. (1970). 'Peripheral physiological variables and emotion: the James-Lange theory revisited', *Psychological Bulletin,* **74,** 411-424.

Ferguson, C.A. (1964). 'Baby talk in six languages', in C.A. Ferguson (1971), *Language Structure and Language Use,* Stanford, California, Stanford University Press.

Ferguson, C.A. (1969). 'Absence of copula and the notion of simplicity: a study of normal speech, baby talk, foreigner talk and pidgins', in C.A. Ferguson (1971), *Language Structure and Language Use,* Stanford, California, Stanford University Press.

Festinger, L. (1957). *A Theory of Cognitive Dissonance,* Evanston, Ill., Row, Peterson.

Festinger, L. (1964). 'Behavioural support for opinion change', *Public Opinion Quarterly,* **28,** 404-417.

Festinger, L. and Carlsmith, J.M. (1959). 'Cognitive consequences of forced compliance', *Journal of Abnormal and Social Psychology,* **58,** 203-210.

202

Fischer, W.F. (1970). 'The faces of anxiety', *Journal of Phenomenological Psychology,* **1**, 31-49.

Fishbein, M. (1967). 'Attitude and the prediction of behaviour', in M. Fishbein, (ed), *Readings in Attitude Theory and Measurement,* New York, Wiley.

Fishbein, M. (1973). 'The prediction of behaviours from attitudinal variables', in C.D. Mortensen and K.K. Sereno (eds), *Advances in Communication Research,* New York, Harper and Row.

Fishman, J.A. (1960). 'A systematisation of the Whorfian hypothesis', in Berry and Dasen (1974).

Fitch, G. (1970). 'Effects of self-esteem, perceived performance and choice on causal attributions', *Journal of Personality and Social Psychology,* **16**, 311-315.

Flapan, D. (1968). *Children's Understanding of Social Interaction,* New York, Teachers College Press, Columbia University.

Flavel, J., Botkin, P.T., Fry, C.L., Wright, J.W. and Jarvis, P.E. (1968). *The Development of Role-taking and Communication Skills in Children,* New York, Wiley.

Fodor, J.A. (1965). 'Could meaning be an r_m?', *Journal of Verbal Learning and Verbal Behaviour,* **4**, 73-81.

Foote, N. (1953). 'Love', in G. Stone and H. Farberman (1970), *Social Psychology through Symbolic Interaction,* Waltham, Mass., Ginn/Blaisdell.

Forgas, J.P. (1976). 'Perception of social episodes: categorical and dimensional representations in two different social milieus', *Journal of personality and Social Psychology,* **34**, 199-209.

Foulds, G.A. (1973). 'Has anybody here seen Kelly?', *British Journal of Medical Psychology,* **46**, 221-225.

Frederiksen, N. (1972). 'Towards a taxonomy of situations', *American Psychologist,* **27**, 114-123.

Freud, S. (1949). 'Instincts and their vicissitudes', in *The Collected Papers of Sigmund Freud* (vol. IV), London, Hogarth.

Frijda, N. (1969). 'Recognition of emotion', *Advances in Experimental Social Psychology,* **4**, 167-223.

Frijda, N. (1970), 'Emotion and recognition of emotion', in Arnold (1970).

Frijda, N. (1973). 'The relation between emotion and expression', in M. von Cranach and I. Vine (1973). *Social Communication and Movement,* New York, Academic Press.

Gallagher, G. (1977). 'Essential and non-essential asymmetries in the doctor-patient relationship,' presented at the Conference on the Phenomenological Analysis of Asymmetrical Interpersonal Relations; Dayton, Ohio, May, 1977.

Gardner, R.A. and Gardner B.T. (1969). 'Teaching sign language to a chimpanzee', *Science,* **165**, 664-672.

Garfinkel, H. (1956). 'Conditions of successful degradation ceremonies', *American Journal of Sociology,* **61**, 420-424.

Garfinkel, H. (1963). 'A conception of, and experiments with, "trust" as a condition of stable concerted actions', in O.J. Harvey (ed) *Motivation and Social Interaction,* New York, Ronald Press.

Garfinkel, H. (1967). *Studies in Ethmomethodology,* New Jersey, Prentice-Hall.

Geertz, H. (1959). 'The vocabulary of emotion: a study of Javanese socialisation processes', in R.A. Levine (1974), *Culture and Personality,* Chicago, Aldine.

Gelman, R. and Shatz, M. (1972). 'Listener-dependent adjustments in the speech of 4 year olds', *Psychonomic Science,* **29**, 267.

Gibson, J.J. (1968). *The Senses Considered as Perceptual Systems,* London, Allen and Unwin.

Gilbert, G.M. (1951). 'Stereotype persistence and change among college students', *Journal of Abnormal and Social psychology,* **46**, 245-254.

Gillin, C.T. (1975). 'Freedom and the limits of social behaviourism: a comparison of selected themes from the works of G.H. Mead and Martin Buber', *Sociology*, **9**, 29-47.

Giorgi, A. (1970). *Psychology as a Human Science: A phenomenologically based approach*, New York, Harper and Row.

Giorgi, A. (1975). 'Phenomenology and the foundations of psychology', in J.K. Cole and W.J. Arnold (eds). *Nebraska Symposium on Motivation, 1975*, Lincoln, Nebraska University Press.

Goffman, E. (1956). 'Embarrassment and social organisation', in E. Goffman (1967), *Interaction Ritual*, Harmondsworth, Penguin.

Goffman, E. (1961). *Asylums*, Harmondsworth, Penguin.

Goffman, E. (1969). *The Presentation of Self in Everyday Life*, Harmondsworth, Penguin.

Goffman, E. (1972). *Encounters*, Harmondsworth, Penguin.

Goffman, E. (1975). *Frame Analysis*, Harmondsworth, Penguin.

Goldstein, D., Fink, D. and Metee, D. (1972). 'Cognition of arousal and actual arousal as determinants of emotion', *Journal of Personality and Social Psychology*, **21**, 41-51.

Gollin, E.S. (1958). 'Organisational characteristics of social judgment: a developmental investigation', *Journal of Personality*, **26**, 139-154.

Gonos, G. (1977). '"Situation" versus "frame": the "interactionist" and "structuralist" analyses of everyday life', *American Sociological Review*, **42**, 854-867.

Goodall, J. (1971). *In the Shadow of Man*, Boston, Houghton Mifflin.

Greene, J. (1975). *Thinking and Language*, London, Methuen.

Greenwald, A.J. (1970) 'When does role playing produce attitude change? Toward an answer', *Journal of Personality and Social Psychology*, **16**, 214-219.

Gregory, S.W. (1977). 'The grammar of motives as elicited by breaching experiments', presented at the Conference on the Phenomenological Analysis of Asymmetrical Interpersonal Relations, Dayton, Ohio, May, 1977.

Grings, W. and Lockhart, R. (1963). 'Effects of "anxiety lessening" instructions and differential set development on the extinction of GSR', *Journal of Experimental Psychology*, **66**, 292-299.

Gross, E. and Stone, G. (1964). 'Embarrassment and the analysis of role requirements', *American Journal of Sociology*, **70**, 1-15.

Grusec, J. (1966). 'Some antecedents of self criticism', *Journal of Personality and Social Psychology*, **4**, 244-252.

Haaf, R.A. and Bell, R.Q. (1967). 'A facial dimension in visual discrimination by human infants', *Child Development*, **38**, 893-899.

Hall, E.T. (1966). *The Hidden Dimension*, New York, Doubleday.

Hall, R.L. and Cobey, V.E. (1976). 'Emotion as the transformation of world', *Journal of Phenomenological Psychology*, **6**, 180-198.

Hallpike, C.R. (1969). 'Social hair', *Man*, **4**, 256-264.

Harney, M. (1978). 'Psychoanalysis and hermeneutics', *Journal of the British Society for Phenomenology*, **9**, 71-81.

Harré, R. (1970). *The Principles of Scientific Thinking*, London, Macmillan.

Harré, R. and Secord, P. (1972). *The Explanation of Social Behaviour*, Oxford, Blackwell.

Hartung, F.E. (1965). *Crime, Law and Society*, Detroit, Wayne State University Press.

Hastorf, A., Schneider, D. and Polefka, J. (1970). *Person Perception*, Reading, Mass., Addison-Wesley.

Heath, A. (1976). *Rational Choice and Social Exchange*, Cambridge, Cambridge University Press.

Heckhausen, H. and Weiner, B. (1972). 'The emergence of a cognitive psychology of motivation', in P.C. Dodwell, (ed), *New Horizons in Psychology 2*, Harmondsworth, Penguin.

Heider, F. (1958). *The Psychology of Interpersonal Relations*, New York, Wiley.

Helmreich, R. and Collins, B. (1968). 'Studies in forced compliance: commitment and magnitude of inducement to comply as determinants of opinion change', *Journal of Personality and Social Psychology,* **10,** 75-81.

Henle, M. (1962). 'On the relation between logic and thinking', *Psychological Review,* **69,** 366-378.

Henley, M. (1973). 'Status and sex: some touching observations', *Bulletin of the Psychonomic Society,* **2,** 91-93.

Herriot, P. (1970). *An Introduction to the Psychology of Language,* London, Methuen.

Hewitt, J.P. and Stokes, R. (1975). 'Disclaimers', *American Sociological Review,* **40,** 1-11.

Hockett, C.F. (1963). 'The problem of universals in language', in J.H. Greenberg (ed.), *Universals of Language,* Cambridge, Mass., M I T Press.

Hohmann, G.W. (1966). 'Some effects of spinal cord lesions on experienced emotional feelings', *Psychophysiology,* **3,** 143-156.

Homans, G. (1962). *Sentiments and Activities: Essays in social science,* London, Routledge and Kegan Paul.

Husband, C. (1977). 'News media, language and race relations: a case study in identity maintenance', in H. Giles (ed), *Language, Ethnicity and Intergroup Relationships,* London, Academic Press.

Inkeles, A. (1959). 'Personality and social structure', in R.K. Merton and colleagues (eds), *Sociology Today,* (vol 2), New York, Basic Books.

Insko, C.A. and Schopler, J. (1967). 'Triadic consistency: a statement of affective-cognitive-conative consistency', *Psychological Review,* **74,** 361-376.

Jaffe, J., Stern, D. and Peery, J.C. (1973). '"Conversational" coupling of gaze behaviour in prelinguistic human development', *Journal of Psycholinguistic Research,* **2,** 321-329.

James, W. (1884). 'What is an emotion?', *Mind,* **9,** 188-205.

James, W. (1892). *Textbook of Psychology. ('Briefer Course'),* New York, Holt.

Janis, I.L. and Gilmore, J. (1965). 'The influence of incentive conditions on the success of roleplaying in modifying attitudes', *Journal of Personality and Social Psychology,* **1,** 17-27.

Jenkins, R.L. (1950). 'Guilt feelings — their function and dysfunction', in M. Reymert (1950), *Feelings and Emotions,* New York, Hafner.

Jersild, A.T. (1951). 'Self-understanding in childhood and adolescence', *American Psychologist,* **6,** 122-126.

Johnson, T.J., Feigenbaum, R. and Weibey, M. (1964). 'Some determinants and consequences of the teacher's perception of causality', *Journal of Educational Psychology,* **55,** 237-246.

Jones, E.E. and de Charms, R. (1957). 'Changes in social perception as a function of the personal relevance of behaviour', *Sociometry,* **20,** 75-85.

Jones, E.E. and Davis, K.E. (1965). 'From acts to dispositions: the attribution process in person perception', *Advances in Experimental Social Psychology,* **2,** 219-266.

Jones, E.E. and Harris, V. (1967). 'The attribution of attitudes', *Journal of Experimental Social Psychology,* **3,** 1-24.

Jones, E.E. and Nisbett, R.E. (1971). *The Actor and the Observer: Divergent perceptions of the causes of behaviour,* New Jersey, General Learning Press.

Jones, R.A. and Rosenberg, S. (1974). 'Structural representations of naturalistic descriptions of personality', *Multivariate Behavioural Research,* **9,** 217-230.

Jourard, S.M. (1963). 'An exploratory study of body accessibility', *British Journal of Social and Clinical Psychology,* **5,** 221-231.

Katz, D. (1960). 'The functional approach to the study of attitudes', *Public Opinion Quarterly,* **24,** 163-204.

Katz, D. (1968). 'Consistency for what?', in Abelson and colleagues (1968).

Katz, D. and Braly, K. (1933). 'Racial prejudice and racial stereotypes', *Journal of Abnormal and Social Psychology,* **30,** 175-193

Katz, D., McClintock, C. and Sarnoff, I. (1957). 'The measurement of ego defence as related to attitude change', *Journal of Personality,* **25,** 465-474.

Katz, D. and Stotland, E. (1959). 'A preliminary statement to a theory of attitude change and structuring', in S. Koch (ed), *Psychology, a study of a science* (vol 3), New York, McGraw-Hill.

Kaye, K. (1977). 'Towards the origin of dialogue', in Schaffer (1977a).

Kelley, H.H. (1952). 'Two functions of reference groups', in H. Proshansky and B. Seidenberg (1965), *Basic Studies in Social Psychology,* New York, Holt, Rinehart and Winston.

Kelley, H.H. (1967). 'Attribution theory in social psychology', in D. Levine (ed), *Nebraska Symposium on Motivation, 1967,* Lincoln, Neb., University of Nebraska Press.

Kelley, H.H. (1971). *Attribution in Social Interaction,* New Jersey, General Learning Press.

Kelley, H.H. (1972). *Causal Schemata and the Attribution Process,* New Jersey, General Learning Press.

Kellogg, R. and Baron, R. (1975). 'Attribution theory, insomnia, and the reverse placebo effect: a reversal of Storms' and Nisbett's findings', *Journal of Personality and Social Psychology,* **32,** 231.

Kelly, G.A. (1955). *The Psychology of Personal Constructs* (2 vols), New York, Norton.

Kelman, H.C. and Baron, R. (1974). 'Moral and hedonic dissonance. A functional analysis of the relationship between discrepant action and attitude change', in S. Himmelfarb and A. Eagly (eds), *Readings in Attitude Change,* New York, Wiley.

Kelvin, P. (1970). *The Bases of Social Behaviour,* London, Holt, Rinehart and Winston.

Kendon, A. (1967). 'Some functions of gaze direction in social interaction', *Acta psychologica,* **26,** 22-47.

Kendon, A. (1978). 'Looking in conversation and the regulation of turns at talk: A comment on the papers of Beattie and Rutter *et al*', *British Journal of Social and Clinical Psychology,* **17,** 23-24.

Kiesler, C., Collins, B. and Miller, N. (1969). *Attitude Change: a critical analysis of theoretical approaches,* New York, Wiley.

Kiesler, C., Nisbett, R. and Zanna, M. (1969). 'On inferring one's belief from one's behaviour', *Journal of Personality and Social Psychology,* **11,** 321-327.

King, B.T. and Janis, I.L. (1956). 'A comparison of the effectiveness of improvised versus non-improvised role-playing in producing opinion changes', *Human Relations,* **9,** 177-186.

Klineberg, O. (1938). 'Emotional expression in Chinese literature', *Journal of Abnormal and Social Psychology,* **33,** 517-520.

Knox, R. and Inkster, J. (1968). 'Post decision dissonance at post time', *Journal of Personality and Social Psychology,* **8,** 319.

Kolb, W. (1944). 'A critical evaluation of Mead's "I" and "me" concepts', *Social Forces,* **22,** 291-296.

Koopman, P.R. and Ames, E.W. (1968). 'Infants' preferences for facial arrangements: a failure to replicate', *Child Development,* **39,** 481-487.

Kothandapani, V. (1971). 'Validation of feeling, belief and intention to act as three components of attitude and their contribution to prediction of contraceptive behaviour', *Journal of Personality and Social Psychology,* **19,** 321-333.

Krauss, R.M. and Glucksberg, S. (1969). 'The development of communication competence as a function of age', *Child Development,* **40,** 255-266.

Krech, D., Crutchfield, R. and Ballachey, E. (1962). *Individual in Society*, New York, McGraw-Hill.

Kuhn, M. (1964). 'Major trends in symbolic interaction theory in the past twenty-five years', *Sociological Quarterly*, **5**, 61-84.

Kuhn, M. and McPartland, T. (1954). 'An empirical investigation of self attitudes', *American Sociological Review*, **19**, 68-76.

Labarre, W. (1947). 'The cultural basis of emotions and gestures', *Journal of Personality*, **16**, 49-68.

Labov, W. (1969). 'The logic of nonstandard English', in P.P. Giglioli (ed, 1972), *Language and Social Context*, Harmondsworth, Penguin.

Lacan, J. (1953). 'Fonction et champ de la parole et du langage en psychanalyse', *Psychanalyse*, **1**, 81-166.

Lacey, J.I. and Lacey, B.C. (1970). 'Some autonomic-central nervous system interrelationships', in Black (1970).

Laing, R.D. (1970). *Knots*, Harmondsworth, Penguin.

Laird, J. (1974). 'Self-attribution of emotion: the effects of expressive behaviour on the quality of emotional experience', *Journal of Personality and Social Psychology*, **29**, 475-486.

La Piere, R. (1934). 'Attitudes versus action', *Social Forces*, **13**, 230-237.

Lashley, K.S. (1951). 'The problem of serial order in behaviour', in L.A. Jeffress (ed), *Cerebral Mechanisms in Behaviour*, New York, Wiley.

Lazarus, R.S. (1966). *Psychological Stress and the Coping Process*, New York, McGraw-Hill.

Lazarus, R.S., Averill, J.R. and Opton, E.M. (1970). 'Towards a cognitive theory of emotion', in Arnold (1970).

Leach, E, (1976). *Culture and Communication*, Cambridge, Cambridge University Press.

Leeper, R.W. (1963). 'The motivational theory of emotion', in Arnold (1970).

Lenneberg, E.H. (1964). 'A biological perspective of language', in E.H. Lenneberg (ed), *New Directions in the Study of Language*, Cambridge, Mass., M I T Press.

Leventhal, H. (1974). 'Attitudes: their nature, growth and change', in C. Nemeth (ed), *Social Psychology: classic and contemporary integrations*, Chicago, Rand McNally.

Levi-Strauss, C. (1968). *Structural Anthropology*, Harmondsworth, Penguin.

Levy, R.I. (1972). 'Tahiti, sin, and the question of integration between personality and sociocultural systems', in R.A. LeVine (1974), *Culture and Personality*, Chicago, Aldine.

Lewis, M. and Rosenblum, L.A. (eds, 1974). *The Effects of the Infant on its Caregiver*, New York, Wiley.

Lichtman, R. (1970). 'Symbolic interactionism and social reality: some Marxist queries', *Berkeley Journal of Sociology*, **15**, 75-94.

Lieberman, S. (1956). 'Effects of changes in roles on the attitudes of role occupants', *Human Relations*, **9**, 385-402.

Linden, E. (1976). *Apes, Men and Language*, Harmondsworth, Penguin.

Linder, D.E., Cooper, J. and Jones, E.E. (1967). 'Decision freedom as a determinant of the role of incentive magnitude in attitude change', *Journal of Personality and Social Psychology*, **6**, 245-254.

Lindesmith, A., Strauss, A. and Denzin, N. (1975). *Social Psychology*, Hinsdale, Ill., Dryden.

Linn, L.S. (1965). 'Verbal attitudes and overt behaviour: a study of racial discrimination', *Social Forces*, **43**, 353-364.

Linton, R. (1945). *The Cultural Background of Personality*, New York, Appleton-Century-Crofts.

Livesley, W. and Bromley, D. (1973). *Person Perception in Childhood and Adolescence*, London, Wiley.

207

Losee, J. (1972). *A Historical Introduction to the Philosophy of Science,* Oxford, Oxford University Press.
Luria, A.R. (1969). 'Speech development and the formation of mental processes', in M. Cole and I. Maltzman (eds), *A Handbook of Contemporary Soviet Psychology,* New York, Basic Books.
Luria, A.R. and Yudovich, F.Ia. (1959). *Speech and the Development of Mental Processes in the Child,* London, Staples Press.
MacCorquodale, K. and Meehl, P. (1948). 'On a distinction between hypothetical constructs and intervening variables', *Psychological Review,* **55**, 95-107.
MacLeod, R.B. (1947). 'The phenomenological approach to social psychology', *Psychological Review,* **54**, 193-210.
Magnusson, D. (1971). 'An analysis of situational dimensions', *Perceptual and Motor Skills,* **32**, 851-867.
Maloy, R. (1977). 'The Don Quixote problem in Schutz and Castaneda', *Journal of the British Society for Phenomenology,* **8**, 28-35.
Malinowski, B. (1927). 'Supplement to Ogden and Richards: *The Meaning of Meaning',* in P. Adams (1972), *Language in Thinking,* Harmondsworth, Penguin.
Mandler, G. (1975). *Mind and Emotion,* New York, Wiley.
May, R. (1950). *The Meaning of Anxiety,* New York, Ronald Press.
McCoy, M. (1975). 'Fould's phenomenological windmill: a reply to criticisms of personal construct psychology', *British Journal of Medical Psychology,* **48**, 139-146.
McDougall, W. (1908). *Introduction to Social Psychology,* London, Methuen.
McGuire, W.J. (1969). 'The nature of attitudes and attitude change', in G. Lindzey and E. Aronson (eds), *Handbook of Social Psychology* (2nd ed, vol. 3), Reading, Mass., Addison-Wesley.
Mead, G.H. (1932). *The Philosophy of the Present,* Chicago, Open Court.
Mead, G.H. (1934). *Mind, Self and Society,* Chicago, Chicago University Press.
Mead, G.H. (1938). *The Philosophy of the Act,* Chicago, Chicago University Press.
Mead, M. (1950). 'Some anthropological considerations concerning guilt', in M. Reymert (1950), *Feelings and Emotions,* New York, Hafner.
Mehrabian, A. (1968). 'Inference of attitudes from posture, orientation and distance of a communicator', *Journal of Consulting and Clinical Psychology,* **32**, 296-308.
Meltzer, B.N. (1964). 'Mead's social psychology', in J.G. Manis and B.N. Meltzer (ed, 1972), *Symbolic Interaction* (2nd ed), Boston, Allyn and Bacon.
Meltzer, B.N., Petras, J.W. and Reynolds, L.T. (1975). *Symbolic Interactionism: Genesis, varieties and criticism,* London, Routledge and Kegan Paul.
Merleau-Ponty, M. (1947). 'The primacy of perception and its philosophical consequences', in M. Merleau-Ponty (1974), *Phenomenology, Language and Sociology,* London, Heinemann.
Merleau-Ponty, M. (1962). *The Phenomenology of Perception,* London, Routledge and Kegan Paul.
Merleau-Ponty, M. (1965). *The Structure of Behaviour,* London, Methuen.
Merton, R. (1957). *Social Theory and Social Structure,* New York, Free Press.
Merton, R., Reader, G. and Kendall, P.L. (1957). *The Student Physician,* Cambridge, Mass., Harvard University Press.
Miller, G.A. (1965). 'Some preliminaries to psycholinguistics', *American Psychologist,* **20**, 15-20.
Miller, N.E. and Dollard, J. (1941). *Social Learning and Imitation,* New Haven, Yale University Press.
Mills, C.W. (1940). 'Situated actions and vocabularies of motive', *American Sociological Review,* **5**, 904-913.
Mischel, W. (1968). *Personality and Assessment,* New York, Wiley.
Moscovici, S. (1972). 'Society and theory in social psychology', in J. Israel and H. Tajfel (eds), *The Context of Social Psychology,* London, Academic Press.

Murphy, C. and Messer, D. (1977). 'Mothers, infants and the pointing gesture', in Schaffer (1977a).

Natanson, M. (1972). 'Phenomenology and social role', *Journal of the British Society for Phenomenology*, **3**, 218-230.

Natanson, M. (1973). *The Social Dynamics of George H. Mead,* The Hague, Nijhoff.

Nel, E., Helmreich, R. and Aronson, E. (1969). 'Opinion change in the advocate as a function of the persuasibility of the audience', *Journal of Personality and Social Psychology*, **12**, 321-327.

Nelson, K. (1973). 'Structure and strategy in learning to talk', *Monographs of the Society for Research in Child Development,* **38**.

Newcomb, T.M., Turner, R.H. and Converse, P.E. (1966). *Social Psychology* (2nd ed), London, Routledge and Kegan Paul.

Newson, J. (1977). 'An intersubjective approach to the systematic description of mother-infant interaction', in Schaffer (1977a).

Newson, J. and Newson, E. (1975). 'Intersubjectivity and the transmission of culture: on the social origins of symbolic functioning', *Bulletin of the British Psychological Society,* **28**, 437-446.

Nisbett, R.E. and Valins, S. (1971). *Perceiving the Causes of One's Own Behaviour,* New Jersey, General Learning Press.

Nowlis, V. (1970). 'Mood, behaviour and experience', in Arnold (1970).

Nuttin, J. (1950). 'Intimacy and shame in the dynamic structure of personality', in M. Reymert (1950), *Feelings and Emotions,* New York, Hafner.

Nuttin, J.M. (1975). *The Illusion of Attitude Change,* London, Academic Press.

Oppenheim, A.N. (1966). *Questionnaire Design and Attitude Measurement,* London, Heinemann.

Ornstein, R.E. (1973). *The Nature of Human Consciousness,* San Francisco, Freeman.

Osgood, C.E. (1952). 'The nature and measurement of meaning', *Psychological Bulletin,* **49**, 197-237.

Osgood, C.E. (1966). 'Dimensionality of the semantic space for communication via facial expression', *Scandinavian Journal of Psychology,* **7**, 1-30.

Pawlby, S.J. (1977). 'Imitative interaction', in Schaffer (1977a).

Peery, J.C. and Stern, D. (1976). 'Gaze direction frequency distributions during mother-infant interaction', *Journal of Genetic Psychology,* **129**, 45-55.

Peevers, B.H. and Secord, P. (1973). 'Developmental changes in attribution of descriptive concepts to persons', *Journal of Personality and Social Psychology,* **27**, 120-128.

Peters, R.S. (1958). *The Concept of Motivation,* London, Routledge and Kegan Paul.

Pfohl, S.J. and Bowman, J.R. (1977). 'Stratified talk: the production of asymmetry in psychiatric diagnosing', presented at the Conference on the Phenomenological Analysis of Asymmetrical Interpersonal Relations, Dayton, Ohio, May, 1977.

Phares, E.J. (1973). *Locus of Control: a personality determinant of behaviour,* New Jersey, General Learning Press.

Phares, E.J., Wilson, K. and Kylver, N. (1971). 'Internal-external control and the attribution of blame under neutral and distractive conditions', *Journal of Personality and Social Psychology,* **18**, 285-288.

Piaget, J. (1926). *The Language and Thought of the Child,* New York, Harcourt, Brace.

Piaget, J. (1972). *Psychology and Epistemology: towards a theory of knowledge,* Harmondsworth, Penguin.

Piers, G. and Singer, M. (1953). *Shame and Guilt,* Springfield, Ill., Thomas.

Plutchick, R. and Ax, A.F. (1967). 'A Critique of "Determinants of emotional state" by Schachter and Singer (1962)', *Psychophysiology,* **4**, 79-82.

Premack, D. (1971). 'Language in the chimpanzee?', *Science,* **172,** 808-822.

Pribram, K. (1970). 'Feelings as monitors', in Arnold (1970).

Reich, B. and Adcock, C. (1978). *Values, Attitudes and Behaviour Change,* London, Methuen.

Richards, M.P.M. (1971). 'Social interaction in the first weeks of human life', *Psychiatria, Neurologia, Neurochirurgia,* **74,** 35-42.

Ricoeur, P. (1970). *Freud and Philosophy: an essay on interpretation,* New Haven, Yale.

Ricoeur, P. (1971). 'The model of the text: meaningful action consider as a text', *Social Research,* **38,** 529-562.

Riezler, K. (1943). 'Comment on the social psychology of shame', *American Journal of Sociology,* **48,** 457-465.

Robinson, E.J. and Robinson, W.P. (1978). 'The relationship between children's explanations of communication failure and their ability deliberately to give bad messages', *British Journal of Social and Clinical Psychology,* **17,** 219-225.

Robson, K.S. (1967). 'The role of eye-to-eye contact in maternal-infant attachment', *Journal of Child Psychology and Psychiatry,* **8,** 13-25.

Roiser, M. (1974). 'Asking silly questions', in N. Armistead (ed), *Reconstructing Social Psychology,* Harmondsworth, Penguin.

Rokeach, M. (1972). *Beliefs, Attitudes and Values,* San Francisco, Jossey-Bass.

Rokeach, M. (1973). *The Nature of Human Values,* New York, Free Press.

Romanyshyn, R. (1971). 'Toward a phenomenology of attitudes', in A. Giorgi, W.F. Fischer and R. von Eckartsberg (eds.) *Duquesne Studies in Phenomenological Psychology* (vol. 1), Pittsburgh, Duquesne University Press.

Rose, A. (1962). *Human Behaviour and Social Processes,* London, Routledge and Kegan Paul.

Rose, A. (1962a). 'A systematic summary of symbolic interaction theory', in Rose (1962).

Rosenberg, M.J. (1965). 'When dissonance fails: on eliminating evaluation apprehension from attitude measurement', *Journal of Personality and Social Psychology,* **1,** 28-42.

Rosenberg, S. and Jones, R. (1972). 'A method for investigating and representing a person's implicit theory of personality: Theodore Dreiser's view of people', *Journal of Personality and Social Psychology.* **22,** 372-386.

Rosenhan, D. (1973). 'On being sane in insane places', *Science,* **179,** 250-258.

Rotenberg, M. (1974). 'Self-labelling: a missing link in the "societal reaction" theory of deviance', *Sociological Review,* **22,** 335-354.

Rotter, J.B. (1966). 'Generalised expectancies for internal versus external control of behaviour', *Psychological Monographs,* **80,** (1) (whole no. 609).

Rotter, J., Seeman, M. and Liverant, S. (1962). Internal versus external control of reinforcement', in N.F. Washburne (ed), *Decisions, Values and Groups* (Vol 2), New York, Pergamon Press.

Rubin, K.M. (1973). 'Egocentrism in childhood: a unitary construct?', *Child Development,* **44,** 102-110.

Rutter, D.R., Stephenson, G.M., Ayling, K. and White, PA. (1978). 'The timing of looks in dyastic conversation', *British Journal of Social and Clinical Psychology,* **17,** 17-21.

Rycroft, C. (1968). *Psychoanalysis Observed,* Harmondsworth, Penguin.

Sarbin, T. (1954). 'Role theory', in G. Lindzey (1954) *Handbook of Social Psychology* (vol. 1), Reading, Mass., Addison-Wesley.

Sartre, J.-P., (1958). *Being and Nothingness,* London, Methuen.

Sartre, J.-P., (1962). *Sketch for a Theory of the Emotions,* London; Methuen.

Scarlett, H.H., Press, A.N. and Crockett, W.H. (1971). 'Children's descriptions of persons: a Wernerian developmental analysis', *Child Development,* **42,** 439-453.

Schachter, S. (1964). 'The interaction of cognitive and physiological determinants of emotional state', *Advances in Experimental Social Psychology,* **1,** 49-80.

Schachter, S. (1970). 'The assumption of identity and phenpheralist-centralist controversies in motivation and emotion', in Arnold (1970).

Schachter, S. and Singer, J. (1962). 'Cognitive, social and physiological determinants of emotional state', *Psychological Review,* **69,** 379-399.

Schaffer, H.R. (1971). *The Growth of Sociability,* Harmondsworth, Penguin.

Schaffer, H.R. (1977a). *Studies in Mother-Infant Interaction,* London, Academic Press.

Schaffer, R. (1977b). *Mothering,* London, Fontana/Open Books.

Schaffer, H.R., Collis, G.M. and Parsons, G. (1977). 'Vocal interchange and visual regard in verbal and pre-verbal children', in Schaffer (1977a).

Scheler, M. (1954). 'Classification of the phenomena of fellow feeling', in G. Stone and H. Farberman (1970), *Social Psychology through Symbolic Interaction,* Waltham, Mass., Ginn/Blaisdell.

Schlosberg, H. (1952). 'The description of facial expressions in terms of two dimensions', *Journal of Experimental Psychology,* **44,** 229-237.

Schlosberg, H. (1954). 'Three dimensions of emotion, *Psychological Review,* **61,** 81-8.

Schuman, H. and Johnson, M.P. (1976). 'Attitudes and behaviour', *Annual Review of Sociology,* **2,** 161-207.

Schutz, A. (1962). *Collected Papers I: The Problem of Social Reality,* The Hague, Nijhoff.

Schutz, A. (1964). 'Don Quixote and the problem of reality', in A. Schutz (1964), *Collected Papers II: Studies in Social Theory,* The Hague, Nijhoff.

Schutz, A. (1972). *The Phenomenology of the Social World,* London, Heinemann.

Schutz, A. and Luckmann, T. (1974). *The Structures of the Life-World,* London, Heinemann.

Scott, M.B. and Lyman, S.M. (1968). 'Accounts', *American Sociological Review,* **33,** 46-62.

Scudder, J.R. (1977). *'Tensions between societal and personal relationships of men and women',* presented at the Conference on the Phenomenological Analysis of Asymmetrical Interpersonal Relations, Dayton, Ohio, May, 1977.

Secord, P. and Backman, C. (1964). *Social Psychology* (1st ed.), New York, McGraw-Hill.

Secord, P. and Backman, C. (1974). *Social Psychology* (2nd ed.), New York, McGraw-Hill.

Selman, R.L. (1971). 'Taking another's perspective: role-taking development in early childhood', *Child Development,* **42,** 1721-1734.

Selman, R.L. and Byrne, D. (1974). 'A structural developmental analysis of levels of role-taking in middle childhood', *Child Development,* **45,** 803-806.

Shantz, C.H. (1975). 'The development of social cognition', in E.M. Hetherington (ed.), *Review of Child Development Research* (vol. 5), Chicago, Chicago University Press.

Shaver, K.G. (1975). *An Introduction to Attribution Processes,* Cambridge, Mass., Winthrop.

Shaw, M.E. and Costanzo, P.R. (1970). *Theories of Social Psychology,* New York, McGraw-Hill.

Shaw, M.E. and Sulzer, J.L. (1964). 'An empirical test of Heider's levels in attribution of responsibility', *Journal of Abnormal and Social Psychology,* **69,** 39-46.

Sherif, M. and Sherif, C.W. (1967). 'The own categories procedure in attitude research', in M. Fishbein (ed), *Readings in Attitude Theory and Measurement,* New York, Wiley.

Simmel, G. (1969). 'Sociology of the senses: visual interaction', in R. Park and E. Burgess (eds.), *Introduction to the Science of Sociology* (rev. ed.), Chicago, Chicago University Press.

Singer, R.D. and Singer, A. (1969). *Psychological Development in Children,* Philadelphia, Saunders.

Skinner, B.F. (1953). *Science and Human Behaviour,* New York, Macmillan.

Skinner, B.F. (1957). *Verbal Behaviour,* New York, Appleton-Century-Crofts.

Skinner, B.F. (1975). 'The steep and thorny way to a science of behaviour', in R. Harré (ed), *Problems of Scientific Revolution,* Oxford, Oxford University Press.

Slobin, D. (1971). *Psycholinguistics,* Glenview, Illinois, Scott, Foresman.

Slobin, D. (1975). 'On the nature of talk to children', in E.H. and E. Lenneberg (eds.), *Foundations of Language Development* (vol. 1), New York, Academic Press; Paris. UNESCO.

Snow, C.E. (1972). 'Mothers' speech to children learning language', *Child Development,* **43**, 549-565.

Spitz, R.A. (1946). 'The smiling response: a contribution to the ontogenesis of social relations', *Genetic Psychology Monographs,* **34**, 57-125.

Spurling, L. (1977). *Phenomenology and the Social World,* London, Routledge and Kegan Paul.

Steiner, G. (1976). 'A note on language and psychoanalysis', *International Review of Psycho-Analysis,* **3**, 253-258.

Stern, D.N. (1971). 'A micro-analysis of mother-infant interaction', *Journal of the American Academy of Child Psychiatry,*. **10**, 501-517.

Stern, D.N. (1977). *The First Relationship: Infant and Mother,* London, Fontana/Open Books.

Stern, D.N., Beebe, B., Jaffe, J. and Bennett, S.L. (1977). 'The infant's stimulus world during social interaction', in Schaffer (1977a).

Stern, D.N., Jaffe, J., Beebe, B. and Bennett, S.L. (1975). 'Vocalising in unison and in alternation: two modes of communication within the mother-infant dyad', *Annals of New York Academy of Sciences,* **263**, 89-100.

Stevick, E. (1971). 'An empirical investigation of the experience of anger', in A. Giorgi, W.F. Fischer and R. von Eckartsberg (eds.), *Duquesne Studies in Phenomenological Psychology* (vol. 1). Pittsburgh, Duquesne University Press.

Stone, G.P. (1962). 'Appearance and the self', in Rose (1962).

Storms, M. and Nisbett, R. (1970). 'Insomnia and the attribution process', *Journal of Personality and Social Psychology,* **16**, 319-328.

Stotland, E. (1969). 'Exploratory investigations of empathy', *Advances in Experimental Social Psychology,* **4**, 271-314.

Streufert, S. and Streufert, S.C. (1969). 'Effects of conceptual structure, failure and success on attribution of causality and interpersonal attitudes', *Journal of Personality and Social Psychology,* **11**, 138-147.

Stringer, P. (1973). 'Do dimensions have face validity?', in M. von Granach and I. Vine (1973), *Social Communication and Movement,* New York, Academic Press.

Strongman, K.T. (1973). *The Psychology of Emotion,* London, Wiley.

Sturtevant, W.C. (1964). 'Studies in ethnoscience', in Berry and Dasen (1974).

Tagiuri, R. (1969). 'Person Perception', in G. Lindzey and E. Aronson (eds.), *The Handbook of Social Psychology* (vol. 3), Reading, Mass., Addison-Wesley.

Tajfel, H. (1972). 'Experiments in a vacuum', in J. Israel and H. Tajfel (eds.), *The Context of Social Psychology,* London, Academic Press.

Tannenbaum, P. (1968). 'Comment: models of the role of stress', in Abelson and colleagues (1968).

Taylor, B. (1976). 'Motives for guilt-free pederasty: some literary considerations', *Sociological Review*, **24**, 97-114.

Taylor, L. (1972). 'The significance and interpretation of replies to motivational questions', *Sociology*, **6**, 23-39.

Tedeschi, J., Schlenker, B., and Bonoma, T. (1971). 'Cognitive dissonance: private ratiocination or public spectacle', *American Psychologist*, **26**, 685-695.

Thinès, G. (1977). *Phenomenology and the Science of Behaviour*, London, George Allen and Unwin.

Thomas, K. (1971). *Attitudes and Behaviour*, Harmondsworth, Penguin.

Thomas, W.I. (1966). *On Social Organisation and Social Personality*, Chicago, Chicago University Press.

Thomas, W.I. and Znaniecki, F. (1918). 'Social environment, attitudes and values', in E.P. Hollander and R.G. Hunt (1972), *Classic Contributions to Social Psychology*, New York, Oxford University Press.

Thurstone, L.L. (1934). 'The vectors of the mind', *Psychological Review*, **41**, 1-32.

Tittle, C.R. and Hill, R.J. (1967). 'Attitude measurement and the prediction of behaviour: an evaluation of conditions and measurement techniques', *Sociometry*, **30**, 199-213.

Totman, R.G. (1973). 'An approach to cognitive dissonance theory in terms of ordinary language', *Journal for the Theory of Social Behaviour*, **3**, 215-238.

Totman, R.G. (1976). 'Cognitive dissonance in the placebo treatment of insomnia — a pilot experiment', *British Journal of Medical Psychology*, **49**, 393-400.

Toulmin, S. (1958). *The Uses of Argument*, London, Cambridge University Press.

Trevarthen, C. (1977). 'Descriptive analyses of infant communicative behaviour', in Schaffer (1977a).

Triandis, H.C. (1964). 'Cultural influences upon cognitive processes', *Advances in Experimental Social Psychology*, **1**, 1-48.

Triandis, H.C. (1964a). 'Exploratory factor analyses of the behavioural component of social attitudes', *Journal of Abnormal and Social Psychology*, **68**, 420-430

Triandis, H. and Lambert, W. (1958). 'A restatement and test of Schlosberg's theory of emotions, with two kinds of subjects from Greece', *Journal of Abnormal and Social Psychology*, **56**, 321-328.

Triseliotis, J. (1973). *In Search of Origins: the experiences of adopted people*, London, Routledge and Kegan Paul.

Truzzi, M. (1973). 'The problem of relevance between orientations for cognitive dissonance theory', *Journal for the Theory of Social Behaviour*, **3**, 239-247.

Tucker, C. (1966). 'Some methodological problems of Kuhn's self theory', *Sociological Quarterly*, **7**, 345-358.

Turner, R.H. (1962). 'Role-taking: process versus conformity', in Rose (1962).

Turner, R.H. (1976). 'The real self: from institution to impulse', *American Journal of Sociology*, **81**, 989-1016.

Urry, J. (1970). 'Role analysis and the sociological enterprise', *Sociological Review*, **18**, 351-363.

Valins, S. (1966). 'Cognitive effects of false heart-rate feedback', *Journal of Personality and Social Psychology*, **4**, 400-408.

Valins, S. (1970). 'The perception and labelling of bodily changes as determinants of emotional behaviour', in Black (1970).

Veblen, T. (1899). *The Theory of the Leisure Class*, New York, Viking Press.

Videbeck, R. (1960). 'Self-conception and the reactions of others', *Sociometry*, **23**, 351-359.

Volosinov, V.N. (1976). *Freudianism: a Marxist critique*, New York, Academic Press.

Vygotsky, L.S. (1962). *Thought and Language*, Cambridge, Mass., MIT Press.

Watson, D. (1967). 'Relationship between locus of control and anxiety', *Journal of Personality and Social Psychology*, **6**, 91-93.

Watson, O.M. and Graves, T.D. (1966). 'Quantitative research in proxemic behaviour', *American Anthropologist,* **68,** 971-985.

Watt, I. (1963). *The Rise of the Novel,* Harmondsworth, Penguin.

Weiner, B. (1972). *Theories of Motivation,* Chicago, Markham.

Weiner, B. and colleagues, (1971). *Perceiving the Causes of Success and Failure,* New Jersey, General Learning Press.

Weinstein, E.A. (1969). 'The development of interpersonal competence', in D.A. Goslin (1969), *Handbook of Socialisation Theory and Research,* Chicago, Rand McNally.

Weissberg, N.C. (1964). 'Commentary on De Fleur and Westies' ''Attitude as a scientific concept''', **42,** 422-425.

Wells, G. (1975). 'The contexts of children's early language experience', *Educational Review,* **27,** 114-125.

Wenger, M.A. (1950). 'Emotion as visceral action', in M. Reymert (ed.), *Feelings and Emotions,* New York, McGraw-Hill.

Whorf, B.L. (1956). *Language, Thought and Reality,* Cambridge, Mass., MIT Press.

Wickens, D., Allen, C. and Hill, F. (1963). 'Effects of instruction and UCS strength on extinction of the conditioned GSR', *Journal of Experimental Psychology,* **66,** 235-240.

Wicker, A.W. (1969). 'Attitudes *vs* actions: the relationship of verbal and overt responses to attitude objects', *Journal of Social Issues,* **25,** 41-78.

Wicker, A.W. (1971). 'An examination of the ''other variables'' explanation of attitude-behaviour inconsistency', *Journal of Personality and Social Psychology,* **19,** 18-30.

Wicker, A.W. and Pomazal, R.J. (1971). 'The relationship between attitudes and behaviour as a function of specificity of attitude object and presence of a significant person during assessment conditions', *Representative Research in Social Psychology,* **2,** 26-31.

Wilkins, W. (1971). 'Perceptual distortion to account for arousal', *Journal of Abnormal Psychology,* **78,** 252-257.

Wish, M. (1976). 'Comparisons among multidimensional structures of interpersonal relations', *Multivariate Behavioural Research,* **11,** 297-324.

Wishner, J. (1960). 'Reanalysis of impressions of personality', *Psychological Review,* **67,** 96-112.

Wolff, P. (1969). 'The natural history of crying and other vocalisations in early infancy', in B.M. Foss (ed), *Determinants of Infant Behaviour* (vol. 4), London, Methuen.

Woodworth, R.S. (1938). *Experimental Psychology,* New York, Holt.

Woodworth, R.S. and Sells, S.B. (1935). 'An atmosphere effect in formal syllogistic reasoning', *Journal of Experimental Psychology,* **18,** 451-460.

Wootton, A. (1975). *Dilemmas of Discourse,* London, Allen and Unwin.

Wrong, D. (1961). 'The oversocialised conception of man in modern sociology', *American Sociological Review,* **26,** 183-193.

Yarrow, M.R. and Campbell, J.D. (1963). 'Person perception in children', *Merrill-Palmer Quarterly,* **9,** 57-72.

Young, P.T. (1961). *Motivation and Emotion,* New York, Wiley.

Zajonc, R.B. (1960). 'Balance, congruity and dissonance', *Public Opinion Quarterly,* **24,** 280-296.

Zillig, M. (1928). 'Einstellung und Aussage', *Zeitschrift für Psychologie,* **106,** 58-106.

Zimbardo, P.G. (1969). *The Cognitive Control of Motivation,* Glenview, Ill., Scott Foresman.

Zimbardo, P.G., Ebbesen, E.B and Maslach, C. (1977). *Influencing Attitudes and Changing Behaviour* (2nd ed.), Reading, Mass., Addison-Wesley.

Author Index

Subject Index